Close That Sale!

Teach®
Yourself

Close That Sale!

Roger Brooksbank

For UK order enquiries: please contact Bookpoint Ltd, 130 Milton Park, Abingdon, Oxon OX14 4SB. Telephone: +44 (0) 1235 827720. Fax: +44 (0) 1235 400454. Lines are open 09.00–17.00, Monday to Saturday, with a 24-hour message answering service. Details about our titles and how to order are available at www.teachyourself.com

Long renowned as the authoritative source for self-guided learning – with more than 50 million copies sold worldwide – the **Teach Yourself** series includes over 500 titles in the fields of languages, crafts, hobbies, business, computing and education.

British Library Cataloguing in Publication Data: a catalogue record for this title is available from the British Library.

This edition published 2010.

Previously published as *Teach Yourself Successful Selling*

The **Teach Yourself** name is a registered trade mark of Hodder Headline.

Typeset by MPS Limited, a Macmillan Company.

Printed in Great Britain for Hodder Education, an Hachette UK Company, 338 Euston Road, London NW1 3BH, by CPI Cox & Wyman, Reading, Berkshire RG1 8EX.

The publisher has used its best endeavours to ensure that the URLs for external websites referred to in this book are correct and active at the time of going to press. However, the publisher and the author have no responsibility for the websites and can make no guarantee that a site will remain live or that the content will remain relevant, decent or appropriate.

Hachette UK's policy is to use papers that are natural, renewable and recyclable products and made from wood grown in sustainable forests. The logging and manufacturing processes are expected to conform to the environmental regulations of the country of origin.

Impression number   10 9 8 7 6 5 4 3 2 1
Year   2014 2013 2012 2011 2010

Peterborough City Council

60000 0000 55837	
Askews & Holts	Feb-2012
658.85	£10.99

Contents

Meet the author

Welcome to _Teach Yourself Close That Sale!_

Over the years I have become internationally known as an author, trainer and speaker in my specialist areas of strategic marketing planning, business promotion, entrepreneurship and professional selling.

In the UK I have previous experience as a salesperson, sales manager, marketing director and business owner, and I have also worked extensively in Europe and Australasia as an independent marketing consultant.

Currently I am an associate professor of marketing with the prestigious University of Waikato Management School in Hamilton, New Zealand.

You can contact me directly on email roger@rogerbrooksbank.com or for further information, please visit www.rogerbrooksbank.com

Roger Brooksbank

Only got a minute?

In a challenging business environment, what do you think is the X factor that differentiates that small group of top-performing salespeople in your industry? Do they work harder than you? Probably not. Are they more self-motivated and self-disciplined than you? Hardly likely. Could it be that they're more knowledgeable about the features and benefits of their products and services? I seriously doubt it. OK, they must be more experienced then – is that it? Not necessarily.

Would you agree that while all these factors are important prerequisites for sales success, none of them gets even close to explaining the true difference between an ordinary salesperson and a top performer?

Let's make no mistake about it. The X factor is a five-letter word: skill. It's a little word that makes a big difference; all the difference, in fact, to a salesperson's performance.

There's no getting away from it. The best way to increase your sales performance is to focus on improving your selling skills, and this book will help you do just that. It provides a concise description of 50 specific selling skills that are essential for any salesperson who sells face to face. Best of all, each skill comes with a 'call-to-action' in the form of a *skill acquisition exercise*. These exercises provide a starting point for taking the skills off the pages of this book and translating them into your day-to-day selling.

Introduction

IS THIS BOOK FOR YOU?

If you are a professional salesperson selling your company's products and services face-to-face with customers, or if you are responsible for training a regional or national sales force, then yes, this book is for you.

FIVE MAIN SKILL AREAS – OIMCO™

On the basis of my extensive involvement in sales training over the past 25 years, I have found that the process of face-to-face selling can be usefully broken down into five sequential phases, or 'skill areas', otherwise known as the O I M C O™ model:

- ▶ O*pening*
- ▶ I*nterviewing*
- ▶ M*atching*
- ▶ C*losing*
- ▶ O*bjection-handling.*

Most importantly, I have observed that whenever a salesperson focuses their efforts on improving their skills in these areas, success inevitably follows. So, let's take a closer look at each of these five areas:

The opening phase
This begins the moment a salesperson comes face to face with a customer. During this phase a salesperson needs the skills to create a favourable first impression and to set the scene for a businesslike and mutually beneficial conversation to take place.

The interviewing phase
A salesperson cannot prescribe a solution for their customer until they have thoroughly diagnosed their buying situation. So, during

this phase of the selling process, a salesperson needs to employ a variety of interviewing skills in order to find out all about their customer's specific needs and wants, and to uncover the key benefits that they are really looking for.

The matching phase
Once a customer's specific requirements have been established, a salesperson needs the skills to match, as closely as possible, that customer's needs and wants to the benefits of their product or service.

The closing phase
Closing is about helping the customer to make up their mind. During this phase of the process a salesperson needs to be able to draw on a wide range of skills for getting the customer's agreement to go ahead with making their purchase, and for ensuring that they are left feeling positive about their decision.

The objection-handling phase
This phase is triggered whenever the customer responds negatively in some way to a salesperson's offer. This occurs when there's an area of 'perceived mismatch' in the customer's mind – a mismatch between what he or she wants and their understanding of what is on offer. So, during this phase of the sale, a salesperson needs the skills to be able to handle the customer's objection to their complete satisfaction and, whenever possible, turn it around into a closing opportunity.

As you can see, in order to progress successfully through each of the five phases of the O I M C O™ model, a salesperson must be able to call upon an array of selling skills at each phase. The purpose of this book is to help you to acquire these skills.

I've divided the book into five chapters, with each chapter corresponding to one of the five phases of the O I M C O™ model, as shown in the diagram opposite. In each chapter I'll take you through a number of specific selling skills that are essential to becoming an expert 'opener', 'interviewer', 'matcher', 'closer' and 'objection-handler'. In total the book covers 50 skills, numbered 1 through to 50 for ease of reference. Each skill is written in a straightforward fashion and clearly spells out the how-to-do-its, concluding with a call to action in the form of a skill acquisition exercise. These exercises are important because they provide a starting point for taking the skills off the pages of this book and putting them into practice in your day-to-day selling.

THE OIMCO™ MODEL OF FACE-TO-FACE SELLING

Opening phase
Set the scene for a businesslike and mutually beneficial conversation to take place between you and the customer.

↓

Interviewing phase
Find out all about the customer's specific needs and wants, and uncover the key benefits that they are really looking for.

↓

Matching phase
Match the customer's needs and wants as closely as possible to the benefits of your product or service offer.

↓

Closing phase
Get the customer's agreement to go ahead, and leave them feeling positive about their purchase decision.

↓

Objection-handling phase
Handle the customer's objection to their complete satisfaction and, if possible, turn it around into a closing opportunity.

At this point you're probably wondering: 'By how much will this book enable me to improve?' Well, of course I can't give you a straight answer to that question because it all depends on your current level of knowledge and expertise. Certainly, not all the 50 skills will necessarily be of equal value or even new to you. However, I can promise you one thing: my book will surprise you if you let it. Providing you read it with an open mind, with a willingness to learn and, above all, with a willingness to try out new ideas and to change your selling habits, you will become a better salesperson and you will close more sales. I've worked with salespeople from some of the world's leading organizations and I've seen it happen. If it works for them, it can work for you too.

GETTING THE MOST FROM THIS BOOK

It isn't just a convenient coincidence that I've included almost the same number of selling skills in this book as there are weeks in a full working year. It's designed to be read S-L-O-W-L-Y – with the intention of acquiring one skill per week for a year. That's all. Except that's not all. Let me explain …

Don't just read it, do something!
This book isn't just for reading – it's for acting upon! In fact, the words on its pages amount to only a tiny fraction of the book's true value. It's what you *do* as a result of reading it that counts. So this is my suggested weekly game plan:

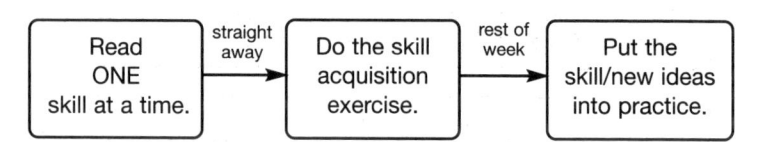

Read ONE skill at a time. → straight away → Do the skill acquisition exercise. → rest of week → Put the skill/new ideas into practice.

Focus your attention solely on reading through one skill at a time; this will take just a few minutes. Then do the *skill acquisition exercise* right away, while it's still fresh in your mind. Doing this exercise is important because it forces you to think about what you could do differently that might help you to sell better. Then for the rest of your working week, take the opportunity to try putting your new ideas into practice during real selling situations, using a process of trial and error to see what works best.

Work systematically through all 50 skills
Regardless of your current level of knowledge and expertise, for optimal results I strongly recommend that you work systematically through all 50 skills in this book. Start with Skill 1 and just keep on going until you've finished Skill 50. Even though you might

already be a seasoned professional, and highly proficient in many of the more 'basic' selling skills, please don't be tempted to skip any of them. Just as the world's top musicians, golfers or dancers never stop working on honing their basic skills, neither do the world's top salespeople and therefore neither should you. By all means spend less time working on some selling skills than on others as appropriate, but please don't short-change yourself. Go through the whole book.

Get yourself a study buddy

A 'study buddy' is another salesperson with whom you join forces as a learning partner. If you can work through this book together, you'll learn a lot more and you'll have more fun doing it. Two heads are better than one, so work closely together comparing notes, providing mutual support and encouragement, and exchanging ideas, knowledge and experience. The ideal study buddy is another member of your sales team who sells the same products and services as you do. However, if this isn't possible, a good choice is any salesperson you know who sells non-competing products or services and who, just like you, wants to keep on improving.

STAY SHARP BY USING THE SELLING SKILLS SELF-ASSESSMENT QUESTIONNAIRE AT THE BACK OF THE BOOK

As time goes by it's all too easy to become a little complacent! Bit by bit, slowly but surely we start to lose our selling 'edge'. So in order to stay sharp, it's important to analyse your level of selling proficiency on a regular basis. For this purpose I've included a diagnostic tool in the form of a self-assessment questionnaire at the back of the book (see page 128). Designed for rapid completion, you'll find it's an easy way to monitor and control your level of selling proficiency. As you will see, each of the 50 questions in the questionnaire corresponds directly with each of the 50 skills featured in this book, thereby enabling you to identify a short list of any selling skills that you need to re-sharpen. You can then turn this list into an 'action-plan' by putting each skill into priority

order and setting yourself a date for re-doing the corresponding
skill acquisition exercise and trying out your new ideas in the field.

ABOUT THE AUDIO PROGRAMME

An audio programme accompanies this book. The audio
programme is structured in accordance with the O I M C O™
model and contains 22 top tips for successful face-to-face selling.
Presented in a lively, fast-moving and entertaining format, it's
ideal for listening to in the car between sales calls. In this context
it will provide plenty of food for thought when reflecting back on
how well you performed during your last sales call. It will also be
a timely source of inspiration and ideas in preparation for the next
one you're about to make. Used in this way, you'll find it's a great
catalyst for self-improvement, either as a stand-alone resource or as
the perfect companion to this book.

You'll find this book quick and easy to read. What's more, it's a
book that you can refer to again and again as a source of new ideas
and inspiration. So, study it, use it, apply it ... and watch yourself
begin to close more sales!

Good luck.

Roger Brooksbank, Hamilton, 2010

Acknowledgements

My sincere thanks go to all of the following for making a contribution in one way or another towards the writing of this book: John Clarke, Jeremy Edwards, Brian Marshall, Steve Kane, Nathalie Giraud, Laurent Besnard-Chantecler, Mike Bottomley, Paul McLaughlin, Fiona McLaughlin, Peter Jones, David Kirby, James McIntosh, Michelle Pinkerton, Michelle Smith, Ning Zhang, Andrew Morgan, Richard Morgan, Zahed Subhan, David Taylor, Alastair Marshall, Sophie Cotter, Mark Lytham, Sally Board, Ed Board, Margaret Brooksbank, Kathryn Borg, Ron Garland, Janet Davey, Lorraine Friend, Marilynne Burton, Quentin Somerville, Neil Lynn, Michele Lynn, Mary FitzPatrick, Merryn Dunsmuir, Renee Railton, Janine Evans and Nikki Leonard.

I would also like to thank my favourite 'selling gurus' – Tom Hopkins, Brian Tracey, Linda Richardson, Robin Fielder, John Fenton and Richard Denny – none of whom I know personally but whose books have sharpened my understanding of professional selling.

Last but not least, special thanks also go to the thousands of salespeople who have attended my sales seminars, training workshops and coaching programmes over the years. It is their positive feedback that inspired me to publish this book.

1

Opening-phase selling skills

In this chapter you will learn:
- *how to set the scene for a businesslike and mutually beneficial conversation to take place between you and the customer*

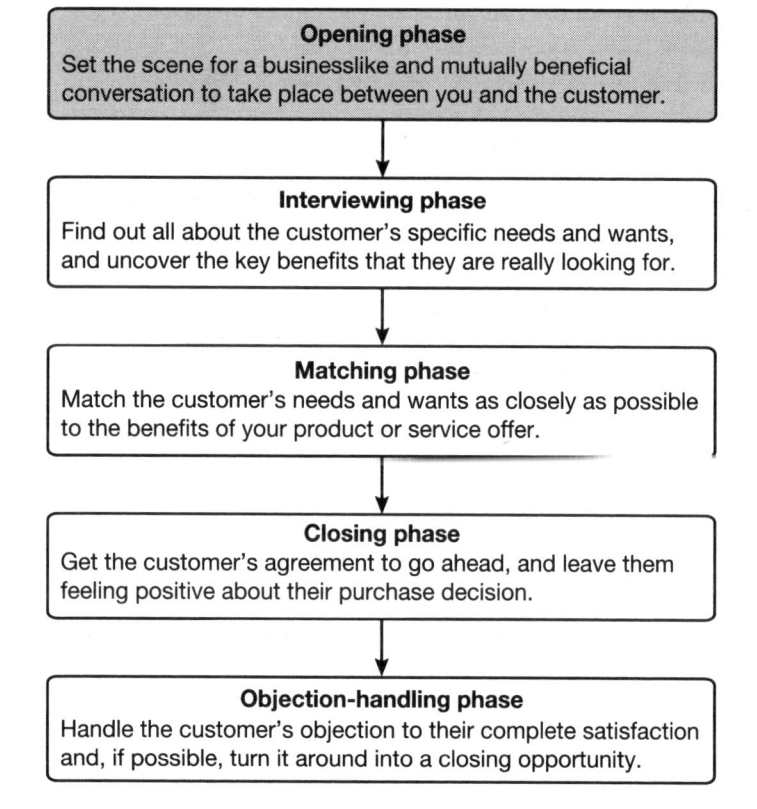

Opening phase
Set the scene for a businesslike and mutually beneficial conversation to take place between you and the customer.

↓

Interviewing phase
Find out all about the customer's specific needs and wants, and uncover the key benefits that they are really looking for.

↓

Matching phase
Match the customer's needs and wants as closely as possible to the benefits of your product or service offer.

↓

Closing phase
Get the customer's agreement to go ahead, and leave them feeling positive about their purchase decision.

↓

Objection-handling phase
Handle the customer's objection to their complete satisfaction and, if possible, turn it around into a closing opportunity.

1 Go through a set-up routine

Picture this. You're fully prepared for an appointment with a prospective customer. You've arrived at their offices with five minutes to spare, parked your car and walked into their reception area. The receptionist tells you that they will be with you shortly and invites you to take a seat. Then it happens. Your mind slips out of the present. Perhaps there is a lot happening in your life and there are other things on your mind. Maybe your head is swimming with nervous anticipation or self-doubt. Whatever the reason, the result is that when the time comes to greet the customer your mind is elsewhere and not focused on the task at hand. Sound familiar?

If you've ever watched an Olympic gymnast or a professional golfer in action you'll know exactly what I mean by a 'set-up routine' (or a 'habitual ritual' as it's sometimes called). Immediately before the gymnast performs a discipline or the golfer hits a shot he or she performs a little ritual that helps to focus the mind and put them in 'the zone' – a place of total concentration and mindfulness in relation to what they are about to do. Of course the routine itself will be different for a salesperson but the principle is the same. Going through a set-up routine in the few moments before meeting a prospective customer is a habit you can acquire to ensure that you're completely focused on performing to the best of your ability every time.

Here are some examples of the set-up routines often used by top salespeople:

- ▶ *Read through any notes you have made relating to the customer you're about to see.*
- ▶ *Access the 'little voice' that's inside your head and use positive self-talk to remind yourself of the value of your offer to the customer.*
- ▶ *Rehearse the exact words you're going to use when greeting the customer by quietly repeating them several times to yourself.*
- ▶ *Do some slow deep-breathing exercises to centre yourself in the moment and become perfectly calm and collected.*

Whenever you have a particularly important sale coming up, I'd recommend a set-up routine called 'mental movie-making'. It works like this: by drawing on the databanks of your memory you already have the ability to make a 'mental movie' of any one of thousands of past experiences, and in such detail that you can quite literally 're-live' that experience inside your head – right? Well, imagine that instead of making a mental movie of the past, you make one of the future – a movie relating to the next sales presentation that you're about to make. That's when mental movie-making can really work for you. By projecting an up-coming sales scenario onto the screen of your mind and making a movie of it, you can 'live out' the experience just as you want it to happen, thereby effectively conditioning yourself for a successful outcome.

Here's how to do it. First, visualize yourself, in detail, successfully 'acting out' your part as the consummate professional salesperson. Second, add the 'sound track', so that inside your head you can hear every single piece of the dialogue between you and your customer, just the way you want it to unfold. Third, add the emotion, so that you can really feel the sense of elation and success you're going to experience as you visualize the sale moving along towards the customer happily deciding to buy. Fourth, now that you have the finished version of your mental movie (complete with moving pictures, soundtrack and emotion), it's important that you 'imprint' it by playing it over and over in your mind prior to going into your next sale.

Insight

The more you can 'live out' a future successful selling experience just as you want it to happen, the more likely it is that it will become your reality.

In developing your set-up routine, do understand that what works for someone else will not necessarily work for you. Everyone must develop their own uniquely personal routine. Use a process of trial and error to find one that just 'feels right' and works for you. While a set-up routine is no substitute for proper preparation and pre-call planning, in those few crucial moments before meeting a customer it's a great way to de-clutter your mind, eliminate negative thinking, banish last-minute nerves and effectively 'program' yourself for a successful outcome.

2 Project your professionalism

First impressions are formed in an instant. Yet their effects can last for a lifetime. Even as you walk towards a new customer, long before you are close enough to shake their hand or engage in conversation, you will have announced your credentials as a professional salesperson simply by the way you look. Just as a book is judged by its cover, in those first few seconds a customer will judge you on the basis of three visual cues:

▶ *the clothes you wear*
▶ *your body language*
▶ *your aura.*

Let's take a closer look at each of these three interrelated aspects of the image you are projecting to your customers:

THE CLOTHES YOU WEAR

The very first thing a customer will notice about you is how you are dressed. In deciding what to wear, the key question to ask yourself is: 'How would my customers expect a top professional salesperson in my industry to be dressed?' – and then dress accordingly. Within these parameters, however, there are a number of general guidelines to bear in mind:

▶ *It's better to dress up than down.*
▶ *Avoid excessively brightly coloured clothes because they can be too distracting. You want a customer to be focused on your face and on what you're saying, rather than on your clothes! In particular, avoid wearing bright red because in a face-to-face selling situation it has all the wrong connotations – it spells 'stop' and is too aggressive.*
▶ *Pay close attention to the standard of your personal grooming.*
▶ *Pay equally close attention to your choice of accessories such as the type and style of briefcase, handbag or hold-all you choose to carry. It's important that accessories complement your overall look.*
▶ *If in doubt about any aspect of your appearance, look to your seniors as role models.*

Insight

Within the first few seconds of meeting up with a new prospective customer, you will have announced your credentials as a professional salesperson simply by the way you look.

YOUR BODY LANGUAGE

The way you move, including your gestures, postures and facial expressions is the next thing your customer will notice. Most experts agree that the non-verbal signals a person communicates through their body language are at least as important as the messages they convey verbally. So, as a salesperson meeting up with a customer for the first time, you should aim to convey openness, enthusiasm and co-operation. This can be achieved by ensuring that your jacket is unbuttoned, that you are smiling frequently, maintaining an upright upper body posture and making plenty of direct eye contact. Above all, as you walk towards a customer, put a spring in your step!

Your aura can be defined as the invisible 'energy' or 'vibes' that surround your body and radiate outwards from it. Make no mistake about it: despite being invisible to the naked eye, upon meeting you for the first time the vast majority of customers will very quickly sense your aura as being either self-centred or customer-centred. Far from being something that just 'is', as many salespeople seem to believe, the aura you project is almost entirely within your control because it springs directly from the attitude that you bring to your job. Fundamentally, a self-centred attitude is epitomized by the stereotypical fast-talking, manipulative salesperson with pound signs in their eyes and shark's jaws for teeth – the kind of salesperson whose only real goal is to satisfy their own needs and wants by making a sale at any cost. In sharp contrast, a customer-centred attitude is the very essence of the modern professional salesperson whose primary goals are to satisfy their customers' needs and wants, and to gain repeat business and referrals through building mutually beneficial long-term relationships. The choice is all yours.

Skill acquisition exercise

On the screen of your mind, create a detailed picture of what a typical customer in your industry would expect a top professional salesperson to look like in terms of their standard of dress, body language and aura. Now stand in front of a full-length mirror and compare this mental image with what you see reflected in the mirror. Ask yourself: in what ways could I improve?

3 Do the handshake one-two-three-four

In a business setting where a handshake is the usual form of greeting between a buyer and seller, doing the 'handshake one-two-three-four' is an excellent habit to acquire. It means you will always be making the most of the opportunity a handshake presents for creating a favourable first impression and building some initial rapport with your customers. So, when shaking hands, there are four things to remember:

ONE-TWO-THREE-FOUR

Look the customer directly in the eye; not just in the general direction of their eyes, but right into the pupils of their eyes. When you do this it usually only takes one or two split seconds before both you and your new customer experience a brief 'twinkle' response in the pupils of each other's eyes. According to human behaviour experts, at this instant a powerful human bonding process takes place that can have a profound effect on the way people instinctively relate to one another.

ONE-**TWO**-THREE-FOUR

Make sure you offer a handshake with a straight, firm grip that's neither too firm nor too limp. This will convey an unspoken message to your new customer that you respect him or her as your equal. Above all, avoid the classic 'I want to dominate you' handshake – shaking too vigorously, applying a vice-like grip, or tilting and rolling your hand so that it's over the top of your customer's hand. Incidentally, if your customer shakes your hand this way, a good method of 'neutralizing' it is to briefly clasp their forearm with your other hand. This double-handed response is usually just enough to let them know that you perceive yourself as their equal, not their subordinate.

ONE-TWO-**THREE**-FOUR

Play the name game. During the act of shaking hands, take the opportunity for personalizing your relationship by asking if you can call your customer by their first name. The best way to do this is to first give your customer permission to call you by your first name before asking for theirs. For example, you might say:

> *Hi, I'm Roger Brooksbank. Please call me Roger ... and may I call you John?*

Once you have the customer's permission to use their first name, you can conclude the handshake by thanking him or her for taking the time to see you:

> *It's good to meet you, John, and thanks for taking the time to see me today.*

Insight

People don't do business with a department, a company or an organization. People do business with people.

Successfully executing the handshake one-two-three-four provides you with the necessary springboard to launch into conducting the rest of your conversation in a businesslike yet friendly manner.

Skill acquisition exercise

Practise the handshake one-two-three-four routine with a colleague or friend until it becomes a natural part of your communication style whenever you meet a customer for the first time.

4 Introduce your company as a 'perfect partner'

Before finding out exactly what you have to offer, most new customers are going to need a little reassurance that your company is the 'right' kind of company to be dealing with. Think of it as being a bit like dating. In exactly the way a young single person is looking for a perfect life-partner, so too a customer is seeking a perfect business partner; for instance, one that has an established track record, is financially secure, or is of a certain size, reputation and standing. That's why during the opening phase of the sale it's wise to say a few words to introduce your company. Simply highlight those aspects of dealing with your company that you feel will be of greatest appeal to your new customer. In other words, treat it as an opportunity to build some rapport between you. Most importantly, keep your company introduction brief and well rehearsed so that it trips easily off the tongue. For example, if you were selling to a local, family-owned business, you might say something like this:

> *We're a family-owned business with a reputation for taking great pride in what we do, and we've been based in Weatherfield for over 10 years now ... very much like your own company, Michael.*

Insight

When telling the customer about your company, make sure you do it with enthusiasm!

Bear in mind that from a customer's point of view your company is not the sum total of the business partnership under consideration. As your company's salesperson, you yourself also come as part and parcel of the package on offer! So, after introducing your company it usually pays to say a few extra words of self-introduction. This should not be too elaborate. Just a couple of well-chosen sentences that will serve to further influence their initial perception of your company and its people as being the 'right' kind of business partner. For example, you might simply say something like this:

> *... and as for myself, I'm in my fourth year with the company. Currently I have over 90 satisfied customers in the Weatherfield region with whom I work very closely on a regular basis.*

In giving a customer a little background information about yourself, always stick to the facts and resist the temptation to be even remotely boastful about your achievements. In exactly the same way as when introducing your company, your aim is simply to highlight what it is about yourself that is likely to be of greatest appeal to your new customer.

5 Build STAR-quality rapport

The term 'rapport' refers to a feeling of personal warmth between you and your customer. If you can build some degree of rapport early on in your sales presentation, then it makes it easy to develop even more as the conversation unfolds. This is important because ultimately, customers only want to do business with someone who they think is an 'OK' person and with whom they feel comfortable. Using the word STAR as an acronym, you can become an effective rapport-builder simply by going through the following four-step rapport-building routine with every new customer you meet:

Insight
People buy people first, and products and services second!

S = SMILE AT YOUR CUSTOMER

A smile, as they say, really is the shortest distance between two people! A relaxed and smiling face lightens the atmosphere and makes you much more friendly and approachable. However, make sure that in putting a smile on your face you do so with sincerity.

A smile that comes from the heart will signal to your new customer that you have a genuine interest in him or her as a person.

T = TELL YOUR CUSTOMER SOMETHING ABOUT YOURSELF

The sooner you let your new customer know a little about who you are on a personal level – something about your background, such as where you were born, where you went to school, or where you live – the sooner they will be able to relate to you as a human being and not 'just another' salesperson. Also, they will be more likely to feel some measure of obligation to tell you a little about themselves in return.

A = ASK YOUR CUSTOMER SOMETHING ABOUT THEMSELVES

Enquire about some aspect of your customer's life: their place of birth, family members, favourite holiday destination, interests and pastimes and so on. However, make sure you do so with as much genuine interest as you can muster. A sure-fire way to kill the sale before you even start is to appear to be just going through the motions of making some small talk without really caring about what your customer is saying.

R = RELATE TO YOUR CUSTOMER

The real key to being able to build great rapport is to find something, anything at all, that you have in common with your new customer. It might be that you share mutual friends or contacts, mutual sporting interests or a mutual love of the arts. It doesn't really matter what it is just as long as it's something that builds a bridge of understanding that you are indeed similar people in some way.

Although extreme care should be taken not to spend too much time giving your customers the STAR treatment, don't underestimate the effectiveness of this simple little rapport-building routine. The trick is to weave it into your initial conversation with each customer and in such a way that it comes across as a natural part of your communication style.

6 Qualify your customer

Have you ever gone through your entire sales presentation only to find out that the person you've been talking to is not the true decision-maker? When this happens, not only is it extremely frustrating but it also means you've wasted a lot of time and risked compromising your professional credibility.

Well, if it's any consolation, I'd wager there are few salespeople who haven't learned the hard way that no matter how well you pre-qualify your prospect as a bona fide customer before setting up an appointment, you should always go through the process of qualifying him or her again when you get there. The fact is, in business-to-business selling there are usually a number of questions well worth asking once you've met up with your customer face-to-face. Here are some example questions to get you thinking:

> *Once we've concluded our discussions today ...*

> *... providing everything is to your complete satisfaction, can you tell me if you're the person who is able to make the final decision?*

> *... what is your role exactly?*

> *... would anyone else be involved?*

… what is their role?

… would it be helpful if we included them in our meeting today?

… how does your company's decision-making process work?

… what would be your next step?

The crucial question, and normally the first question you must ask, relates to whether or not the person in front of you has decision-making authority. If the answer is unequivocally in the affirmative, then you probably won't need to ask many more qualifying questions. If, on the other hand, you receive a guarded or negative response, then you'll have to find out more by asking some or even all of the above questions.

Insight

Before proceeding with your sales presentation, check *your new* customer has the necessary purchasing authority.

Some salespeople worry that by asking such questions they risk offending their customer by implying that he or she might not have sufficient seniority to make a purchase decision. Others doubt the wisdom of asking these questions at all for fear of providing their customer with a ready-made 'escape route' before the meeting even gets started. However, unless you know for sure that the person you've gone to see has sole decision-making authority, the reality is that you can't afford *not* to ask them. By all means, be as tactful as you can with regard to the manner in which you ask your questions, but don't leave these issues hanging in the air because they're not going to go away. You know it and your customer knows it. Indeed, most customers will respect you for tackling these issues up front. Better still, it's precisely because you ask them that they'll be more likely to perceive you as the kind of salesperson who has the experience, industry knowledge and confidence they're looking for. It's what a customer expects of a professional salesperson.

7 Take control of your selling space

Providing you visit your customers at their place of business, at some point within the first few minutes of the opening phase of the sale it is always necessary to make an assessment of the space the customer has set aside for your meeting. Is it going to be conducive to carrying out your presentation and is there anything you should do to improve it?

In carrying out your assessment there are all sorts of environmental factors to look out for, all of which could seriously compromise your chances of delivering a great sales presentation. For example, is there going to be sufficient privacy for your customer? Does it look as though there is going to be a lot of background activity or noise that will be distracting for your customer? Will there be enough desk or table-top space available? Is the seating arranged to your liking? Will it be too warm or too cold to be comfortable, and will there be sufficient ventilation and lighting?

Insight

Ensure that the space your customer has set aside for the meeting will be suitable for your purposes.

If, having scanned your selling space, you decide it is not as good as it could be, then you should move quickly to do something about it before proceeding with your sales presentation. This is not a time to be faint-hearted! Simply go right ahead and suggest to the customer how you think the conditions for your meeting could be improved, perhaps by rearranging some furniture, opening a window, turning on the lights or whatever. If necessary you could even suggest moving to an adjacent office or ask if there is another room available that would be more suitable. For example, you might say:

Since we're going to be exchanging a lot of commercially sensitive information, is there another office we could use that would give us some privacy?

As long as you put it in such a way that you are obviously showing care and consideration for your customer and acting as much in their best interests as your own, they will usually be only too happy to let you take control of your selling space in this way. In fact, most customers will appreciate your candour and it will probably have the effect of enhancing their perception of your professionalism.

Sometimes your customers will be well versed in the art of 'persuasive buying'. This is something of a double-edged sword. On the one hand it means the space set aside for your meeting will undoubtedly be functional and adequate for your purposes – they will have made sure of that. On the other hand, it also means they will have 'stage-managed' it to their advantage. Commonly referred to as the use of 'territory power', I'm talking about a customer's deliberate use of the familiar surroundings of their office to undermine a salesperson's aspiration levels and to play on any insecurities they might be feeling about their prices being 'too high'. Here's a typical scenario:

Example

As you walk into the customer's office he or she stands up to greet you from behind a huge, expensive-looking desk before sitting back down on a plush swivel chair. In the meantime, you are invited to be seated on the only other chair in the room across the desk. It's a small chair that's less than comfortable, and puts you on a lower level

(Contd)

> than your customer. Then, as the conversation begins, you notice that he or she is silhouetted against a large window, which makes it very difficult to see the detail of their facial expressions. What's more, you can't help but notice that their desk is littered with your competitors' brochures and price lists ...

Clearly, this sort of situation is designed to intimidate and the customer has purposely left you with very little scope, if any, for influencing your selling environment. So it's important to be able to recognize the use of territory power for what it is and not to let it faze you. It's a buying tactic that only works if you let it, which is why the best way to counter it is to ignore it. While under such circumstances you might not be able to take control of your selling space, you can, at least, control your reaction to it.

Skill acquisition exercise

Imagine the ideal setting in which you would like to be able to conduct all your sales presentations and develop a mental checklist of your 'must have' requirements. Decide how you intend to communicate this to your customers whenever it becomes necessary.

8 Use an appropriate attention-grabber

Would you like to double your sales in the next twelve months?

Have you ever heard of an attention-grabber? Yes, you're right. I just used one! Admittedly it was not a very original one perhaps, but nonetheless it was an attention-grabber.

Just about every model of selling states that before you can sell anything to anybody you must first get their undivided attention. So an 'attention-grabber' is a device for doing just that. Here's an example:

Example

Tom sells refrigerated display cabinets to small convenience stores. He walks into a store and introduces himself to the owner, then takes a 1 m^2 piece of folded-up fluorescent yellow paper out of his inside pocket and proceeds to unfold it, fold by fold, in front of the store owner. Then he puts it down on the floor by the counter and gets the owner to stand on it, before asking a question that goes something like this:

Tell me, how would you like that spare piece of floor space you're standing on to earn you an extra £3500 next year?

So let's take a closer look at the main types of attention-grabber that are typically used by top salespeople. As you can see, your choice of an appropriate attention grabber is limited only by your imagination:

▶ *a benefit-loaded question*

How would you like to cut your telephone bill by up to 45 per cent next month?

▶ *a striking factual statement*

Did you know that, according to the latest government statistics …

- ▶ *a reference to someone they know*

  Fred Smith from the XYZ Company suggested I should see you because …

- ▶ *a reference to a news item*

  Congratulations! I see from this month's trade magazine that your company has just won a big export order …

- ▶ *an unexpected gift*

  On behalf of the ABC Corporation please accept this small gift … it's yours to keep with our compliments …

- ▶ *an unusual photograph or exhibit of some kind*

  Take a look at this …

- ▶ *a dramatic mini-demonstration*

  Here … drop this piece of our super-strength shatterproof glass and watch it bounce …

In choosing to use an attention-grabber, always remember that it must be both *appropriate* to the nature of your product or service and *credible* to your target customers. For example, if you sell merchant banking services to company directors in the boardroom then it would hardly be appropriate to use an attention-grabber that was too 'flashy' or too rich in entertainment value. Another important consideration is that you must plan ahead. Just as with any other selling tool, the success with which you deploy an attention-grabber will always be dependent on a flawless execution – and that can only be achieved by meticulous planning, preparation and rehearsal.

Skill acquisition exercise

Devise an appropriate attention-grabber that you could use at a certain point during the opening phase of your sales presentation. Practise carrying it out.

9 Set an agenda

You have just met your prospective customer. You've introduced
yourself and made a good first impression. Next, you've
been through the ritual of chatting a little and have taken the
opportunity of building some rapport. So now what? Well, now
is the time to take control of the conversation by providing the
customer with a 'road-map' of how you intend to proceed. In other
words, you should suggest an outline agenda for the meeting and
get the customer's agreement to it so that you can get started in
a businesslike way. There's no need for anything too elaborate.
Simply say you'd like to cover this, then that, and so on, in order
to make the best use of your time together. For example, you could
say something like this:

> *Susan, I want to make sure that we make the very best use of
> the time we've set aside for our meeting today. So I'd like to
> start off by asking you a few questions to find out all about
> you and your requirements. Then providing I think we can
> help, I'd like to explore with you exactly how we could go
> about doing that ... does that sound OK to you?*

Insight

At an appropriate point during the opening phase of the sale,
provide the customer with a 'road-map' of what you intend
to cover during the rest of the meeting.

If you sell a highly customized and/or a particularly complex
product or service, it might be preferable to provide your customer
with a pre-prepared written agenda that itemizes all the key topics
for discussion. At the appropriate time you simply hand it to your
customer while saying something like this:

> *Since we have a lot of items to discuss today, I've taken the
> liberty of preparing a brief outline agenda ... please Susan ...
> take a moment to read through it and let me know if you
> think it looks OK ...*

Setting an agenda for your meeting with a customer has a number of advantages. Not only does it come across as being highly professional but it also provides you with an element of control throughout the rest of the meeting so that whenever necessary you are able to refer back to it and move things along to the next stage.

10 Size up your customer

In business-to-business selling, the vast majority of customers will fall into one of two broad categories: 'purchase maximizers' or 'purchase satisficers'.

A purchase maximizer is the kind of customer who is always aiming to get as near as is humanly possible to making a 'perfect' purchase. As such, these types of customers will typically hold a full-time buying position with a job title that reflects this responsibility, such as 'Chief Buyer', 'Purchasing Officer' or 'Procurement Manager'. A purchase satisficer, on the other hand, is a very different animal. As the term implies, this kind of customer is only really aiming to make a purchase that's good enough (will *suffice* to *satisfy* their requirements). As long as a product or service is going to do a good job in serving its purpose, they're happy. These types of customers will usually have only an occasional responsibility for buying because it's just something else they do as and when required, alongside their everyday responsibilities. As such, purchase satisficers will typically hold a senior position within their company with a job title such as 'Managing Director', 'Company Director' or 'Owner-Manager'.

Insight

Correctly 'sizing up' the customer enables you to adapt the content and delivery style of your presentation accordingly – and to maximum effect.

Figure A encapsulates the very essence of the differences between the buying styles of these two customer types. The purchase maximizer will spend more time researching their options and deliberating over their decision. They'll place a higher priority on facts and figures and on using a rigorous, systematic decision-making process. They'll tend to be more measured, quietly spoken and analytical. By contrast, a purchase satisficer will spend less time collecting information. They'll quickly make up their minds, relying more on trusting their instincts and sense of judgement than anything else. They'll tend to be more talkative, forceful and opinionated.

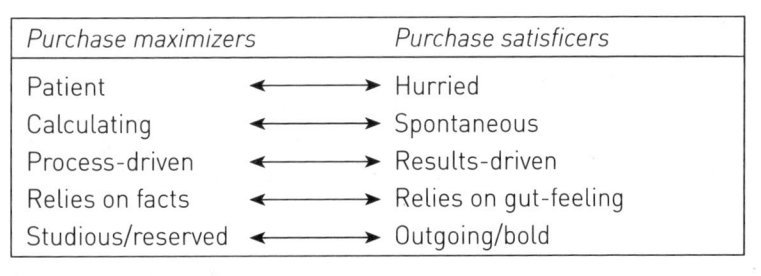

Purchase maximizers		Purchase satisficers
Patient	←——→	Hurried
Calculating	←——→	Spontaneous
Process-driven	←——→	Results-driven
Relies on facts	←——→	Relies on gut-feeling
Studious/reserved	←——→	Outgoing/bold

Figure A. Customer buying styles.

Clearly, these two types of customer have completely different buying styles, so in order to be able to sell to each type effectively you're going to have to size up your customer and adapt your selling style accordingly, as shown in Figure B.

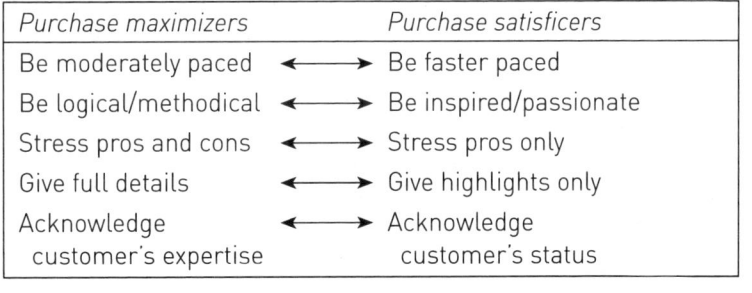

Purchase maximizers		Purchase satisficers
Be moderately paced	←——→	Be faster paced
Be logical/methodical	←——→	Be inspired/passionate
Stress pros and cons	←——→	Stress pros only
Give full details	←——→	Give highlights only
Acknowledge customer's expertise	←——→	Acknowledge customer's status

Figure B. Appropriate selling styles.

For a purchase maximizer, you should aim to come across as the kind of salesperson who is 'the controlled, cool-headed thinker'. This means your manner is going to be rational, deliberate and methodical. Using a calm, moderated speaking voice you're going to deliver a detailed, factual and well-balanced but persuasive sales presentation that clearly acknowledges their technical knowledge and expertise.

By contrast, for a purchase satisficer, you should aim to come across as 'the expressive, quick-witted straightshooter' kind of salesperson. This means your manner is going to be more animated, warm and engaging, and using a brisk, matter-of-fact speaking voice, you're going to deliver a no-frills sales presentation that clearly accommodates your customer's 'must have' purchase goals.

What I'm suggesting is that there's no such thing as a one-size-fits-all selling style – at least not one that's going to be effective anything close to 100 per cent of the time.

Skill acquisition exercise

Prepare and rehearse two variations of your sales presentation that differ in both their content and in your delivery style: one that is tailored to suit purchase maximizers, the other tailored to suit purchase satisficers.

10 THINGS TO REMEMBER

1 *Go through a set-up routine.*

2 *Project your professionalism.*

3 *Do the handshake one-two-three-four.*

4 *Introduce your company as a 'perfect partner'.*

5 *Build STAR-quality rapport.*

6 *Qualify your customer.*

7 *Take control of your selling space.*

8 *Use an appropriate attention-grabber.*

9 *Set an agenda.*

10 *Size up your customer.*

2

Interviewing-phase selling skills

In this chapter you will learn:

- *how to find out all about the customer's specific needs and wants, and uncover the key benefits that they are really looking for*

Opening phase
Set the scene for a businesslike and mutually beneficial conversation to take place between you and the customer.

↓

Interviewing phase
Find out all about the customer's specific needs and wants, and uncover the key benefits that they are really looking for.

↓

Matching phase
Match the customer's needs and wants as closely as possible to the benefits of your product or service offer.

↓

Closing phase
Get the customer's agreement to go ahead, and leave them feeling positive about their purchase decision.

↓

Objection-handling phase
Handle the customer's objection to their complete satisfaction and, if possible, turn it around into a closing opportunity.

11 Ask plenty of open-style questions

If there is one characteristic shared by just about every customer on the planet, it is their need to feel that a salesperson thoroughly understands their purchase situation. Experienced salespeople fully appreciate this and always take their time to interview each customer about every aspect of their individual requirements. They know that the quickest way to kill a sale is to start trying to sell their product or service prematurely, without having first made an effort to really understand their customer's requirements.

It's only by asking open-style questions that you can find out about a customer – what sort of person they are, their needs and wants, hopes and fears, and their vision of the future. To put it another way, it's only by asking open-style questions that you are able to unlock the detailed information you're going to need in order to satisfy a customer and make a sale. In interviewing a customer, there are a number of different open-style questions to employ.

THE SIX 'CLASSIC' INFORMATION-SEEKERS

There are six 'classic' open questions, and the easiest way to remember them is to refer to Rudyard Kipling's famous verse from *The Elephant's Child*:

> **I keep six honest serving-men**
> **(They taught me all I knew);**
> **Their names are What and Why and When**
> **And How and Where and Who.**

So, the six 'classic' open and information-seeking questions are simply those that start with *what, why, when, how, where* or *who*, because they demand a full and expansive answer. Examples include:

- ▶ *What are your key buying criteria?*
- ▶ *Why is that so important to you?*
- ▶ *When will the new factory be completed?*

- *How reliable is your existing system?*
- *Where are you going to relocate your workshop?*
- *Who is involved in operating your machines?*

THE 'DIRECT-REQUEST' METHOD

This style of open questioning requires that you make a 'direct request' for certain information. The beauty of this method is that it focuses the interview on a specific topic area of your choice. Here are some examples:

- *Tell me more about ...*
- *Describe to me ...*
- *Explain to me ...*
- *Give me an example of ...*

THE 'INSTANT-REPLAY' TECHNIQUE

This is when you repeat back to your customer, like an 'instant-replay', a key word or phrase they have just used, but with a quizzical upward inflection in your voice so as to indicate that you would like them to tell you more. For example:

> **Customer:** *I'm concerned about the safety issues ...*
> **Salesperson:** *The safety issues ... ?* (quizzical voice inflection)

THE 'FILL-IN-THE-BLANKS' APPROACH

Using an enquiring tone of voice, this is when you deliberately encourage the customer to 'fill-in-the-blanks' and tell you more about the topic at hand by using the following types of 'tag on' words and phrases to feed off something that's just been said:

- *Which is ... ?*
- *Such as ... ?*
- *And so ... ?*
- *And then ... ?*
- *Because of ... ?*

Although each of the four open-style questioning methods above is powerful in its own right, the real key to effective interviewing is to use a combination of them as necessary. For example, if your customer seems a little timid or reserved, then you need to ask an easy-to-answer 'classic' open question to get them talking more freely. If, on the other hand, he or she has a tendency to ramble, then a 'direct-request' for more information on a specific point will help to keep the conversation focused. If a customer is being a little evasive or unforthcoming on a particular issue, however, then an 'instant-replay' question or a 'fill-in-the-blanks' style of question can be a good way to force their hand and find out what is really on their mind.

Skill acquisition exercise

Using as wide a range of open-style questions as you possibly can, interview a friend or colleague about their favourite hobby or pastime. Continue this exercise until you begin to acquire the habit of using various combinations of open-style questions that draw from them more and more about it, and from every conceivable angle.

12 Trigger your customer's imagination

Cast your mind back to the last time you made a major purchase of some kind – perhaps a decision to buy a new home or to go on the holiday of a lifetime. Now ask yourself this: before making your decision, isn't it true that you allowed yourself the luxury of imagining just how good it would feel once you owned that new home or were actually on that holiday? Of course you did! That's why one of the skills of professional selling is an ability to help your customers to engage their own imagination.

Insight

You can trigger your customer's imagination simply by asking a question that requires him or her to step out of reality and be creative.

Here are three examples showing the types of questions you can ask and the words and phrases you can use to trigger your customer's imagination:

▶ *Imagine the perfect xxx machine had been up and running in your factory since the start of the year. Let me ask you, in what ways do you think you'd have benefited from it so far?*

▶ *Just pretend the perfect xxx service is already in place right now. Tell me, what unnecessary work would it eliminate for you and your staff?*

▶ *Let's say it's the end of the financial year and with the help of the perfect xxx system you've actually achieved your projected sales target on budget. May I ask, what would that mean to you personally?*

A popular approach is to package your question using the 'Let's assume … What happened …?' format. This is a great technique because it accommodates just about any type of product or service, and once you've asked it, there's only one place your customer can go to come up with an answer: their imagination. Here's how it goes:

Let's assume *you've already owned the perfect xxxx for the last 12 months.* **What happened** *during that 12 month period to convince you it was a good buy?*

In triggering your customer's imagination the key is to ask them to assume ownership of your product or service and to live out the benefits in the theatre of their mind – a place which is full of the possibilities of how good life could be once they've made the decision to buy. The moment your customer starts to imagine a world in which they already own your product or service then you can be sure your job will have instantly become a lot easier.

Skill acquisition exercise

Devise a question that you would feel comfortable asking which would enable you to successfully trigger your customer's imagination. Work out the exact phrasing. Memorize and rehearse it.

13 Use closed questions with pinpoint precision

A 'closed question' is a form of question that demands only a one-word answer – usually a 'yes' or a 'no'. As such, it's a very specialized form of question that should always be used with great care during a sales interview. By forcing a customer into giving you only a one-word answer, you are preventing a flowing two-way conversation from taking place. Worse still, the injudicious use of closed questions can easily lead to too many 'nos'. Not that the odd 'no' is necessarily a bad thing, but as a general rule too many 'nos' introduces a disproportionate amount of negativity and this can have the effect of 'freezing you out' of a sale.

Used correctly, however, closed questions can be an extremely effective selling tool. It's just a matter of knowing when and how to use them with pinpoint precision. Let's take a closer look at the two main types of closed question.

THE STRAIGHT CLOSED QUESTION

This is the type of closed question that starts with a verb conjugated in the affirmative. Here are some examples:

- *Are you … ?*
- *Can you … ?*
- *Could you … ?*
- *Do you … ?*
- *Would you … ?*
- *Have you … ?*
- *Will you … ?*
- *Is it … ?*
- *Does it … ?*
- *Are there … ?*

This type of closed question is called 'straight' because it's a totally unbiased and genuine question that simply aims to establish either a 'yes' or a 'no' response. The beauty of asking a few well-chosen straight closed questions is that they can provide you with a lot of factual information in a very efficient and authoritative manner, while at the same time giving you the necessary feedback to be able to steer the subject matter of a conversation in an appropriate direction. Take, for example, the question: 'Do you have any particular colour preferences?' If the customer replies 'no' then you have succeeded in establishing an important fact, enabling you to refocus and direct your next question to some other aspect of their requirement. If, however, the customer says 'yes', then obviously you will need to immediately follow up with a line of open questions in order to find out exactly what colour(s) he or she prefers, for what reasons, and so on.

Insight

When used at the right time and in the right way, closed questions can be an extremely effective selling tool.

THE LOADED CLOSED QUESTION

It's a good idea to get as many 'yes' responses as possible from a customer during the course of a sales presentation, *isn't it?* It works really well to build a sort of 'staircase of agreement' between you, *doesn't it*? In fact, I'm building one now, *aren't I*? What's more, you can see exactly how I'm doing it, *can't you*? I'm making a positive statement and then seeking to wrap up your agreement by tagging on to the end of it a verb conjugated in the negative. Otherwise known as the 'wrap-up' technique, this is a classic method of asking a loaded closed question. However, I could have sought to wrap up your agreement just as easily by putting the verb at the beginning of each statement instead of at the end. I could have said: *Isn't it* a good idea to get as many 'yes' responses as possible from a customer? or *Doesn't it* work really well to build a sort of 'staircase of agreement' between you?

Examples of loaded closed questions include:

Aren't you ... ?	or	... aren't you?
Can't you ... ?	or	... can't you?
Couldn't you ...?	or	... couldn't you?
Don't you ... ?	or	... don't you?
Wouldn't you ... ?	or	... wouldn't you?
Haven't you ... ?	or	... haven't you?
Won't you ... ?	or	... won't you?
Isn't it ... ?	or	... isn't it?
Doesn't it ... ?	or	... doesn't it?
Aren't there ... ?	or	... aren't there?

This type of closed question is 'loaded' because it is deliberately designed to elicit a 'yes' response. So, they're a great way to cement the customer's agreement to minor points as you go through the interviewing phase of your sales presentation and beyond. However, don't be too trigger-happy in using them. They may come across as somewhat manipulative and controlling in nature, which means they can very easily irritate the customer. One loaded closed question too many at the wrong time and the whole tone of a conversation may quickly turn from being warm and co-operative to very cold and confrontational. The trick is to use them sparingly and, most importantly, only ever at those times when you can sense sufficient positive stimuli coming back from the customer to feel confident that he or she is likely to respond with genuine agreement.

Skill acquisition exercise

Decide upon the exact wording of a number of (a) straight closed questions, and (b) loaded closed questions, that you could usefully employ during the interviewing phase of your sales presentation.

14 Employ the SPOTS interviewing framework

Just as a chat show host on radio or TV needs to have prepared a list of meaningful questions to ask their guest before 'going live', so it is for you as a salesperson. There is no substitute for a well-prepared, well-structured interview with a line of questioning that starts off with a few general questions and then follows up with more searching 'piggybacked' questions that feed off the answers given and become increasingly focused on your customer's particular buying situation.

Insight
The sequencing, quality and relevance of your questions will always reveal to the customer your level of experience and expertise as a sales professional in your industry.

One way of planning the scope and sequencing of your questions is to employ the SPOTS interviewing framework. SPOTS stands for:

▶ *Situation*
▶ *Problem*
▶ *Opportunity*

- *Threat*
- *Summary.*

The idea is to develop a number of key questions in each area before moving on to the next.

S = SITUATION

Situation questions enable you to gain a thorough understanding of all relevant background information relating to the customer's current situation. For example:

What quality control systems do you use at the moment?

P = PROBLEM

Problem questions enable you to identify any worries, problems, difficulties or 'pain' the customer is experiencing. For example:

How well is your current system performing?

O = OPPORTUNITY

Opportunity questions enable you to find out what the customer's ideal situation would be and how he or she would benefit from solving their problem. For example:

What level of improvement do you see as being achievable?

T = THREAT

Threat questions enable you to explore the downstream consequences and implications of the customer continuing on their current path without taking any action whatsoever. For example:

How will quality control affect your company's ability to compete in your new export markets?

S = SUMMARY

Summary questions enable you to gain the customer's agreement to your understanding of their needs and wants, and benefits sought. For example:

So as I understand it, what you need is xxx in order that you can xxx. Have I got that right?

Skill acquisition exercise

Using the SPOTS framework, brainstorm with one or more of your colleagues or friends to develop a sequence of questions that will encourage your customers to talk freely and tell you all about their requirements.

15 Mirror the customer's 'personal vocabulary'

Most of us use a vocabulary of about 2,500 words in our everyday conversations. Although we think of the vast majority of these words as being nothing more than 'just a word', a few become especially significant to us. Certain words and phrases take on a special significance because at some point in our lives, and for some good reason, they have become associated with a particular emotion, and that association has become ingrained. While these words and phrases are not necessarily special to anyone else, they are to us. In short, the importance we attach to these words and phrases helps to define us as the unique individuals that we are.

In the world of professional selling, any words or phrases that seem to hold a special significance for a customer are referred to as their 'personal vocabulary'. It's a sort of language-within-a-language that you should tune in to with every new customer. In so doing, your customers will feel as though you better appreciate and understand them and you will also experience a greater sense of customer rapport.

Insight

The more you can talk the customer's language, the more you'll be enhancing the quality of your interpersonal communications.

There are three main types of personal vocabulary to pick up on and 'mirror' back to a customer as your sales presentation unfolds:

▶ *'pet' words*
▶ *favourite sayings*
▶ *industry buzz-words and jargon.*

So that you can be sure of exactly what I'm talking about, let's consider a few examples of each type:

'PET' WORDS

Most customers have at least one or two favourite words. Typically, they're easily recognizable if for no other reason than how often we hear a customer use them! However, another tell-tale sign is that they're often slightly unusual words. Here's an example:

Example

I had been with a prospective customer for just a few minutes when it became apparent that one of his pet words was 'acknowledge'. He wanted to 'acknowledge' the fact that his business was losing market share and to 'acknowledge' that the time had come to hire-in some

(Contd)

marketing expertise. Having picked up on his pet word, I was then able to use it myself on a number of occasions during our conversation. In particular, when I got around to summing up the customer's needs I was able to say 'you acknowledge that ...'

Sometimes, a customer's pet word isn't a real word at all but one that he or she has made up. In these cases don't correct or question your customer's use of this word. As long as the meaning behind the word is entirely understandable then there's no reason why you shouldn't use it yourself. For example:

Example

Steve sells specialist computer systems to retailers. He once told me the story of a customer who said he wanted to 'electronify' his stock control records. Steve knew that what the retailer really meant was to 'computerize' his stock control system, but wisely chose to use the customer's made-up word from that point onwards in his sales presentation.

FAVOURITE SAYINGS

If you notice that a customer is particularly fond of a certain saying, such as 'time flies', or 'as sure as night follows day', then use these terms yourself as the sale progresses. In fact, because sayings often carry a message of universal truth, they can be especially useful as a sales tool – made all the more powerful because you can be sure your choice of language will resonate loud and clear with your customer. For example:

INDUSTRY BUZZ-WORDS AND JARGON

Every industry has its own buzz-words and jargon. For example, in the advertising industry people talk about 'advertorials', 'advergaming', 'psychographics' and 'IMCs', to mention but a few. This type of language signifies that the person using it is an industry 'insider' with special knowledge. For this reason, some salespeople believe they should use a lot of these words. Certainly, they should be familiar with them. However, more often than not a salesperson's gratuitous use of this kind of lingo has a negative effect on a customer because it is seen merely as an attempt to impress. That's why the best time to use a particular buzz-word or piece of industry jargon is when you notice your customer is in the habit of using it as part of their own 'personal vocabulary'. When you observe this simple rule, it becomes a rapport-maker instead of a rapport breaker.

16 Signal your questions

Have you ever noticed how the top current affairs journalists and other professional interviewers on radio or TV have a tendency to 'signal' their questions immediately prior to asking them? For example, they commonly use the most basic form of signalling, which is simply to indicate that they are about to ask a question by using a phrase such as:

- ▶ *Let me ask you ...*
- ▶ *Tell me ...*
- ▶ *My next question is ...*
- ▶ *I'd like to ask you ...*
- ▶ *Another question is ...*
- ▶ *May I ask you ...*

Alternatively, they may signal their questions by telling their interviewee what topic they are going to ask about next. For example:

- ▶ *Let's turn now to the question of globalization ...*

Sometimes they signal a question by alerting their interviewee to the advantage of answering a particular question by saying something like this:

- ▶ *I want to give you the opportunity to publicly state your position on this issue ...*

Similarly, they might signal a question by referring to its importance. For example:

- ▶ *One question that's of immense public interest at the moment is ...*

Insight

Professional interviewers always take the time to 'signal' to their interviewee that they're about to ask another question.

When a particular question is right at the heart of the matter, then as a means of adding further emphasis you'll often hear a professional interviewer double-signal or even triple-signal a question. In other words, they might use a combination of two or three different signals in their build-up to asking a certain question. Here's an example of a double and then a triple-signalled question:

▶ *Let me ask you* [first signal] *one question that's of immense public interest at the moment* [second signal] ...
▶ *Let's turn now to the question of globalization* [first signal]. *I want to give you the opportunity to publicly state your position on this issue* [second signal]; *tell me* [third signal] ...

As a professional salesperson, you should do exactly the same when interviewing a customer about their needs and wants, and for good reason. Signalling provides your customer with a sense of context and helps them to focus on the question at hand. It also serves as a 'signpost' to lead your customer smoothly through the interviewing phase of your sales presentation, promoting a crystal clear exchange of information. As long as you don't dilute its effects by over-using any one phrase, you'll soon discover signalling can be an effective communication tool that gives you a greater degree of authority during your sales interviews.

Skill acquisition exercise

Identify all the key topics that you cover during the course of your sales interviews. Determine the exact words you could use to signal your intention to question your customers in each of these areas.

17 Listen actively

The flip-side of asking questions is listening to the answers given. In fact, listening actively rather than passively (showing that you are listening rather than giving a deadpan response) is every bit as important as asking questions.

Being an active listener means making the effort to show that you are comprehending and interested in what is being said. This is a basic skill all salespeople should master because when customers are talking about themselves and their business, to them it's the most important subject under the sun. Active listening demonstrates concern, builds trust and helps reduce any 'sales resistance'. Moreover, it turns you into a brilliant conversationalist. After all, it's often said that people who want to talk about themselves are boring, but people who want to talk about me are brilliant conversationalists!

Insight
Whenever customers are talking about themselves and their business, to them it's the most important subject under the sun.

You can become an expert 'active listener' by acquiring the habit of using the following techniques to show the customer you are listening carefully:

PROVIDE PLENTY OF BRIEF VERBAL FEEDBACK

Use small utterances that encourage the customer to keep on talking but without interrupting their flow. For example:

- *Hmm*
- *Ah-ah*
- *Huh-huh*
- *I see*
- *Oh really*
- *I understand.*

PROVIDE PLENTY OF NON-VERBAL FEEDBACK

Use your eyes, face and body language to show the customer you're interested in what's being said. For example, nod, smile, tilt your head, stroke your chin, lean forward and so on.

PERIODICALLY PARAPHRASE AND RESTATE

Use summary statements and restatements to check your level of understanding and comprehension. For example:

So if I understand correctly, what you're saying is ...

ASK REACTIVE QUESTIONS

Use thoughtful and reflective open questions to request clarification or further information whenever appropriate. For example:

- ▶ *How do you mean, exactly?*
- ▶ *Tell me more about that ...*

Before asking a reactive question, a good tip is to count to three silently to yourself. This creates a short pause which indicates to your customer that you have been listening attentively and given due consideration to your next question.

TAKE NOTES

Making notes not only helps you to concentrate on what's being said but it also reinforces your role as a problem-solver. However, be sure to ask your customer's permission before taking any notes. For example, you might say:

I have some more questions about that. To ensure I don't miss anything would you mind if I take notes?

Then, subsequently, whenever you want to stop to make some notes you can say:

Thanks, that's most helpful ... just give me a moment and I'll make a note of it.

Finally, remember to listen with your brain at all times – and not just with your ears! In other words, learn to listen to what the customer does not say. For example, listen for hesitations and omissions, or words tinged with sarcasm or insincerity, and try to understand the true meaning behind the actual words being spoken.

18 Read your customer's body language

Face-to-face communication always has two components – the audible and the inaudible. The audible component relates to what people say and the words they use. It is the spoken language of communication. The inaudible component, on the other hand, relates to the unspoken 'silent' messages conveyed through the 'body language' of facial expressions, gestures, eye contact, body posture, hand, arm and leg movements, and so on.

Most experts agree that since the majority of signals communicated through a person's body language happen spontaneously and at a subconscious level, they are likely to be a more accurate representation of what someone is really thinking than what they might actually be telling you verbally. So, being able to read your customer's body language is a vital selling skill. You can use it to get some sense of your customer's underlying mood and to gain greater insight into what they are really thinking. You can also use it to help minimize any ambiguity or misunderstandings and to provide for a greater clarity of information exchange.

Insight
Body language is likely to be a more accurate representation of what someone is really thinking than what they might be telling you verbally.

It is useful to think of the signals a customer communicates through their body language as being a bit like the signals on a set of traffic lights: there are green ones, amber ones and red ones.

GREEN SIGNALS

These signals indicate that your customer is fully engaged in and responding favourably to your sales presentation. Some classic examples of the main types of green signals to look out for are when your customer is:

▶ *sitting upright or leaning slightly forwards in their chair*
▶ *making lots of direct eye contact*
▶ *nodding periodically*
▶ *looking at you with a relaxed and pleasant facial expression*
▶ *stroking their chin in a thoughtful way*
▶ *sitting or standing relatively still while talking.*

So what should you do when observing 'code green' body language? Well, just keep on doing what you're doing because you're definitely going well and are on the right track!

AMBER SIGNALS

These signals suggest that your customer is a little unclear about some aspect of the conversation or perhaps a touch bored or even impatient with it. Examples of amber signals to look out for are when your customer:

▶ *begins to slump down in their chair or starts to lean slightly away from you*
▶ *blinks rapidly as if they are struggling to maintain mental focus*
▶ *has a blank or perplexed facial expression*
▶ *is doodling with their pen or fiddling with their bracelet or ring.*

So what should you do when observing 'code amber' body language? Well, clearly you need to proceed with great care because you're probably in danger of losing your customer's attention. Depending on the specific situation at hand, it might be appropriate to quickly move the conversation along to a different topic, suggest a stretch break, begin to signal your questions more clearly or to re-double your efforts as an active listener.

RED SIGNALS

These signals show that your customer is responding negatively to your sales presentation. They may have lost interest in it or even become disapproving of it. Some examples of red signals to look out for are when your customer:

▶ *shuffles in their chair so that their entire body is tilted away from you*
▶ *avoids making eye contact*
▶ *has a tense or frowning facial expression*
▶ *folds their arms across their chest*
▶ *crosses their legs in a direction that's away from you*
▶ *clenches their hands or starts to drum their fingers on the desktop.*

So what should you do when observing 'code red' body language? Well, you'll certainly need to act quickly and decisively because a total communication breakdown is imminent. This means you have little option but to stop your presentation dead in its tracks and let your customer know that you're well aware that there's a problem. Ask him or her what it is, apologize for anything untoward you might have inadvertently said or done, and do whatever it takes to re-establish rapport before continuing.

Please note that the key to learning to accurately read your customer's body language is to look out for a *pattern* of signals. Be aware that an isolated gesture is probably meaningless. As soon as you notice a number of signals occurring, however, especially when you can see that they are forming a familiar pattern, then it's time to act.

Select a TV channel featuring a serious interview. Hit the 'record' button and with the sound turned off try to sharpen your ability to read the body language of both the interviewee and interviewer. Then turn on the sound and replay the interview to see how well you've done.

19 Provide information-affirmation

Here's the story of how I learned about this powerful little selling skill:

Example

Many years ago I made an appointment to see a personal financial planner to help sort out my financial affairs. I arrived at his office at the agreed time, and after we had exchanged the usual pleasantries he explained to me that before he could work out a plan he would need to spend our first meeting interviewing me in some depth in order to gain a thorough understanding of my life situation, financial priorities and so on. Consequently, he began to fire away with a seemingly endless barrage of increasingly detailed and very personal questions. At first I didn't mind answering his questions. After all, it was in my interests to help him do his job. However, as time wore on, the intensity of his questioning and the feeling of being under a microscope started to take its toll on my patience and motivation levels. I even began to resent what seemed, at times, to be an almost gratuitous intrusion into some of

(Contd)

the most private areas of my life. So, after being on the receiving end of almost a full hour of relentless questioning, it was with great relief that the interview finally came to an end. Driving away from his office, I felt both exhausted and more than a little irritated. However, as I had a professional interest in the interviewing process itself, I reflected on our meeting and tried to make sense of my negative reaction to his technique. It certainly wasn't that the guy was a bad interviewer; in fact he'd been a great listener, had taken copious notes and had 'signalled' most of his questions. But something had been missing and, infuriatingly, I just couldn't put my finger on it.

A few months later when I was recounting my story to a friend, the penny finally dropped. There was one key skill, one facet of the financial planner's interviewing style, that was lacking that day. A skill that I've since realized is fundamental to any in-depth sales interview because it helps to keep a customer interested and motivated to answer questions: during a lengthy sales interview, you owe it to your customer to provide him or her with frequent 'information-affirmation', i.e. plenty of positive feedback about the value of the information you are being given.

It seems so obvious, doesn't it? But I am convinced that most salespeople routinely fail to appreciate the importance of providing their customers with this kind of feedback.

Insight

Providing information-affirmation is a key skill because it helps to motivate the customer to keep on answering your questions.

There are two types of information-affirmation that you can feed back to your customers – simple and complex. During the course of an interview you should aim to provide your customer with an appropriate and varied mix of both types.

SIMPLE INFORMATION-AFFIRMATION

Simple information-affirmations involve using a few stock phrases to acknowledge the value of the information you're receiving, such as:

- ▶ *Thanks, that's very interesting.*
- ▶ *Thanks, that's most helpful.*
- ▶ *Thanks, that's really useful.*
- ▶ *Thanks, that's extremely valuable.*

COMPLEX INFORMATION-AFFIRMATION

A complex information-affirmation is used more sparingly. It goes one step further than a simple information-affirmation in that it requires that you go on to give your customer a specific explanation or reason as to *why* you think their information is 'interesting', 'helpful', 'useful' or 'valuable'. You can turn a simple information-affirmation into a complex one just by adding the word 'because' and then filling in the blanks, like this:

- ▶ *Thanks, that's very useful, because …*
- ▶ *Thanks, that's most helpful, because …*
- ▶ *Thanks, that's really useful, because …*
- ▶ *Thanks, that's extremely valuable, because …*

At this point, if you're thinking to yourself 'that's all very well, but often my customers don't give me the quality of information I need', then please remember that poor information quality is not your customer's fault; it's your fault for not asking the right questions in the first place! To put it another way, as a professional salesperson it's your responsibility to ensure that you get the quality of information you need – and when you do you should always take the time to affirm it with gratitude, sincerity and enthusiasm.

20 Keep control of the interview

With some customers it's all too easy to find yourself losing control of the sale almost before you've had a chance to get started! I'm talking about the ones who just don't seem to want to be questioned about their needs and wants and instead seem determined to turn the tables on you by becoming your interview*er* rather than interview*ee*. As a young salesperson I can still remember dreading the thought of coming across these customers because I felt powerless to stop them from totally dominating the conversation, undermining my confidence and compromising my chances of making a sale. Then one day, quite by chance, I discovered the secret of controlling a sales interview. Here's what happened:

to see was this door-to-door salesperson. Sure enough though, he eventually started walking down my driveway carrying two huge suitcases full of his wares. So, in an effort to get rid of him as quickly as possible, I kicked open the garage door and shouted in my roughest and most aggressive-sounding tone of voice: 'What are you selling?' to which, with a twinkle in his eye and an extra spring in his step, he replied: 'What do you want?' Now as it happened, at that precise moment what I really wanted was a certain type of screwdriver to enable me to undo a particularly obstinate engine screw, and needless to say, he was able to sell one to me! Later on that morning as I drove to my appointment I reflected on his technique. I realized that by answering my question with a question he'd been able to sidestep almost certain rejection while at the same time putting himself in total control of the sale, and to my ultimate benefit. What a brilliant piece of selling!

Let's review the lessons I learned from that door-to-door salesperson. The first lesson is to understand that when two people are having a conversation, it's the person asking the questions who's actually in control of the subject matter of that conversation and *not* the one who's doing all the talking. The second lesson is to appreciate that the moment you find yourself beginning to lose control of a sales interview, you must immediately seize back the initiative by answering their question with a question. You should even be prepared to 'question wrestle' with your customer if that's what it takes. Yes, learning to execute this technique will feel a little uncomfortable (and even impolite) at first but it can and must be done, because the more a customer pushes you into assuming the role of an interviewee, the harder it becomes to re-establish an appropriate level of authority over the sale as the interviewer. Please note, however, that there is plenty of scope for delivering this technique with varying degrees of subtlety. If needs be, it can be softened considerably by adopting a friendly manner and providing your customer with a brief answer to their question prior to asking one back. For example, in a computer store:

Customer: *What sort of printers do you have in stock?*

Salesperson: *Well, we have an extremely wide range, Madam [big smile] ... tell me, what sort of printing do you want to be able to do?*

Insight

The moment you find yourself beginning to lose control of a sales interview you must immediately seize back the initiative by answering their questions with a question.

A third and final lesson is to realize that you won't be doing your customers any favours by allowing them to control your sales conversations. Look at it like this: if you haven't been able to find out all about their buying requirements, your customer is being deprived of the opportunity to take advantage of all your knowledge, experience and expertise in helping him or her to make the best possible purchase decision.

Skill acquisition exercise

Recall a previous sales conversation when you lost control by readily answering too many of the customer's questions. Now imagine yourself in the same situation in the future. What could you say to prevent this from happening again?

10 THINGS TO REMEMBER

1 *Ask plenty of open-style questions.*

2 *Trigger your customer's imagination.*

3 *Use closed questions with pinpoint precision.*

4 *Employ the SPOTS interviewing framework.*

5 *Mirror the customer's 'personal vocabulary'.*

6 *Signal your questions.*

7 *Listen actively.*

8 *Read your customer's body language.*

9 *Provide information-affirmation.*

10 *Keep control of the interview.*

3

Matching-phase selling skills

In this chapter you will learn:
- *how to match the customer's needs and wants as closely as possible to the benefits of your product or service offer*

Opening phase
Set the scene for a businesslike and mutually beneficial conversation to take place between you and the customer.

↓

Interviewing phase
Find out all about the customer's specific needs and wants, and uncover the key benefits that they are really looking for.

↓

Matching phase
Match the customer's needs and wants as closely as possible to the benefits of your product or service offer.

↓

Closing phase
Get the customer's agreement to go ahead, and leave them feeling positive about their purchase decision.

↓

Objection-handling phase
Handle the customer's objection to their complete satisfaction and, if possible, turn it around into a closing opportunity.

21 Apply the SELL formula

If there's one phrase that all salespeople should commit to memory it's got to be the three Bs: **Buyers Buy Benefits.**

As a professional salesperson you don't sell the *features* of your product or service, you sell the *benefits* that those features represent to the customer. Most customers' benefits relate to one or more of the following areas:

- ▶ *saving money*
- ▶ *making money*
- ▶ *saving time*
- ▶ *reducing effort*
- ▶ *obtaining peace of mind*
- ▶ *satisfying an ego*
- ▶ *experiencing sensory pleasure*
- ▶ *improving health*
- ▶ *exercising a social conscience*
- ▶ *achieving personal growth.*

So, whereas the term 'features' refers to the characteristics of your product or service, such as its level of quality or its technical configuration, the term 'benefits' refers to what the product or service can do for your customer.

Insight

Whereas a 'feature' answers the customer's question, 'What is it?', a 'benefit' answers the customer's question, 'What's in it for me?'

However, effective benefit selling does not mean that you emphasize the benefits of your product or service to the exclusion of mentioning features at all! In fact, describing selected features is important because they provide the means by which you can convince the customer that your product or service is indeed capable of delivering the particular benefits that they are looking for. That's why an ability to link a feature to a benefit lies at the very heart of effective benefit selling. Using the acronym SELL, let's look at how to do it.

S = SHOW YOUR CUSTOMER A RELEVANT PRODUCT OR SERVICE FEATURE

Draw your customer's attention to a specific feature that you know will enable them to experience a particular benefit from owning or using your product or service, and one that will be well matched to their requirements. For example, the telephone system salesperson might say:

> *Take a look at this feature, Jim ... it's called a multiaxis facility ...*

E = EXPLAIN THE FEATURE IN FULL DETAIL

Aim to enhance your customer's understanding of the feature by explaining, in detail, how it works, how it can be used, and especially what it does – its advantages/performance characteristics. To continue our example:

> *It's a computer chip that automatically routes international calls down the cheapest available telephone line ...*

L = LINK

Use a simple link phrase such as 'and what this means for you is ...' or its equivalent. To continue our example:

> *... which means that ...*

L = LAY OUT THE BENEFIT TO THE CUSTOMER

Go beyond a generic, one-size-fits-all approach and spell out the benefit in a way that it makes it as relevant and as meaningful as possible for your customer. To continue our example:

> ... based on your current calling profile, you'll save around 27 per cent off your monthly phone bill ... and that's about £280 less than you're paying at the moment.

As this example clearly shows, the use of a 'link phrase' is fundamental to being able to sell benefits because it forces you to go on to interpret exactly how a particular feature will benefit your customer. To put it another way, it provides the necessary underlying rationale to ensure that each of your selling points will really make sense and sound credible and attainable to your customers.

Skill acquisition exercise

Make a list of all the features that describe your product or service. Then take each feature on your list and write down the benefit that it represents from the customer's point of view. Next, apply the SELL formula to work out the exact phrasing you're going to use to sell each feature and benefit as effectively as possible. Memorize and rehearse.

22 Sell matching benefits

There are two sorts of salespeople: 'feature creatures' and 'benefit beasties'. Let me explain exactly what I mean by telling you about the day I went shopping for a DVD player to replace my old video cassette player. All I wanted was a basic model that would be very easy to operate and compatible with my existing TV set. Here's what happened:

Example

In the first store I visited, the salesperson was a classic 'feature creature' – the sort who thinks their job is to sell products rather than to help their customers to buy benefits. As soon as I'd expressed an interest in buying a DVD player, I was shown a particular model and was assured that it was the 'best value buy' in the store because it had a whole raft of technical features for doing this, that and the other. However, as each feature was being pointed out at breakneck speed and in excruciating technical detail, I found myself becoming increasingly inattentive and losing interest. There was no way I would use all those features, and in any case I was sure it would be far too complicated to operate. So, at the earliest opportunity I made my excuses, said goodbye and was glad to make a speedy getaway.

Five minutes later I was in a different store across the street. Once again I expressed an interest in buying a DVD player but this time the salesperson was a 'benefit beastie' and her response was very different. She started out by asking me a range of questions to find out how much I knew about DVD players, the type of TV set I had at home, how often I would be using it and so on. Eventually she recommended a particular model and took the time to carefully explain two or three of its main features and benefits that were well matched to my requirements. When I mentioned it seemed to meet my needs perfectly, she promptly closed the sale. Another satisfied customer!

Well, I'm sure my story has a familiar ring to it! It certainly serves to remind us that customers are not interested in buying the features of a product or service. They are only interested in buying benefits – such as obtaining peace of mind, saving time, and so on. Most importantly, however, my story also reminds us that successful selling is NOT about selling the same benefits to all customers all of the time. Rather, the key is to focus on selling *matching* benefits, because the same product or service will almost always benefit different customers in different ways, depending on their individual circumstances.

Insight

Put the focus on selling those benefits that are well matched to your customer's specific needs and wants.

What makes your product or service superior to another is not the fact that it has more features, and consequently more benefits, but that it does more of what a particular customer wants it to do. So in a competitive market, if you want to 'snatch' more than your fair share of all those customers out there then you will have to become a 'benefit beastie' and match more customers. It's that simple.

Skill acquisition exercise

Spend a few moments every day repeating the following affirmation to yourself, until it becomes your personal mantra for successful selling:

If I'm going to snatch 'em, I've gotta match 'em!

23 Demonstrate your benefits

The ancient Chinese philosopher Confucius is reputed to have said:

Tell me and I'll forget
Show me and I'll remember
Involve me and I'll understand

We all relate to the world through the five senses of sight, sound, touch, smell and taste – and that includes our customers! Consequently, if you can demonstrate the benefits of your product or service in a way that stimulates as many as possible of your customer's five senses, the more they will experience a sense of involvement in the purchase process and the more appealing your product or service is likely to become. Anyone who has ever experienced buying a new car from their local dealership will know exactly what I'm talking about. The sheer thrill of sitting in the driving seat for the first time and then going for a test-drive is what makes the purchase process so enjoyable and the thought of owning the new car so irresistible.

Regardless of what you sell, there's usually a way to demonstrate at least one or two key benefits through harnessing the power of customer involvement. All it takes is some imagination and creative thought. Here are three examples to get you thinking:

▸ *The marine equipment salesperson demonstrates the unique benefit of a new battery-powered navigation device by insisting that their customer drops it over the side of their yacht! After a couple of seconds it bobs back up to the surface and floats. The salesperson then retrieves the device from the water with a small net before handing it over to the customer to inspect it. Amazingly, it hasn't let in water and continues to operate normally.*
▸ *The water-softening-equipment salesperson demonstrates the soap cost savings of dishwashing in soft water to a hotel owner by issuing a challenge. Two test tubes are filled half full: one with the hard water straight from the tap in the hotel kitchen and the other with treated tap water. One droplet of liquid soap is then dispensed into each test tube and the hotel owner is asked to vigorously shake the contents of each one until an equal head of lather is achieved in both test tubes. Whereas a single shake is*

*enough to produce an overflowing head of suds in the
test tube containing the soft water; no amount of agitation
has any effect whatsoever on the hard water in the other
test tube.*

▶ *The financial services salesperson demonstrates the projected
profits of a new savings plan by inviting the customer to enter
their investment details into a laptop computer, and then to
sit back and watch the year-on-year interest figures appear
on screen.*

Insight

There's usually a way to demonstrate at least one or two
key benefits through harnessing the power of customer
involvement.

In planning a demonstration, you can maximize its effectiveness by
paying close attention to the following points:

1 *Before you begin the demonstration, create a little anticipation
and intrigue. Tell the customer what is about to happen, what
you want them to do, and why.*

2 *Set the 'stage'. Clear away and keep out of sight anything that
could possibly distract the customer from focusing exclusively
on taking part in your demonstration.*

3 *Put the customer 'in the driving seat'. In other words,
maximize the potential for the customer to be able to taste,
smell, touch, see, hear and experience the benefits of using
and/or owning your product or service.*

4 *Encourage your customer to spend as much time as possible
getting involved with your demonstration. Make encouraging
remarks. Tell them they're 'catching on fast', 'doing well' or
whatever is appropriate.*

5 *During the demonstration, keep the benefits in the spotlight
at all times by relating them to your customer's situation.*

6 *At the conclusion of the demonstration, be sure to summarize
all the key points.*

24 Translate benefits into pounds and pence

Just because you tell a customer that a particular feature of your product or service means that they will be able to benefit by 'increasing their sales', 'reducing their costs' (or whatever) it does NOT mean you've done your job as a salesperson. You see, the problem with this sort of 'benefit telling' is that it's just too generalized. It ignores the fact that every business customer views their circumstances as unique and that what he or she really wants to know, specifically and in financial terms, is by *how much* you can help to increase their sales or reduce their costs and by *how much* your offer is more cost-effective relative to their alternatives. The point is, 'benefit telling' often amounts to little more than parrot-fashion selling because it requires very little effort and usually means that the salesperson has failed to 'go to work' for the customer. By contrast, 'benefit selling' means that you go one step further and really spell out the full value to the customer of each benefit and that you do so in specific and measurable financial terms relative to their individual business situation.

Insight

In the end, you've simply got to get down to the nitty-gritty of translating benefits into pounds and pence. It's what business-to-business selling is all about.

Clearly, some types of benefits more readily lend themselves to being translated into financial terms (such as increasing sales or reducing costs), whereas others (such as saving time or obtaining peace of mind) aren't quite so easy to convert. Nonetheless, even in the difficult cases I'd strongly encourage you to rise to the challenge. Through adopting a customer perspective and a little creative thinking, you'll almost always be able to find a way. Here's a good example:

Example

Time saving is a major benefit of the stock control software packages that Jeremy sells to retail owner-managers. Here's his take on benefit selling: 'At a certain point in my sales presentation I ask my customers to write down a ballpark figure of their net annual earnings. I then ask them to divide it by their estimate of the total number of hours they work during a year in order to work out an approximation of their hourly rate. Once people can see exactly how much their time is worth to them, it's amazing how quickly they get serious about wanting to free up some of their valuable time so that it can be spent more productively in other areas of the business ... and it's my job to talk them through exactly that.'

Helping a customer to measure the financial value of your proposition usually means that you will have to work closely with them to go through every aspect of their cost–benefit equation. This is an exacting process that demands a great deal of skill, experience, expertise and judgement. However, it is well worth the effort. Make no mistake about it, this is the highest level of service a salesperson can perform for a customer and when it's done in a professional manner it is always appreciated. After all, how else can your customer be expected to make a fully informed purchase decision?

25 Substantiate your claims

No matter how well you explain a benefit, your assertion alone is not necessarily going to be proof enough for the customer. To put it another way, customers are often sceptical about the claims salespeople make and either consciously or subconsciously they are likely to be questioning the validity of your proposition. So you should always be ready to support your case by providing the customer with as much proof as possible. For this purpose you should carry a sales presentation folder and/or laptop computer files containing at least some of the following sales aids.

PHOTOGRAPHS

Some of the best photographs to show a customer are:

- ▶ *'amazing but true' photographic evidence of a dramatic demonstration taking place*
- ▶ *a pair of 'before' and 'after' photographs presented side by side*
- ▶ *a sequence of photographs that show the methods and processes involved in making your product or carrying out your service*
- ▶ *close-ups showing the detail of some aspect of your product or the materials from which it is made*
- ▶ *a series of 'in action' shots showing the different situations and places where your product is being used.*

ILLUSTRATIVE DRAWINGS

Illustrative drawings or artist's impressions are invaluable if you are selling a design service or a product that is still at the concept stage. For example, a real estate salesperson would typically use an artist's impression of a planned residential development to great effect as a way of communicating key features and benefits to a prospective home owner.

TECHNICAL DRAWINGS

Technical drawings can be particularly useful when you want to explain certain aspects of your product. For example, a black and white line-drawing or a 3D computer graphic would be ideal for showing your customer the details of a specific feature and benefit associated with the internal mechanics of a new type of fork-lift truck.

STORYBOARDS

A cartoon strip or storyboard can be a superb way to explain a sequence of events, especially if there is an element of education involved. For example, a salesperson I know sells an ingenious mobile display stand by referring to a cartoon strip as a means of showing how easy it is to unpack, erect and then dismantle again, and all within a 20-minute timeframe.

VIDEO CLIPS

Moving pictures with a soundtrack can be an extremely useful way of substantiating your claims, especially when, for logistical or safety reasons, you are unable to demonstrate them 'live'. For example, a bullet-proof-vest salesperson I know shows dramatic footage of his CEO shooting himself in the stomach as a means of demonstrating the effectiveness of his product!

LETTERS OF RECOMMENDATION OR THANKS

A signed letter of recommendation or a thank-you letter from a satisfied customer is a brilliant sales aid, especially when it's the original copy written on their company notepaper.

PUBLISHED ARTICLES AND REPORTS

If a journalist has ever 'road-tested' your product or service, or written any type of feature article or report in which he or she has independently assessed your product or service and made some favourable remarks about it, then of course this represents an invaluable source of proof relating to the features and benefits of your offer.

RESEARCH DATA

For products or services that are technical or scientific in nature, then the provision of hard evidence in the form of research-based data can be especially convincing, particularly if it has been independently certified by someone in a position of authority, such as a doctor or a university professor.

CUSTOMER LISTS

The old adage that 'hundreds of customers can't be wrong' is still a powerful argument that carries a lot of weight with prospective customers.

One way to draw your customers' attention to the above sales aids is to simply 'show and tell' (i.e. show it to them and then tell them about it). However, whenever possible, the best way is to ask an involvement question first, *before* you show and tell. To illustrate what I mean, let's take the example of a salesperson selling a new type of industrial wastewater purification system. When the time comes for the salesperson to substantiate the claim that this system is capable of dramatically improving the purity of a particular customer's wastewater, the conversation unfolds like this:

> **Salesperson:** *As a matter of fact, we've just had the system independently tested by Professor Jones and his team at City University. Tell me, just out of curiosity, what would be your guess of the best possible percentage output of water purity achievable for the throughput levels you're talking about?* (Asks)

> **Customer:** *Oh, I don't know, maybe about 90 per cent.*

> **Salesperson:** *Well, take a look at the data for yourself.* (Shows) *It shows that with our new system, water purity is recorded at an incredible 97 per cent!* (Tells)

Make no mistake about it, every time you substantiate your claims with proof and evidence, you'll be magnifying your credibility in the eyes of the customer. Pure dynamite!

Skill acquisition exercise

Assemble a range of sales aids that will enable you to prove, as far as possible, each of your benefits to the customer. Decide how you can use each one to maximum effect.

26 Master the art of storytelling

Telling a story dramatizes your selling points and makes them more memorable, real and believable. It can also make the buying process a more pleasurable experience for your customers.

Customers are just like everyone else – they enjoy hearing a good story!

Depending on the situation at hand there are two types of story that can be effective as a selling tool: a success story and a failure story.

A SUCCESS STORY

A success story is when you tell a story about a previous customer who, for some particular reason, was extremely glad they bought from you. This is a particularly useful type of story to tell when you need to support your claims about how a customer would benefit from using your product or service. For example, a tractor salesperson could tell the story of a nearby farmer who has been able to save himself more than six hours of work per week since purchasing a certain model – going into detail about exactly how he used the tractor, and, of course, what he does with all his extra spare time!

A FAILURE STORY

A failure story is when you tell the story of a previous customer who decided not to buy from you and then, for some particular reason, later regretted that decision. This would be an appropriate story to tell if a customer seems uncertain about their level of requirement relative to one or more aspects of your offer. For example, the tractor salesperson could tell the story of another farmer who only six months earlier had decided not to buy and then later on regretted not having the benefit of various features during a particularly wet winter season – going on to explain how it had ended up costing him a great deal of money in lost revenues.

A useful approach to storytelling is the 'feel–felt–found' method because it indicates that, at least to some extent, you are able to relate to your customer's circumstances. With this approach you use the words 'feel–felt–found' as the structure for telling the story. For example:

> *I think I know how you **feel** Michael.*
>
> *Mr Smith from the ABC Company **felt** the same way,*
>
> *but once he bought it (or decided not to buy), what he **found** was that …*

Note that for maximum effectiveness you should always tell the relevant parts of a story in as much detail as you can. Include names and dates and quote as many facts and figures as possible. Above all, remember that a story should always be totally and completely true. Nothing a salesperson can ever say will be more compelling or convincing to a customer than the truth.

Skill acquisition exercise

Identify at least one success story and one failure story that would be useful for you to be able to tell from now on, as and when required.

27 Handle your product with pride

Cast your mind back to the last time you went to a jewellery store to buy a necklace or a bracelet. Do you recall how the salesperson carefully handled each piece of jewellery they showed to you as if it were the most precious piece in the world? Well of course this is brilliant salesmanship and for at least two good reasons. Firstly, it inspires great confidence in the expertise and professionalism of the salesperson. After all, surely only someone who is genuinely knowledgeable and enthusiastic about their work would handle their products with such obvious pride – right? Secondly, it serves to enhance the perception of product quality and value in the mind of a customer. Surely only something that is well worth having and paying good money for would be worthy of such reverence and respect – right?

Your customers will be similarly impressed if you handle your product or samples with this kind of pride and appreciation. It doesn't matter if it is an industrial product or one that is 'positioned' at the lower end of a market, because every customer wants to believe in both the salesperson and the value-for-money of their offer. Even if you don't sell a tangible product this principle still applies. For example, if you sell a pure service such as insurance, then it is more important than ever to handle your company's documentation, brochures and other sales materials with a similar show of respect and pride because, in effect, these resources are your only means of 'showcasing' your offer to the customer.

Insight

Every customer wants to believe in both the salesperson and the value-for-money of their offer.

My research has shown that after a customer has bought an item of jewellery from a top jewellery salesperson, some of the key words that they use to describe how the salesperson handled their product are:

- ▶ *loving*
- ▶ *caring*
- ▶ *admiring*
- ▶ *expert*
- ▶ *respectful*
- ▶ *mesmerizing*
- ▶ *impassioned*
- ▶ *confident*
- ▶ *knowledgeable*
- ▶ *enthusiastic*
- ▶ *professional.*

If your product-handling methods could elicit responses like these from your customers, just think what it might do for your sales figures!

Skill acquisition exercise

Brainstorm with your colleagues or friends to work out the best way to handle your product and/or sales materials in front of the customer. Rehearse your new methods until you feel entirely comfortable using them.

28 Power-pack your benefits

FedEx, the worldwide courier company, has one of my favourite business slogans: *Absolutely, positively, overnight.*

I like it because it says exactly what a customer wants to hear and in no uncertain terms: I will enjoy the total peace of mind that comes with knowing that no matter where in the world I want to send my package, I can be sure it will be delivered within 24 hours. No ifs, no buts, no maybes. How's that for a power-packed benefit!

Now ask yourself – when you're explaining the benefits of your offer to customers, can you honestly say that you do so in an equally powerful and unequivocal fashion? That is, in a way that doesn't leave a single trace of doubt in their mind as to the depth of your conviction? Well, if you're anything like most salespeople there's probably room for improvement because the nature of benefit selling is such that you're either totally convincing or you're not. If a customer detects even the slightest hint of uncertainty in your communication style then they will almost inevitably seize upon it and respond with a degree of scepticism.

You can power-pack your benefits by paying close attention
to two interrelated components of your communication style:
what you say (i.e. the choice of words and phrases you use) and
how you say it.

POWER-PACK WHAT YOU SAY

With regard to *what* you say, be careful not to fall into the
trap of using any words and phrases which could sound even
remotely weak or which could be open to misinterpretation.
Instead, take a leaf out of Federal Express's book and use only
powerful and emotionally charged words and phrases that will
convey an uncompromising belief in the benefits of your offer.
Some examples are as follows:

Don't say	Do say
I think …	*I am totally and utterly convinced …*
I have little doubt …	*I have absolutely no doubt …*
I guess …	*I know for sure …*
I'd say …	*I'd strongly recommend …*

POWER-PACK HOW YOU SAY IT

With regard to *how* you should communicate a benefit, once again
there can be no room for misinterpretation. Everything about your
manner should convey an air of unswerving confidence in what
you have to offer as well as a passionate belief in its value to your
customer. I'm talking about every aspect of your body language,
and especially your tone of voice, your facial expression and the
look in your eye. Indeed, the intensity of your conviction should be
almost palpable to the customer. If you're going to say it anyway,
you might as well say it with every ounce of conviction that you
can muster.

29 Know when and how to mention the competition

In these days of rapidly increasing competition, we salespeople might be forgiven for being more than a little confused about the wisdom of referring to our competitors during the course of a sales presentation, and especially when it comes to the part when we are explaining the unique benefits of our offer to the customer. The key questions are: 'Should the existence of competitors be acknowledged?' and if so, 'How should we refer to them?' So here are the rules for when and how to mention the competition.

RULE ONE

If your customer does not mention the competition then neither should you. *Never* discuss the competition in any way unless you have to. Just carry on with your sales presentation as if they do not exist.

RULE TWO

If your customer mentions the competition in passing, not by naming them specifically but in such a way that it signals to you that he or she is aware of their choices, then you should simply refer to them as 'all the others' or 'all the rest'. Don't give away free advertising for any of your competitors by mentioning their names.

RULE THREE

If your customer tells you that you are up against a specific competitor, ask the customer to tell you which one before proceeding to acknowledge this competitor as being a good company with a reputable product or service. Then go on to point out the superior benefits to the customer of your offer compared with theirs. Never put your rival company down.

Insight

Always put the focus on selling the superiority of your offer, not the inferiority of your competitor's offer.

RULE FOUR

If yours is a relatively small company and the customer mentions that he or she is considering buying from the largest and most well-known company in the market, then feel free to mention the name of this competitor as often as you like because by comparing yourselves with the market leader your company will only gain further credibility. So, acknowledge their status as the market leader but then go on to sell the benefits of buying from a small specialist company like yours: one with greater agility and flexibility to be able to better meet their needs, one that will provide a far more personalized service, and one that has to work harder to prove themselves and to keep their customers satisfied.

RULE FIVE

If during the course of your sales presentation it becomes apparent that due to an unusual set of circumstances your product or service will not satisfy a particular customer's requirements in some fundamental way, then by all means go ahead and recommend a competitor's product that will. You may not win the sale but you will win the customer's respect for being a highly professional salesperson working for a highly professional company. Gold-dust!

Skill acquisition exercise

Commit to memory the five rules outlined above and resolve that from now on you'll apply them to the letter.

30 Sell your secret weapon

Guess what? You have a secret weapon! One that is totally under your control and that can provide you with an extra competitive edge whenever you need it. Think about it. Whatever else your competitors might have to offer ... they don't have YOU! They don't have a salesperson with your dedication and commitment to providing customers with the best possible after-sales personal service – someone who is prepared to 'go the extra mile' on their behalf to ensure all goes smoothly. What I'm suggesting is that no matter how well you sell your company's reputation for providing great service, this will not be anything like as convincing as your personal assurances that you yourself will make a special effort to look after them post-sale.

Insight

A customer will often be more convinced by the depth of your conviction to serve him or her to the very boot of your ability than by anything else.

Here's a list of some of the many types of after-sales services that you could consider offering to your customers; services that go over and above the norm for a salesperson to offer, and as such encourage a customer to want to buy from you and not from your competitors:

▶ *Offer to speed up the processing of your customer's order by tracking order status, checking shipping and delivery schedules and so on.*

- ▶ *Offer to personally oversee product installation and set-up, including operator training.*
- ▶ *Offer to liaise between your people and theirs, ensuring good communication, co-ordination, co-operation and collaboration as appropriate.*
- ▶ *Offer to monitor the ongoing performance of your product or service post-sale, relative to your customer's original purchase goals.*
- ▶ *Offer to be available 24/7 as a first point of contact in case of an emergency or urgent requirement of any kind.*
- ▶ *Offer to keep your customer updated regarding any useful new research information, product application techniques and so on.*

In offering any of these types of additional services, don't simply tell your customer about them – *sell them*! This can be done by addressing your customer's concerns one-by-one (as necessary) and by asking him or her a specific 'straight' closed question which begins with the words:

Tell me, Michael, would it set your mind at rest if I promise to …

This is a magical little formula because you can tag onto the end of it any additional service you are prepared to offer that you think would be likely to inspire a greater confidence in buying from you. What's more, it makes it perfectly obvious that what you're offering is something you yourself are prepared to do specifically for that customer.

Showing a customer that you are prepared to go the extra mile can be very compelling. In fact, in a competitive situation, a customer will often be more convinced by the depth of your conviction to serve him or her to the very best of your ability than by anything else. It's a great way to differentiate yourself from the competition, add value, win your customer's confidence and tip the balance of their decision in your favour.

Skill acquisition exercise

Ask yourself this question: 'Over and above my company's standard offer, what additional services could I offer that would be of high value to my customers but would be something I could do at a low or no cost to me?'

10 THINGS TO REMEMBER

1 *Apply the SELL formula.*

2 *Sell matching benefits.*

3 *Demonstrate your benefits.*

4 *Translate benefits into pounds and pence.*

5 *Substantiate your claims.*

6 *Master the art of storytelling.*

7 *Handle your product with pride.*

8 *Power-pack your benefits.*

9 *Know when and how to mention the competition.*

10 *Sell your secret weapon.*

Closing-phase selling skills

In this chapter you will learn:

* *how to get the customer's agreement to go ahead, and leave them feeling positive about their purchase decision*

> **Opening phase**
> Set the scene for a businesslike and mutually beneficial conversation to take place between you and the customer.

> ↓

> **Interviewing phase**
> Find out all about the customer's specific needs and wants, and uncover the key benefits that they are really looking for.

> ↓

> **Matching phase**
> Match the customer's needs and wants as closely as possible to the benefits of your product or service offer.

> ↓

> **Closing phase**
> Got the customer's agreement to go ahead, and leave them feeling positive about their purchase decision.

> ↓

> **Objection-handling phase**
> Handle the customer's objection to their complete satisfaction and, if possible, turn it around into a closing opportunity.

31 Tune in to buying signals

Question: When is the right time to ask that closing question?

Answer: When the customer gives you a buying signal. A buying signal is anything a customer says or does which suggests they have an interest in going ahead with making a purchase.

> **Insight**
> When people talk about the need for 'good timing' in selling, what they are referring to is the salesperson's ability to recognize and respond appropriately to a buying signal.

Since most customers are reluctant to come right out and say 'OK, I'm getting close to making a decision now and I'd like you to help me to make up my mind', it's useful to think of a buying signal as being a sort of coded language for telling you they're interested. Here's a list of some classic examples. It's by no means a definitive listing of all the buying signals you could ever receive but it does give you a flavour of what to look out for. It's a buying signal when the customer:

- ▶ *exclaims 'It looks perfect!'*
- ▶ *asks 'So how much is it?'*
- ▶ *starts to talk 'past the sale', i.e. as if they already own your product or service*
- ▶ *offers you an additional argument to support your case*
- ▶ *picks up the agreement form to read some of the fine print*
- ▶ *uses a calculator to check the numbers relating to a particularly important element in their decision*
- ▶ *enquires about the potential for modifying a certain product specification*
- ▶ *makes a thoughtful sounding 'hmm …' in response to your discussions on a specific purchase variable.*

Notably, some of the buying signals above are stronger than others in that they indicate a greater degree of interest. Perhaps you've already spotted that I've put four stronger ones in the top half of my list and four weaker ones in the bottom half. Nevertheless, during the course of a sales presentation, it is imperative that you're tuned in to watching and listening for any and every type of buying signal because each time you miss one you're throwing away a precious opportunity to ask an appropriate closing question. This is very easily done, especially when you are preoccupied with trying to get your sales points across.

Please also note that many salespeople make the unfortunate mistake of assuming that a buying signal is only ever going to crop up towards the end of their sales presentation. Although this is often the case, it could occur at any time. Your customer might well be getting ready to make their purchase decision sooner than you think!

Finally, if due to the unusual nature of your type of business, you believe you get less than your fair share of buying signals, then please consider this fact: *good salespeople get more buying signals!* I'm afraid there's nowhere to hide. Nine times out of ten, when a customer gives you a buying signal it's actually a reflex response to good selling. In other words, the more successful you become at stimulating the desire to buy, the more buying signals you'll receive.

Skill acquisition exercise

Prepare a comprehensive list of all the various buying signals you might get from customers. Memorize your list so that you will be able to instantly recognize every buying signal that you receive from now on.

32 Trial close after a weak buying signal

A trial close is a conditional closing question such as an 'If … then …' or 'Let's just suppose …' type question, and the time to ask it is when you receive your cue from the customer in the form of a weak buying signal. A weak buying signal is anything a customer says or does which suggests a tentative interest in making a purchase. For example, let's say the customer gives you a weak buying signal by expressing a cautious interest in taking advantage of some special finance terms. It comes in the form of a thoughtful sounding 'hmm ... ' just after you've explained that your company's finance options mean that longer repayment periods will not necessarily incur higher interest rate charges. Then at this point, you might say:

> *If we could work out a way of extending your repayment period at no extra charge **then** would you be happy to go ahead on that basis?*

or

> ***Let's just suppose** that we could work out a way of extending your repayment period at no extra charge. Would you consider going ahead on that basis?*

Insight
A weak buying signal is anything a customer says or does which suggests a tentative interest in making a purchase.

Please bear in mind that sometimes it will be inappropriate to pose a trial closing question in this way. This is because from the customer's point of view there's always a fine line between a trial-closing question that sounds assertive and 'fair' and one that just sounds too controlling and manipulative. Consequently, depending on your reading of the situation you might prefer to soften the delivery of a trial close just to make sure it isn't going to irritate your customer. This can be done by signalling to him or her that you don't wish to offend, immediately prior to asking the question. Here are three examples of the types of phrases that can be used:

- ▶ *I don't mean to put you under any pressure; nevertheless, may I ask you ...*
- ▶ *It's not my intention to play hardball; nonetheless, please tell me ...*
- ▶ *I'm not trying to be pushy; however, let me ask you ...*

The key advantage of a trial-closing question is that a negative response does not lock you out of the sale because it is conditional upon something. If you get a positive response, however, then this is great news because all you have to do now is to satisfy the condition and the sale is closed. In this way trial closing questions avoid showdowns while still moving you closer to a sale. In short, they're dynamite! Use them liberally throughout your sales presentation as a means of 'testing out the temperature of the sale' whenever you receive a weak buying signal from the customer. You'll create more closing situations and you'll make more sales.

Skill acquisition exercise

Identify the weak buying signals you typically receive from your customers and work out the best type of trial-closing question you could ask in response to each one. Role-play with a colleague or friend until your trial closing questions become a reflex response.

33 Full close after a strong buying signal

A full-closing question is when you ask for the sale outright, and the time to ask it is when you receive your cue from the customer in the form of a strong buying signal. A strong buying signal is anything a customer says or does which suggests a clear interest in making a purchase. When a customer gives you a strong buying signal it usually means they are more or less ready and waiting for you to ask a full-closing question. So don't disappoint your customer! Look them straight in the eye, lean forwards a little and lower your voice to draw them in, and then with an air of confident expectation, ask for the sale.

There are two main types of full close: the direct close and the
alternative-choice close.

THE DIRECT CLOSE

The direct close is when you simply go right ahead and ask the
customer if he or she would like to buy. Here are a couple of
examples:

> **Customer:** *It looks perfect! (**strong buying signal**)*
> **Salesperson:** *Great! Can I write up your order? (**direct close**)*

> **Customer:** *So how much is it? (**strong buying signal**)*
> **Salesperson:** *It's £499. Would you like one? (**direct close**)*

I am absolutely convinced that there's no better close than
the direct close. It might not be very sophisticated, but it's
straightforward, assertive, positive, plain and simple. Therein
lies its power.

THE ALTERNATIVE-CHOICE CLOSE

Another type of full close is the alternative-choice close. This close
is most effective when the amount of positive stimuli coming across
from your customer is so overwhelming that you can be sure that
their strong buying signal indicates that they have already made
up their mind to buy. So, rather than asking directly if they would
like to buy, instead you ask about their preference regarding some
relatively minor aspect of their purchase, such as their preferred
method of payment, their preferred date of delivery or their
preferred colour. It really doesn't matter what aspect of your
product or service you ask about, just as long as it provides the
customer with an opportunity to express their preference between
two genuine alternative purchase choices. To go back to our

previous buying-signal examples, here's how the alternative-choice close could be used:

> **Customer:** *It looks perfect! (**strong buying signal**)*
> **Salesperson:** *Great! Would you prefer to take delivery this Thursday or next Thursday? (**alternative-choice close**)*
>
> **Customer:** *So how much is it? (**strong buying signal**)*
> **Salesperson:** *It's £499. Would you prefer the white or the satin finish? (**alternative-choice close**)*

The beauty of the alternative-choice close is that whichever option the customer chooses represents a watertight commitment to go ahead with their purchase. Sold!

Skill acquisition exercise

Identify the strong buying signals that you typically receive from your customers and work out the best type of full-closing question that you could ask in response to each one. Role-play with a colleague or friend until your full-closing questions become a reflex response.

34 'Manufacture' a close

When it comes to the number and quality of buying signals that you will receive throughout your career as a professional salesperson, the good news is that you are in charge! This is because just about every buying signal you get from a customer (whether a strong one or a weak one) will be the result of good selling on your part. To put it another way, when you sell well and trigger a customer's interest in making a purchase, he or she will almost always 'reward' you with a buying signal – thereby providing you with the perfect opportunity to ask a closing question of one type or another.

Now for the not-so-good news. Sometimes, no matter how well you sell, that all-important buying signal just isn't forthcoming! This is because from time to time you will inevitably encounter one of those difficult customers who could be described as the 'strong and silent' personality type. Such customers tend to be unresponsive during the course of a sales presentation, typically displaying nothing more than the merest hint of a buying signal. So in these situations you need to be able to 'manufacture' for yourself a legitimate closing opportunity. This can be done by using an approach known as the 'three-question closing sequence'.

Insight
'Manufacture' a closing opportunity whenever a buying signal is unforthcoming.

The best time to deploy this approach is normally towards the end of a sales presentation after you have explained all the benefits and when, having received very little by way of meaningful feedback from your customer, there's no apparent reason why they should not go ahead with their purchase. So, after a short pause, the three-question closing sequence goes like this:

Salesperson's first question: *Tell me Andrew, have I given you all the information you need?*

Customer: *Yes, I think so.*

Salesperson's second question: *Good, and are you happy with everything?*

Customer: *Well, er ... yes, I think so. Yes.*

Salesperson's third question: *Excellent! Can we go ahead then?'* (**direct close**)
or

Salesperson's third question: *Excellent! So, when would you prefer to take delivery ... this Thursday or next Thursday? (alternative-choice close)*

The beauty of the three-question closing sequence is that providing your customer responds positively to each of the first two questions then you have effectively succeeded in 'manufacturing' for yourself a strong buying signal and the opportunity to ask a full-closing question. Better still, a 'yes' response to each of the first two questions means that, to all intents and purposes, your customer is already committed to saying 'yes' to your third question and to going ahead with their purchase. If, however, your customer responds negatively to either of the first two questions then at least you're in a great position to be able to find out exactly what else you have to do to make the sale. Here's your script:

▶ *If you get a negative response to your first question:*

  OK, so tell me, what additional information do you need?

▶ *If you get a negative response to your second question:*

  OK, so tell me, what exactly is it that you're not happy about?

I firmly believe that all salespeople should learn to master the three-question closing sequence. It's easy to use and when executed in the right way and at the right time it always moves you closer to a sale. Best of all, by enabling you to 'manufacture' a closing situation it can help to unlock a sale with even the most unresponsive and difficult of customers.

Skill acquisition exercise

Study the precise wording of the three-question closing sequence as outlined above and check that you feel entirely comfortable with it. If not, feel free to modify it a little. Then memorize it word for word.

35 Deploy the summary-of-benefits close

The longer a sales meeting takes and the more involved it becomes due to the range and complexity of the customer's requirements, the greater the potential effectiveness of this close.

A summary-of-benefits close is when you reflect back on the course of your discussion and pull things together by reminding the customer of all the benefits of your offer that match their specific buying needs – thereby setting yourself up to ask for the sale using a full-closing question. So this close relies completely on being able to accurately recall, in detail, all the key points of your preceding discussions with a customer! That's why in order to ensure that you don't forget anything, immediately prior to deploying this close, it's extremely useful to be able to refer back to some brief notes you made earlier in your discussion.

Insight

Deploy the summary-of-benefits close whenever the customer's benefits-sought are particularly complex, varied and numerous.

The first stage in successfully executing this close is to signal to your customer what you're about to do. Let's take the example of a salesperson selling specialist computer systems. While beginning to flick back through their notes, he or she might say:

> *OK Heather, we seem to have covered everything. So, let's review all the key points we've discussed ...*

Depending on the situation, the next stage is then to use either a single-step or multi-step approach. Let's take a closer look at each one:

THE SINGLE-STEP APPROACH

The idea behind this approach is to summarize all the key benefits to the customer in a concisely worded statement. Without stopping to pause, you then simply go ahead and ask a full-closing question. The best time to use a single-step approach is when your customer has already given you their explicit agreement to each of the main matching benefits on offer during the course of your previous discussion, leaving you with the simple task of re-stating them. So, in our example, the specialist computer system salesperson might say:

> *You estimated the YP3000 system will save about eight hours per week of staff time, representing an instant reduction in your annual wages bill of £3,000. You also calculated that the eradication of human error saves you about £25 per week, which translates into a further £1,300 of annual savings. Most of all you say you want the total peace of mind that comes with our unique five-star service programme. So ... would you like to go ahead?*

THE MULTI-STEP APPROACH

Just as with the single-step approach, the idea behind the multi-step approach is to summarize all the key benefits to the customer that have been discussed. The difference is that with this approach you're going to wrap up the customer's agreement to each benefit one by one as you run through your summary. This approach is sometimes referred to as the 'continuous-yes' close because by re-stating each benefit in the form of a loaded 'say yes' question and stacking them all up one after the other your customer will be encouraged to say 'yes' when you conclude your summary with a full-closing question.

The best time to use a multi-step approach is when, up to this point, your customer has only given you their tacit agreement to each of the main matching benefits, leaving you with the need for him or her to affirm them before you feel you can legitimately go for a full close. So, to go back to our example, the specialist computer salesperson might say:

> **Salesperson:** *You estimated the YP3000 system will save about eight hours per week of staff time, representing an*

instant reduction in your annual wages bill of around £3,000, didn't you?

Customer: *Yes, I did.*

Salesperson: *OK, and you also calculated that the eradication of human error saves you about £25 per week, which translates into a further £1,300 of annual savings ... is that right?*

Customer: *Yes, that's right.*

Salesperson: *Right, and most of all, you say you want the total peace of mind that comes with our unique five-star service programme ... don't you?*

Customer: *Yes, I do.*

Salesperson: *Excellent! So ... would you like to go ahead?*

Skill acquisition exercise

Paying close attention to your use of appropriate body language (gestures, posture, facial expressions, etc.) and to your use of an appropriate tone of voice, role-play both versions of the summary-of-benefits close with a colleague or friend.

36 Perfect the art of silence

The golden rule of closing is this:

Once you have asked a full-closing question, keep quiet and make sure it is the customer who speaks next.

The subtle pressure of silence is the only type of pressure that's perfectly acceptable in customer-oriented selling. After all, you've probably worked hard to 'earn' the opportunity to ask a full-closing question, so why shouldn't you be entitled to a reply?

Believe me, you don't want to break this golden rule. Let's look at what happens if you do by taking the example of a fleet-car salesperson. After a long meeting he or she is attempting to close an order for 20 new cars with a large corporate customer:

> **Customer:** *Hmmm ... I must say your overall offer looks very tempting ... (**strong buying signal**)*

> **Salesperson:** *Yes, and with good reason, Michael. It meets all your company's requirements and much more. So ... would you like to go ahead? (**full close**)*

> **Customer:** *(Takes a deep breath but says nothing – at this point there's a long and drawn-out silence.)*

> **Salesperson:** *Or ... perhaps you're still uncertain about the period of lease? (**breaks the silence**)*

> **Customer:** *Yes, maybe you're right. I should think some more about that and anyway, I don't have to make a final decision until the end of the month ... (**The customer's thoughts are now fully re-focused away from having to make a decision.**)*

Can you see what just happened? When the salesperson in our example broke the silence simply because they had become a little impatient and twitchy, the customer's mind was effectively deflected away from having to make a final decision. To put it bluntly, at the critical moment the salesperson let their customer off the hook. So, once you've asked a closing question, you should always keep quiet and give your customer all the time he or she needs to respond.

Maintaining a silence in those critical moments after a close might sound easy but it is not! If a customer doesn't give you an answer straight away, don't be too surprised if your nerves begin to jangle, your confidence evaporates and you start to experience a powerful urge to say something – anything – in order to relieve the uncomfortable feeling that grows within you as the silence continues. The fact is, the ability to stay cool, calm and confident having asked a closing question is something we have to learn.

At the risk of contradicting myself, it has to be said that occasionally, when a silence has gone on for so long that you can actually see the customer begin to struggle with the strain of having to make their decision, then it may well be appropriate to break the silence yourself. If this is the case, then simply put a big grin on your face and say:

> *Michael, I've always believed that silence is equal to consent … am I right?*

It's a cheeky way of momentarily relieving the tension for your customer while simultaneously re-focusing them on having to make a decision.

Skill acquisition exercise

Compose a short affirmation that you can repeat silently to yourself immediately after you ask a closing question. One that will encourage you to keep quiet and give your customer plenty of time to make up their mind.

37 Help your customer to make up their mind

If a customer is genuinely experiencing some real difficulty in making up their mind, this approach can work wonders. Also known as the 'weigh-up' close, it's when you suggest to the customer that perhaps the best way to resolve their dilemma is to weigh up all the positives against all the negatives of their decision by writing them down. For example:

> *Susan, I can understand that this is a tough decision for you so I'd like to suggest that we go through the process of weighing up all the positives and negatives of your decision ... just to see if we can clear the fog one way or the other ... shall we give it a try?*

Then take a blank sheet of paper and draw a vertical line straight down the middle. In large letters at the top of the right-hand column write *'Yes, I'll buy'* and at the top of the left-hand column write *'No, I won't buy'*. (Note: it is important to use these exact words because this makes it perfectly clear to your customer that they will be expected to make a final decision one way or the other.) Next, your task is to tactfully and skilfully direct the customer's thinking so that his or her list of reasons for going ahead with a purchase clearly outweigh the list of reasons against.

If your customer is struggling to make up their mind between buying from you or buying from one of your competitors, you could try using an adaptation of this approach. Once again take a large blank sheet of paper and draw a vertical line down the middle. This time, however, the column headings should read *'I'll buy from (write in your own name)'* in the right-hand column and *'I'll buy from them'* in the left-hand column. Once again, it is important that you use these exact words because in a subtle way it personalizes their decision. As before, it is then up to you as the salesperson to encourage your customer to end up with more reasons why they should buy from you instead of the competition.

Here's a little tip: this close works best if you hand over to your customer the responsibility for filling out the two columns so that they feel in control of the 'weighing-up' process. It's also important to start off by asking your customer to list all the positive reasons first, while still fresh in their mind. Put it like this:

> *Let's start off by writing under the right-hand column all the reasons you can think of for placing your business with me today.*

Clearly, the key to your success with this technique is being well prepared. Not only will you need to know about all the benefits and potential drawbacks of your product or service but you will also need to be exceptionally adept and well rehearsed in the way you assist your customer through the list-making process. The fact is, using this approach is only believable to a customer if they perceive that you are genuinely considering both sides of the equation and have their best interests at heart. It's a real skill to be able to help a customer to come up with a comprehensive list of reasons without seeming to apply any pressure or being too pushy. However, it can be done and when, in the final analysis, a 'yes' decision clearly outweighs a 'no', the sale is effectively closed.

Skill acquisition exercise

Write out (a) all the benefits, and (b) all the potential drawbacks of your product or service. Then rehearse how you will lead your customer through the list-development process, and in such a way that they will feel as though it's their list, not yours.

38 Cultivate the right closing vocabulary

When you're about to gain a customer's agreement, it's always worth remembering that every word you say counts. Let's take a look at why it's better to use some words in preference to others.

DON'T SAY 'CONTRACT', SAY 'AGREEMENT FORM' OR 'PAPERWORK'

Think about the word 'contract' from a customer's point of view. Most people are extremely wary of a contract. It just sounds too formal and legalistic. So, instead, call it an 'agreement form' or 'the paperwork' because these terms sound a lot less scary.

Insight
Always employ a closing vocabulary that is as customer-friendly as possible!

DON'T SAY 'SIGN', SAY 'AUTHORIZE' OR 'AUTOGRAPH'

People tend to feel a little nervous if they are asked to 'sign' something (especially if it's a 'contract'). It just sounds too serious. That's why it's preferable to ask a customer to 'authorize' or 'autograph' the agreement form. These terms are more customer-friendly. What's more, by using these terms it's as if, as a matter of courtesy, you are acknowledging their buying authority or status.

DON'T SAY 'PAY', SAY 'INVEST'

The word 'pay' has negative connotations for most customers because it puts the emphasis on the amount that your product or service will cost them. The word 'invest', on the other hand, has more positive connotations because it puts the emphasis on the value that your price represents and on the benefits that your product or service will provide. Somehow it seems much more sensible to invest in something than to pay for it.

DON'T SAY 'PRICE', SAY 'TOTAL INVESTMENT'

The word 'price' can easily strike the wrong chord with some customers because it has connotations of sacrifice or loss. The term 'total investment' on the other hand, is much more positive because it infers desirability and worth.

DON'T SAY 'BUY', SAY 'OWN'

It is usually wise to avoid the word 'buy'. It's a word that can easily touch the wrong nerve for customers simply because it reminds them of the need to exchange their hard-earned money in order to obtain your product or service. So it's preferable to ask your customers if they would like to 'own' it. Deep down in a customer's psyche, the thought of 'owning' something triggers a much warmer feeling than the thought of buying something.

Skill acquisition exercise

Identify the key words and phrases that you habitually use when seeking a customer's agreement and finalizing a sale. Make an assessment of them and decide which ones could be usefully substituted with a more customer-friendly choice.

39 Ensure the sale is properly CLOSED

A well-closed sale is one that leaves your customer feeling great about having chosen to do business with you. The acronym CLOSED is a good way to remember the ideal sequence of events for ensuring this happens every time. It goes like this ...

C = CONGRATULATE YOUR CUSTOMER

As soon as your customer has said 'yes' to going ahead with a purchase (and I mean the precise moment the word has left their lips) you should put a big smile on your face and offer your heartfelt congratulations. For example:

That's fantastic, John. Congratulations.

L = LEGITIMIZE THEIR DECISION

Make a point of reinforcing the wisdom of their decision. This is especially important if they have had a tough time making up their mind to buy from you. For example:

I'm absolutely certain you've made the right decision.

O = OFFER A CONGRATULATORY HANDSHAKE

The simple act of offering to shake the customer's hand demonstrates how pleased you are that they have made the right decision and communicates that you are genuinely appreciative of their business. At the same time the symbolic value of 'shaking hands on a deal' has the effect of locking in your customer's commitment to their decision.

S = SAY THANK YOU

Said with genuine sincerity, these words are among the most powerful in any salesperson's toolkit, and the time to say them is right now. For example:

… and thanks very much for placing your order with us. I really appreciate it.

E = EXPLAIN WHAT HAPPENS NEXT

Depending on the type of product or service you sell there may well be a number of follow-through steps post-sale. If so, at this point it will be necessary to briefly run through them one more time in order to confirm all the details. For example:

> *Within 48 hours you'll receive a written confirmation of your order. As we've agreed, your machine will be scheduled for delivery on the 15th of November and our installation team will arrive the next day. They'll set it up, and take you through all the operating instructions.*

Insight

Leave every new customer who says 'yes' feeling great about having chosen to do business with you.

D = DEAL WITH THE PAYMENT

Now you can go ahead and take your customer's payment. For example:

> *Now, I just need you to authorize the paperwork and then we can get the ball rolling.*

Skill acquisition exercise

Role-play the CLOSED sequence with a colleague or friend. Repeat it over and over again so that the next time a customer says 'yes' it will trigger a reflex response.

---

40 Time your exit

There are three rules for timing your exit to perfection. Let's take a look at each one:

RULE ONE

The moment a sale is successfully completed it is only natural for both you and your new customer to experience a mild sense of euphoria. Any tension quickly dissipates, which means there's often a strong temptation to accept an offer of another cup of coffee and to stay for a little while longer. However, at this point it is important to observe the first rule of timing your exit:

> **When I close a sale, the best time to say goodbye is while we're both still on a high.**

Once you have congratulated your customer on his or her decision, made arrangements for delivery as necessary and finalized the payment, there's nothing left to do except to say goodbye and make a swift exit. By staying even a moment longer than necessary, there's always a danger that you could mess things up and undo all your good work. You never know. The customer might have a sudden afterthought or ask an awkward question. Worse still, you might unconsciously say or do something which causes them to reconsider their decision. You cannot improve on 100 per cent success. That's why there are no exceptions to this rule – no matter how friendly your customer appears to be and no matter how sure you are that the sale is watertight!

RULE TWO

The second rule of timing your exit relates to a different set of circumstances. It's very tempting only ever to think of 'closing' in terms of closing the sale. However, while this is certainly your primary objective, restricting your thinking in this way can dramatically reduce your overall sales performance. The fact is that sometimes (for a variety of customer-related reasons) it is just not possible to close a sale. So under these circumstances you must trust your instincts and choose the right moment to switch direction and attempt to close on your next best secondary or 'fall-back' objective. A good secondary objective at least takes you one step closer to a sale at a later date. Some classic examples include:

- ▶ *Arrange for a full product demonstration.*
- ▶ *Agree to submit a formal written proposal.*
- ▶ *Organize a factory visit.*
- ▶ *Arrange to do a comprehensive cost–benefit survey.*
- ▶ *Promise to find out more information.*
- ▶ *Agree to renew contact at a future point in time.*

Insight
In choosing the right moment to close on a secondary objective – trust your instincts!

Since some secondary objectives are preferable to others, you'll need to be crystal clear about your priorities. That way, if for some good reason you can't achieve your best secondary objective then you can shoot for your next best and so on. This ensures that you will always walk away from a sale secure in the knowledge that you have achieved the best possible outcome. So here's the second rule of timing your exit:

> **When I can't close a sale, the best time to say goodbye is as soon as I've achieved my best secondary objective.**

RULE THREE

Occasionally, in the middle of a sales presentation you will realize that your product or service is not at all well matched to that particular customer's requirements. In these situations there's simply no point in continuing with the sale, even if, as is sometimes the case, your customer is blissfully unaware of the extent of the problem! The only ethical course of action is to explain the situation to your customer straight away, recommend a different solution if you can, and then pack up your things and say goodbye. So the third rule of timing your exit goes like this:

When I realize it's not a good buy for my customer, it's time to say 'goodbye' to my customer.

Skill acquisition exercise

Identify three potentially useful secondary objectives. List them in priority order. Memorize your list and resolve that you'll act upon it whenever you find yourself unable to achieve your primary objective of making a sale.

10 THINGS TO REMEMBER

1 *Tune in to buying signals.*

2 *Trial close after a weak buying signal.*

3 *Full close after a strong buying signal.*

4 *'Manufacture' a close.*

5 *Deploy the summary-of-benefits close.*

6 *Perfect the art of silence.*

7 *Help your customer to make up their mind.*

8 *Cultivate the right closing vocabulary.*

9 *Ensure the sale is properly CLOSED.*

10 *Time your exit.*

5

Objection-handling-phase selling skills

In this chapter you will learn:
- *how to handle the customer's objection to their complete satisfaction and, if possible, turn it around into a closing opportunity*

Opening phase
Set the scene for a businesslike and mutually beneficial conversation to take place between you and the customer.

↓

Interviewing phase
Find out all about the customer's specific needs and wants, and uncover the key benefits that they are really looking for.

↓

Matching phase
Match the customer's needs and wants as closely as possible to the benefits of your product or service offer.

↓

Closing phase
Get the customer's agreement to go ahead, and leave them feeling positive about their purchase decision.

↓

Objection-handling phase
Handle the customer's objection to their complete satisfaction and, if possible, turn it around into a closing opportunity.

---

41 Condition yourself positively to objections

An objection is when a customer responds negatively to your proposition. Objections typically relate to an aspect of your product, your service or your price that a customer perceives to be mismatched to their requirements in some way – either in absolute terms or by comparison to a competitor's offer. Here are some classic examples:

- ▶ *The control panel on your machine is too complicated ...* (product-based objection stated in absolute terms)
- ▶ *The control panel on your machine is more complicated than the XYZ Company's machine ...* (same objection stated in comparative terms)
- ▶ *I don't think your firm has sufficient technical expertise in this area ...* (service-based objection stated in absolute terms)
- ▶ *I don't think your firm has as much technical expertise in this area as the XYZ Company ...* (same objection stated in comparative terms)
- ▶ *Your price is very expensive ...* (price-based objection stated in absolute terms)
- ▶ *Your price is a lot more expensive than the XYZ Company ...* (same objection stated in comparative terms)

Many salespeople live in fear of objections because they believe customers use them to deliberately block a sale. The trouble is, when salespeople condition themselves negatively to objections in this way, their insecurity inevitably reveals itself during their sales presentations. They often become visibly pale at the mere thought of an objection, let alone at the mention of one, and so do everything possible to avoid having to confront them. This usually means they talk far too much, hardly letting their customers get a word in edgeways. They'll even ignore an objection altogether if they think they can possibly get away with it. Then when they finally reach the point where they have no option but to answer an objection, they do so almost apologetically. Under these circumstances a customer's faith in both the salesperson and in their offer quickly dissipates.

The point is, for these salespeople, losing the sale actually becomes a self-fulfilling prophecy.

By contrast, top salespeople adopt a completely different mindset. Unlike their lesser-performing counterparts they condition themselves positively to objections, to the point where they actually welcome them as opportunities to dispel any doubts in their customer's mind, and to clear a path towards the sale. This attitude similarly translates across into their sales presentations. They readily and confidently discuss their customer's objections and as a result, they earn their customer's trust and close more sales.

The key to conditioning yourself positively to objections is to look at them from a customer's perspective. Ask yourself 'If I were a customer, why would I want to raise an objection?'. As soon as you do this you'll realize that it's perfectly natural for a genuine buyer to want to raise an objection and for any number of good reasons. For example, most people become hesitant and critically evaluative of an important purchase decision because they have to be able to fully justify the expenditure to themselves and sometimes to others too. Quite understandably, they also feel the need to have a thorough comprehension of all aspects of an offer before they will feel comfortable about making a decision to buy. In fact, when you really think about it, the more genuine a customer is, the more likely it is that he or she would want to raise an objection. Wouldn't you agree?

Insight
The key to conditioning yourself positively towards objections is to look at them from a customer's perspective.

So, from now on, choose to see every objection for what it really is: a buying signal! Although it's extremely well 'disguised' or 'encoded' as an objection, nine times out of ten, this is what it really is:

- ▶ *a request for more detailed information*
- ▶ *a need for further clarification and explanation*

- *a sign that a specific area is of special importance or interest*
- *a misconception or misunderstanding that needs clearing up*
- *a request for help and advice in making a more informed decision*
- *a need for additional reassurance about something.*

Armed with this mindset you can look forward to welcoming your customer's objections because each and every one is a golden opportunity to put your customer's mind at rest and to clear a path towards closing the sale.

Skill acquisition exercise

Repeat the following affirmation quietly to yourself, over and over, until it becomes a deeply held belief:

Beneath every objection under the sun, lies an opportunity for a sale to be won.

42 Pre-handle predictable objections

Pre-handling an objection means that you yourself raise the objection. The advantage of doing this is twofold. Firstly, you get to control the timing of the objection. The whole point of pre-handling an objection is to get a particular issue out of the way early on in your sales presentation when it is less likely to interfere with the customer's final purchase decision. Secondly, a customer does not feel as though he or she 'owns' an objection that was raised by the salesperson, which means that your customer is less likely to feel the need to 'dig their heels in' and defend it – because you raised it. Here's an example:

Example

Mary sells accountancy services for a large firm. One of her target customer groups are small-business entrepreneurs. With these customers she knows there's one objection that's guaranteed to crop up every time. For a variety of reasons they are always extremely nervous about the idea of doing business with a large firm. However, with experience, Mary has learned that the best way to deal with this objection is to pre-handle it, and at a very early stage in her presentation. The dialogue goes something like this:

Mary: *... Incidentally, I know that some of my small-business clients, entrepreneurs like yourself, have initially felt a little uncomfortable with the idea of handing over their company records to a large accountancy firm like ours. So may I ask you, is that something that concerns you at all, Michael?*

Customer: *Frankly, yes, maybe it does a little ... let's just say we're naturally cautious about giving away any commercially sensitive information.*

Mary: *Fair enough, I can certainly understand your reservations. However, what our small-business clients soon discover is that it's precisely because of our size that we've been able to develop state-of-the-art data protection systems for ensuring that our client information is always kept completely and totally secure. Tell me, does that help to put your mind at ease, Michael?*

Customer: *Well yes, when you put it like that, I suppose it does.*

Mary: *Good, and is there anything else that concerns you about that ... because if so, perhaps we should discuss it now before we go any further?*

Customer: *No, I guess not.*

(Contd)

> Mary: *That's great. I'm glad I've had a chance to put your mind at rest on that one. Now, where were we ... ?* (Mary now resumes her presentation.)

Let's review the finer points of executing this technique:

1 *Make it perfectly clear that you're only bringing it up because in the past you've found it to be a common concern among customers.*
2 *Enquire if the issue is similarly a matter of concern for your customer, and in such a way that makes it easy for him or her to say 'yes' without feeling foolish or embarrassed.*
3 *If the customer admits that it is a concern for them, cover it by referring to past customers' experiences.*
4 *Check that the customer agrees with what you've said and that there aren't any other surrounding concerns.*
5 *Make a point of putting the subject firmly behind you before continuing with your presentation.*

Insight

This technique should only ever be applied to 'predictable' objections – those which you know for a fact will come up because they always do.

Finally, as in the above example, this technique should only ever be applied to 'predictable' objections – the last thing you want is to bring up an objection that your customer wouldn't have otherwise considered because this would only result in making your job even more challenging than it is already!

Skill acquisition exercise

Identify the predictable objections that you could usefully pre-handle from now on. In each case, decide upon the best way to go about it.

43 Play CATCH with every objection raised

Successful objection-handling is not like being in a boxing match! Your aim is not to hit the customer back as hard as you can in the hope that you can quickly eliminate their concern with one knockout counter-punch! On the contrary, it's about going through a step-by-step objection-handling process to slowly but surely dismantle any doubt in your customer's mind, and, whenever possible, turn it around into a closing opportunity. That's why it's a lot more like playing a game of catch-the-ball with your customers than it is about trading punches with them. Your aim is to CATCH every objection raised and then throw it back and forth a few times in order to be able to handle it in a respectful, customer-friendly and professional manner. Using the acronym CATCH, here's how:

C = CLARIFY IT

First make sure that you fully understand the objection. This can be done by encouraging the customer to tell you as much as possible about it. Most people find it difficult to communicate the precise nature of their concerns within their first few sentences, so it is important to realize that you'll often need to question the objection in order to make it specific. That way, you'll have something much more concrete to work with. For example:

> **Customer:** *I don't like the sound of that kind of deal ... I never have. (This objection is couched in general terms only.)*

> **Salesperson:** *Tell me more Bob, what exactly is it you don't like the sound of?*

An alternative technique is simply to repeat back to the customer your understanding of the specific point(s) being made in order to check that you have interpreted it correctly. For example, you may say:

> *Let me just check I've understood you correctly, Bob, are you saying that ... ?*

Sometimes it becomes apparent that there is actually more than one objection being raised. In these cases you have no choice but to go ahead and help the customer to articulate the exact nature of their concerns. Even if this results in the identification of two or three separate objections, so be it. At least you will have found out the precise nature of the objections you are going to have to deal with in order to make a sale.

A = AGREE WITH THE LOGIC BEHIND IT

The second step is always to tell the customer that you think their point is a valid one, and why. This does not mean you should agree with the objection itself, only with the logic behind it. By doing this you are investing in the customer's self-esteem and thereby helping to soften your counter-response and make it easier for him or her to accept. Some useful phrases are:

- *Yes, I do understand your concern because ...*
- *Yes, I can appreciate your logic because ...*
- *Yes, in theory you're quite right because ...*
- *Yes, in a way that is perfectly true because ...*

T = TRIAL CLOSE ON IT

As we have already noted, a top salesperson regards every genuine objection as if it were a subtle buying signal (although often very well disguised!) around which to wrap a trial-closing question. So, whenever appropriate, the third step is to trial close on the objection before going on to counter it. For example, you might say:

> *Bob, just supposing I could answer that point to your complete and total satisfaction, then would you be happy to go ahead?*

If the customer agrees, then the sale is effectively closed subject to the objection being handled to their satisfaction. On the other hand, if the customer responds negatively you must probe further to find out what else is holding them back, and then trial close again on both points.

A top salesperson regards every genuine objection as if it were a subtle buying signal!

C = COUNTER IT

The fourth step in handling an objection is to counter it. This can be done in one of three ways:

1 *You can* **drown it**, *by explaining how in their situation the advantages would by far outweigh the disadvantages.*
2 *You can* **dilute it**, *by explaining how, in practice, it would not prove to be such a serious problem for them.*
3 *You can* **dissolve it**, *by explaining how it would not apply in their particular case.*

There is no reason why you should not be able to anticipate virtually all the objections you are likely to encounter, and rehearse your counter responses to perfection. It's up to you to make sure you are well prepared.

H = HARVEST IT

The final step is to ask the customer whether you have answered their objection to their complete and total satisfaction. If the answer is 'no' then you have no option but to find out why and try once again to answer it in a way that satisfies them. If, on the other hand, the answer is 'yes' then you have two options:

1 *If, when the objection was first raised, you chose not to trial close on it for some reason, then you should 'bury' the objection once and for all so that he or she may never raise it again, before returning to your presentation. For example, you might say:*

   I'm glad we've cleared that up, Bob ... Now, where were we?

2 *If, when the objection was first raised, you had decided to wrap a trial-closing question around it (i.e. subject to their*

complete satisfaction with your answer, they had agreed to go ahead), then you've made a sale. All you have to do now is take the order!

44 Flush out the real objection

Some customers have a tendency to reel off any number of 'smokescreen' objections. They're so called because in reality they're not that important to the customer. The truth is they're usually just convenient excuses that serve only to camouflage a customer's genuine indecision about a much deeper, underlying concern; an issue that he or she doesn't want to tell you about for fear of having to confront it and actually make a decision. Since it's very easy to end up wasting a lot of time trying to answer what are effectively 'fob off' objections, you have to learn to trust your instincts. If you can sense a customer isn't being entirely candid about their concerns then the only way forward is to try and cut through the smokescreen and find out what's really holding them back. One way to do this is to put a smokescreen objection 'on ice' in order to try and winkle out the real objection. For example, you might say:

Janet, I do understand the point you're making, but leaving it to one side just for the moment ... I just get the feeling there's something else that's stopping you from going ahead ... may I ask what it is?

Insight

If you are not too careful, it is very easy to end up wasting a lot of time trying to answer what are effectively 'fob off' objections.

No matter how hard you try to get a customer to reveal their true objection, occasionally he or she will simply go quiet – and you're left with the feeling that they must be holding back some deep-seated irrational fear that they either can't or won't tell you about. Maybe it's the fear of making a commitment, of what someone else might think, or of trying out something new. Regardless, you have little option but to probe for the fear and help your customer to voice it and confront it. Understandably, it's not easy for people to reveal the underlying fears and anxieties that affect their decisions, so you'll need to probe for them with great tact and sensitivity. Here's how to go about it.

First, you need to ask for the customer's permission to be perfectly candid and open about something that is on your mind. This shows respect for your customer and signals to him or her that you would like to take the conversation onto a deeper and more intimate level. Second, you need to go ahead and probe for the fear. In order to do this, I believe a straight closed question works best because by being direct, honest and specific about your suspicions, a customer is much more likely to respond than if you ask a more searching open-ended style of question. In phrasing the question, it's also important that you use the kind of language that seeks to 'connect' with your customer on an emotional level. For example, you could say:

> *I'm sensing that there's something really bothering you Janet … tell me, is it the fear of trying out something new?*

or

> *I'm concerned that you seem to be worried about something Janet … tell me, is it the fear of learning to use a new technology?*

Sometimes the only way to unlock a difficult sale is to 'go fishing' in the hope that you can flush out the customer's underlying concerns. The great thing about using these techniques is that when your customer finally reveals their real objection, it usually comes complete with flashing lights and a siren. In other words, by reading the customer's body language and other cues the chances are that it will be very obvious that you've succeeded in flushing it out. At this point, at last, both you and your customer will have taken a giant leap towards being able to conclude the sale one way or the other.

Skill acquisition exercise

Create a list of all the 'fob off' objections you're likely to encounter. In each case, decide how you can cut through the smokescreen and flush out your customer's real, underlying concerns.

45 Use arithmetic to handle price objections

There are two keys to successfully handling price objections. The first key is to accept responsibility for the fact that your customer has seen fit to raise a price objection. This means adopting the attitude that you obviously haven't yet convinced the customer of the true value-for-money that your price represents for them. The second key is to go ahead and do the convincing. This can be done most effectively by using one or more of the four calculation tools of adding, dividing, subtracting and multiplying.

Adding and dividing are the perfect tools to use whenever a customer raises a price objection stated in absolute terms, such as 'Your price is very expensive.' Here's how:

ADD

Add up every feature and benefit to justify and defend the financial value of your price right down to the last penny. For example:

> *So you can be sure of exactly what you'd be getting for your money, let's run through each of the key features and benefits, and the financial value they'll bring to your business ...*

DIVIDE

Divide your price by the life expectancy of your product – then 'reduce to the ridiculous', such as the price per day. Once you've done this then you can go on to make it sound trivial by comparing it with an everyday purchase such as a cup of coffee or a newspaper. For example:

> *You said you'd expect our machine to last for about five years, so your total investment of £1,250 works out to be £250 per year. When divided by 50 working weeks per year that works out to be £5 a week ... and that's the equivalent of only a pound a day ... about half the price of a cup of coffee!*

Now let's consider subtracting and multiplying. They're the perfect tools to adopt whenever a customer raises a price objection stated in comparative terms, such as 'Your price is a lot more expensive than the XYZ Company.' Here's how to use them:

SUBTRACT

Subtract the features and benefits the customer wants but will not get by buying cheaper from your competitor. For example:

> *Let's take a closer look at all the features and benefits you've said you wanted, but won't get by buying cheaper ... firstly, you won't get the total peace of mind that comes with our unique five-star customer-service programme; secondly, you won't get ... (and so on).*

Multiply the hidden costs of buying a cheaper product or service in the mind of the customer. In other words, heighten the customer's apprehensions and uncertainties about the implications of buying cheaper. For example:

> *Tell me Michael, next time there's a breakdown emergency in your factory and you urgently need a service engineer, then what price is the peace of mind that comes with a reputation for dependability like ours?*

Insight
Nine times out of ten the customer will get no more and no less than what they pay for!

By using these tools of basic arithmetic you have the means to overcome virtually any price objection. However, the real power of these tools lies in your ability to use them creatively and imaginatively – and if necessary, in combination with each other – to put your customer's mind totally at rest about the true value-for-money that your price represents.

Skill acquisition exercise

Anticipate all the price objections you're likely to encounter and then use the four tools of adding, dividing, subtracting and multiplying to prepare your best responses in advance. Rehearse carrying them out, and commit them to memory.

46 Seek out your customer's advice

Do you remember Murphy's Law? It states that, in life, just when you least expect it, if something can go wrong, it will – and usually at the most inopportune moment. Here's how it comes up in sales:

Example

I'd been in with an important customer for quite some time. Everything seemed to have gone well and I'd been able to resolve two or three major customer concerns during the course of my presentation and to her total satisfaction. Then, without warning – Murphy's Law – I could hardly believe my ears as she suddenly came up with an unusual yet authentic-sounding objection that I'd never encountered before and to which I hadn't a clue how to respond.

It's just a fact of business life that from time to time an unusual objection will crop up that takes you completely by surprise – and yes, infuriatingly, it only ever seems to happen in those situations when everything else meets with the customer's approval and it's apparently the only remaining obstacle preventing them from going ahead! So, here's what to do about it: look your customer directly in the eye, and in a disarmingly forthright way, simply tell the truth and ask for their help. For example:

Heather, that's a very good point you raise and quite honestly I just don't know what to suggest ... so let me ask you, have you yourself got any ideas as to what could be done about it ... what would you suggest?

The beauty of this approach is that you will soon find out how important the objection really is. You see, if it is genuinely important, your customer will probably go deep into thought and do their level best to come up with a solution. This in itself is an excellent sign because irrespective of whether or not he or she comes up with a solution on the spot, at least you now know exactly what you have to do to successfully close the sale. If it is relatively unimportant, however, then after a brief moment of reflection the customer will probably just dismiss it as something minor, removing the need for you to have to deal with it and so clearing your path towards closing the sale.

> **Insight**
> The beauty of asking the customer for their advice is that you will soon find out how important the objection really is!

Incidentally, if it transpires that the objection is important and there's no obvious way to resolve it, tell the customer that you'll return to your office to consult with your colleagues, and that you'll do your very best to come up with a solution. Most importantly, arrange a date and time for a return visit when you can report back to your customer, and always take the opportunity to trial close on the objection before leaving. Here's your script:

> *Heather, providing I can resolve this issue to your complete satisfaction when I come back to see you, then can I take it that everything else is OK and you'll be happy to place your business with me at that time?*

Skill acquisition exercise

In the event that a customer should raise an unusual objection that would be impossible to anticipate, decide upon the exact wording of a question you could comfortably ask that would seek their advice for dealing with it. Practise and memorize it.

47 Trade a minor price concession

Do you ever encounter a type of customer known as a 'priceshaver'? Despite the fact that you've matched all their requirements and addressed all their concerns, this is the type of customer who persists in pushing you to shave a few pounds off the price, almost as if their life depends on it!

In handling the priceshaver, your initial response should always be to defend the value-to-the-customer that your price-package represents and to maintain the integrity of your company's pricing policy. Unfortunately, however, it's the very nature of a priceshaver to 'dig their heels in' and to just keep on pushing for a price concession, regardless. It's a pig-headed attitude that defies all logic. There's something else about a priceshaver customer that you should know: the moment an unsuspecting and inexperienced salesperson buckles under the pressure and agrees to an unqualified price concession, no matter how small it might be, the priceshaver will simply take it, say 'thanks very much', and then keep on pushing for even more until the salesperson has been well and truly taken to the cleaners.

Let's assume then, that you've justified your price to the hilt and that, true to form, your priceshaver customer still refuses to buy without a discount. What now? Well, under these circumstances you could suggest a 'trade' whereby you agree to make a small price concession but only on the condition that you modify your offer accordingly. This approach is based upon the time-honoured principle of sales negotiation: *A slightly different price buys a slightly different package.*

Of course, whatever it is that you propose to deduct from your offer must be of about equal value, in financial terms, to the price concession you're making. Most importantly, it must also be something that your customer won't mind letting go of as a part of your package. In fact, the real key to success when trading a minor price concession is to offer to trade it off against some equally minor element of your package which, to that particular customer at that particular time, is of only minimal value. For example, imagine you were a specialist computer system salesperson. If, during your discussions you'd learnt that your customer is already an experienced computer user, then this would mean they would not necessarily require the full training that is included in your standard price-package. So in this case you could agree to a minor price concession but only on the understanding that he or she spent less time with your computer system trainer.

Insight

Always maintain the integrity of your company's pricing policy!

At this point you might be thinking 'Yes, but what if there is no scope whatsoever for modifying my package – then what?' Well, there is one other trading opportunity that you might want to consider as a last ditch effort: you could try trading a minor price concession for a final agreement. In other words, you could agree to grant your priceshaver customer a minor discount but only on the condition that they give you a 'yes' decision right there and then; no more ifs or buts. As a never-to-be-repeated, take-it-or-leave-it final offer, this can be a useful way, perhaps the only way, to hook a priceshaver. It's your call.

Skill acquisition exercise

Identify the non-price variables that you could suggest to a 'priceshaver' customer as a trade-off against a slightly lower price. Prepare your script for suggesting the trade.

48 Use the ATTACK formula

After a long and hard sales presentation, some customers will just thank you for your time and insist they'll be in touch after they have 'had a chance to think about it'. This is one of the most frustrating and difficult objections to overcome because the customer is not really objecting to the substance of your offer at all. Consequently, you have two basic choices. Depending on your reading of the situation, you can either adopt a defensive stance, which means taking the customer at their word, or you can decide to go on the offensive by using the ATTACK formula.

Insight

The ATTACK formula cannot compensate for a poor sales presentation. It is simply a means of encouraging a customer not to procrastinate and, hopefully, to make a positive decision.

Each letter of this acronym stands for an action in a series of steps that can help you to successfully turn this situation around to your advantage. It goes like this:

A = ASK WHAT AREAS OF DOUBT STILL REMAIN

For example:

> *I agree that you should think about it, Michael, although in my experience when people say this it usually means they are still unsure of a few things. May I ask what's on your mind ... ?*

T = TRANSCRIBE

Transcribe each of the customer's areas of doubt onto a master list, making sure that you write down every single one, no matter how many there are. For example:

> *OK, let's list them all out and see what we're talking about. Your first concern is X, have I got that right?* (**and so on**)

T = TRIAL CLOSE BEFORE ATTEMPTING TO ANSWER THE POINTS ON THE LIST

For example:

> *So in a perfect world, if I could deal with all these points to your complete and total satisfaction, then can I take it that you'd be happy to place an order?*

A = ANSWER

Answer each point, and be sure to check that you have handled it to the customer's complete and total satisfaction. Then ask if you can cross it off the list. For example:

> *That's great! I'm glad we've cleared that one up Michael, so can I cross it off the list now?*

C = CLOSE

When you've crossed the last item off the list, close the sale by using the alternative-choice close. For example:

> *Fantastic! That's everything covered! So, when would you like to take delivery Michael: this Thursday or the following Thursday?*

K = KEEP QUIET

Keep quiet and don't deflect the customer's mind from making their final decision.

Skill acquisition exercise

Role-play with a colleague or friend until you feel confident in being able to use the ATTACK formula the next time a customer insists 'I want to think about it'.

49 Resort to a tactic of last resort

At the end of a sales presentation there are two nightmare scenarios that can all too easily unfold. Let's call them scenario Y and scenario Z. The word 'nightmare' sums them up perfectly because these are situations when your customer suddenly and unexpectedly says something that appears to slam the door firmly shut on any remaining hope you had of being able to close the sale. It seems all is lost. Well, perhaps not. In each of these scenarios there is a tactic of last resort that's worth a try.

SCENARIO Y

If a corporate customer has been unusually quiet throughout your meeting and then coldly informs you they have decided to buy from a major competitor instead of from you … but is extremely evasive about telling you why, then it's likely there's some form of skulduggery going on. Perhaps he or she is receiving an under-the-table payment in return for placing the order with your competitor, or something of that sort. Unfortunately, regardless of what it is that they are not telling you, by being starved of information you are in a virtually impossible situation and the sale is effectively lost. There is, however, one last-ditch question you could ask:

Tell me Sam, in an ideal world, if there was one thing I could do to get you to buy from me instead, what would it be?

The power of this question lies in its phrasing. Providing it is asked in all sincerity, it's a question that always comes across as non-accusing and non-confrontational because your customer can answer safe in the knowledge that whatever he or she says is conditional upon there being an 'ideal world'. Moreover, the fact that you only ask for 'one thing' tends to focus their mind and make it a lot easier to answer than a more general style of question. As soon as you have asked this question you must remain silent and wait patiently for the customer to respond. Chances are you'll probably still receive the same 'stonewall' treatment, but on those occasions when you do get a reply at least you will be in a position to consider your options. With a bit of luck you just might be able to find a way forward to make the sale.

Insight

Knowing when and how to resort to a tactic of last resort can make a big difference to your sales figures.

At the conclusion of a long and laborious sales presentation some customers just say 'no' and insist that you leave without giving you any reason at all for their decision. Typically, however, this has nothing to do with your abilities as a salesperson. More than likely it happens because the customer has a phobia about salespeople. Some people are extremely wary of salespeople. They never let their guard down or allow themselves to enter into a meaningful conversation about their requirements for fear of losing control of their own purchase decision. This creates an extremely frustrating situation! Without the necessary feedback there comes a point when you are powerless to do anything but say goodbye and head for the door. However, since at this point you have absolutely nothing left to lose, there is another tactic of last resort that's worth a try. Here's what to do. Just as you approach the door to leave, turn your head to look back at the customer one last time, and in a tone of voice that suggests it is an afterthought, ask this question:

> *Sam, I wonder if you would be kind enough to do me a big favour … just so I know exactly where I've gone wrong … what was the* **main reason** *you decided not to buy from me today?*

You never know, when the customer's guard is down because they think you've accepted their decision, you might just get a reply that gives you an opportunity to recover the situation.

Skill acquisition exercise

Check that you feel entirely comfortable with the wording of the two questions of last resort outlined above. If not, modify them to suit. Then memorize them word for word, and practise your delivery of each question.

50 Bring your customer back down the mountain

If you've ever had the frustrating experience of having a sale cancelled completely 'out of the blue' within a few days because the customer has had second thoughts, then you'll already be familiar with a phenomenon known as PPCD – which stands for Post-Purchase Cognitive Dissonance. The words 'post-purchase' meaning after the moment when the purchase decision was made, 'cognitive' meaning perceiving or being aware of, and 'dissonance' meaning discord or uncertainty.

Generally speaking, a customer will experience PPCD in direct proportion to the degree of importance that he or she has attached to their purchase. That's why (i) the more expensive it is in financial terms, (ii) the more competitive your marketplace is, and (iii) the more complex your products and services are, the more likely it is that a customer will start to question the wisdom of their decision – almost from the moment they authorize the order form! So it's important to have a plan of action at the ready that's capable of 'neutralizing' the threat of PPCD and bringing a customer safely 'back down the mountain' from the heady heights of making a big purchase decision.

Insight

Sometimes, working to keep a sale closed is every bit as important as securing it in the first place.

In devising a plan to bring your customers 'back down the mountain', you could consider employing one or more of the following actions:

REAFFIRM THEIR DECISION

At the time of making a sale, as soon as you have congratulated the customer on their purchase, make a point of reinforcing the wisdom of their decision by reaffirming all the positive reasons why it's the right choice. Then go on to encourage them to remember those reasons should they have any doubts after you've gone.

BE ACCESSIBLE

Just before saying goodbye, get the customer's assurance that he or she will contact you if they have any further questions, afterthoughts or concerns. Make a point of ensuring that they have all your contact details and especially your 'after hours' telephone number. Tell them that you see it as your job to ensure that your customers always feel 100 per cent happy with their decision.

MAKE A FOLLOW-UP TELEPHONE CALL

The day after the sale, telephone your customer to thank them for their order, to check the details of it, and to double-check that they are still totally committed to going ahead with their purchase.

SEND A LETTER

Post or email a thank-you letter to be received by your customer within 24 hours of their purchase decision. In your letter say how much you appreciate their order, confirm the details and go on to take the opportunity to reassure the customer that they have made the right decision. If necessary, mention the many hundreds of satisfied customers who are already using your product or service.

USE A GO-BETWEEN

Within a day or two of the sale, arrange for one of your existing customers who knows your new customer to telephone and congratulate him or her on their new purchase and, most importantly, to endorse the wisdom of their decision.

Skill acquisition exercise

Develop a detailed action plan for keeping a sale closed whenever you anticipate that a new customer is going to experience PPCD.

10 THINGS TO REMEMBER

1 *Condition yourself positively to objections.*

2 *Pre-handle predictable objections.*

3 *Play CATCH with every objection raised.*

4 *Flush out the real objection.*

5 *Use arithmetic to handle price objections.*

6 *Seek out your customer's advice.*

7 *Trade a minor price concession.*

8 *Use the ATTACK formula.*

9 *Resort to a tactic of last resort.*

10 *Bring your customer back down the mountain.*

Where to from here?

I trust this book has been a stimulating read and that you're already successfully closing more sales. But please don't put it down just yet. Now is the time for further action!

Go to the selling skills self-assessment questionnaire (page 128) and follow the instructions. The questionnaire has been designed to provide you with a quick and easy method of reviewing your level of selling proficiency – something you should be doing on a regular basis in order to ensure that you stay sharp. As you will see, each of the 50 questions in the questionnaire corresponds directly with each of the 50 skills featured in this book, thereby enabling you to identify a short list of those selling skills that require additional work. You can then turn this list into an 'action-plan' by putting each skill into priority order and setting yourself a date for re-doing the corresponding *skill acquisition exercise* and trying out your new ideas in the field.

Looking ahead, in your quest to become a more successful salesperson, your mission is to be constantly striving to improve your selling skills. This can only be done through the discipline of ongoing learning and self-development. As the saying goes:

If I want to earn more, I've got to learn more.

However, as well as the core face-to-face selling skills you've been developing by working through this book, I'd like to encourage you to widen the focus of your learning in the future so that it embraces the full spectrum of selling skills. Specifically, I'm talking about learning how to:

- *develop the mindset of an elite salesperson*
- *become an expert sales prospector*
- *book more sales appointments by phone*

- *master the art of sales negotiating*
- *build strong and rewarding customer relationships.*

In the ultra-competitive world of professional selling, if you don't keep on learning you'll soon get left behind by your competitors. So, resolve to become a life-long student of your craft. Keep on reading books, attending training programmes, listening to CDs and watching DVDs. Above all:

Let every customer be your teacher!

Well, you have reached the end of the book but I hope that it marks just the beginning of an exciting new era of successful selling for you and your company. I wish you every success.

Selling skills self-assessment questionnaire

Instructions

Answer these 50 questions in one of the following three ways, and award yourself either two, one or zero percentage points accordingly:

- ▶ *Frequently (2 percentage points)*
- ▶ *Sometimes (1 percentage point)*
- ▶ *Seldom/Never (zero percentage points).*

When you have answered all 50 questions, add up your score, and evaluate your current level of selling proficiency as follows:

- ▶ **90% or more** *You are a highly skilled professional salesperson.*
- ▶ **50–89%** *You are an average salesperson with room for improvement.*
- ▶ **10–49%** *You are a poor salesperson, with plenty of room for improvement.*
- ▶ **0–9%** *You are a hopeless salesperson and should probably pursue an alternative career path.*

[NB: Each of the following five sections (A, B, C, D and E) contains 10 questions, so to evaluate your skills relative to any one of the five 'phases' or 'skill areas' of the selling process, simply multiply your total score for that section by five].

Section A: Opening-phase selling skills

1 *Do you go through a little ritual of some kind that helps to focus your mind and put you 'in the zone' immediately before meeting up with a new prospective customer?*

2 *Do you project the visual image of a top sales professional with every new prospective customer you meet?*

3 *Do you make the most of the opportunity an introductory handshake presents for creating a favourable first impression?*

4 *Do you introduce the company you represent as if it were the 'perfect business partner' for your new prospective customer?*

5 *Do you quickly manage to build a good rapport and feeling of personal warmth between yourself and your new prospective customer?*

6 *Do you qualify your new prospective customer as having the necessary purchasing authority before proceeding with your sales presentation?*

7 *Do you recognize when a professional buyer deliberately uses their office 'territory power' in an effort to undermine your confidence in the price-competitiveness of your company's offer?*

8 *Do you use an appropriate 'attention-grabber' that will arouse your customer's curiosity and make them want to learn more about what you have to offer?*

9 *Do you set an agenda that ensures you and your customer will make the best use of the time set aside for your meeting?*

10 *Do you know how to 'size up' your customer's personality type, so that you can vary the content and delivery style of your sales presentation accordingly?*

Section B: Interviewing-phase selling skills

11 *Do you ask enough open-style questions to gain a thorough understanding of your customer's purchase requirements?*

12 Do you deliberately ask selected questions that will help your customer to 'live out' the benefits of your offer in the theatre of their imagination?

13 Do you use closed-ended questions with pinpoint precision, and to maximum effect?

14 Do you plan the scope and sequencing of your needs-analysis questions?

15 Do you pick up on and mirror-back your customer's 'personal vocabulary' as a means of building rapport as your conversation unfolds?

16 Do you 'signal' the topic area/reason behind all your key questions immediately prior to asking them?

17 Do you listen actively when the customer is talking?

18 Do you pay sufficient attention to reading your customer's body language?

19 Do you give your customer plenty of positive feedback about the value of the information he or she is giving to you?

20 Do you keep control of your needs-analysis interviews?

Section C: Matching-phase selling skills

21 Do you link the features of your product or service to the benefits they represent to your customer?

22 Do you focus your efforts on selling just those benefits that are well matched to each individual customer's particular needs and wants?

23 Do you harness the principle of 'customer involvement' by demonstrating, in some interactive way, one or more of the major benefits-to-the-customer of your offer?

24 Do you, as far as possible, spell out the full value-to-the-customer of each key benefit and in financial terms relative to their individual business situation?

25 Do you, as far as possible, substantiate your claims by providing proof of their validity?

26 Do you make the most of the 'art of storytelling' to dramatize your selling points?

27 *Do you handle your product/samples/sales materials and other documentation with reverence and pride?*

28 *Do you use a rich and colourful vocabulary to power-pack your selling points?*

29 *Do you refer to your competition in the right way and at the right time during your sales conversations?*

30 *Do you sell yourself as an integral part of your overall offer, and to maximum effect?*

Section D: Closing-phase selling skills

31 *Do you consciously identify, in real time, all the 'buying signals' you typically receive from a customer?*

32 *Do you ask a trial closing question in response to every weak buying signal you receive from a customer?*

33 *Do you ask a full closing question in response to every strong buying signal you receive from a customer?*

34 *Do you 'manufacture' a closing opportunity whenever buying signals are unforthcoming?*

35 *Do you deploy the summary-of-benefits close whenever the customer's benefits-sought are particularly complex, varied and numerous?*

36 *Do you, once you've asked a closing question, keep quiet and make sure it is the customer who is the next person to speak?*

37 *Do you deploy the 'weigh-up' close whenever it becomes necessary to help a 'procrastinator' customer to make up their mind?*

38 *Do you employ a 'closing vocabulary' that is as customer-friendly as possible?*

39 *Do you leave every new customer who says 'yes' feeling great about having chosen to do business with you?*

40 *Do you time your exit (irrespective of the outcome of your customer visit) to perfection every time?*

Section E: Objection-handling-phase selling skills

41 *Do you condition yourself positively towards receiving objections?*

42 *Do you pre-handle 'predictable' objections?*

43 *Do you employ a step-by-step and customer-friendly objection-handling process?*

44 *Do you manage to cut through 'smokescreen' objections by finding out what's really holding the customer back from going ahead?*

45 *Do you successfully handle price objections?*

46 *Do you handle unexpected and unusual objections well?*

47 *Do you maintain the integrity of your company's pricing policy, no matter what?*

48 *Do you make the most of the opportunity that the 'I want to think about it' objection presents?*

49 *Do you know when and how to unleash the 'last resort' question tactic?*

50 *Do you counter the threat of 'buyer's remorse' whenever you feel it might be necessary to do so?*

Postscript

A CODE OF ETHICS FOR THE PROFESSIONAL SALESPERSON

My code of ethics is to:

1 Do no harm, knowingly, to others.
2 Know and follow all relevant laws.
3 Represent my company and its products and services as truthfully and as accurately as possible.
4 Represent myself as truthfully and as accurately as possible, including all aspects of my industry knowledge, qualifications, training and experience.
5 Sell only to those customers who have a genuine requirement for my products and services.
6 Act without prejudice or bias, conflict of interest, or the undue influence of any other interested parties.
7 Carry out my duties in a manner consistent with the very highest professional standards that all customers have the right to expect.

Signed: ....

Dated: ....

Index

NB: Selling skills are listed in *italic* together with their reference numbers.

How Horses Learn

How Horses Learn

EQUINE PSYCHOLOGY
APPLIED TO TRAINING

Jeanna Fiske Godfrey, DVM

DRAWINGS BY

Elayne Sears

AN AUTHORS GUILD BACKINPRINT.COM EDITION

How Horses Learn
EQUINE PSYCHOLOGY APPLIED TO TRAINING

AN AUTHORS GUILD BACKINPRINT.COM EDITION

Published by iUniverse, Inc.

For information address:
iUniverse, Inc.
2021 Pine Lake Road, Suite 100
Lincoln, NE 68512
www.iuniverse.com

Originally published by Stephen Greene Press

ISBN-13: 978-0-595-37933-0
ISBN-10: 0-595-37933-8

Printed in the United States of America

Contents

Introduction

IT IS OFTEN SAID there are as many ways to train a horse as there are trainers. One has but to pick up any horse magazine to read the varied ideas and opinions of horsepeople on a baffling array of training techniques. The novice horse owner can easily develop a defeatist attitude about horse training: it's as though the ability to train a horse (or any animal, for that matter) is a capacity granted to a select few.

But any trained horse is an "educated" horse—an animal that has learned a repertoire of responses through the application of basic learning principles. Conversely, the horse trainer is simply a teacher, someone who has developed an understanding of these principles either through reading and observation, experience, or more often, both.

The purpose of this book, then, is to look at learning in the horse from a scientific viewpoint. Most of the principles of learning brought out in this book will be recognizable to the successful trainer, for he or she has used them extensively in training horses, although perhaps not calling them by their scientific names. For the novice trainer, these principles may provide insight and interest into the complex area of horse training.

The horse industry is increasing dramatically each year and the horse population is estimated to reach 8 million by 1980. Thousands of dollars are invested each year in horses both for business and pleasure pursuits, and more and more people are joining the ranks of horse owners. With renewed interest in the horse has come a demand for knowledge about horse nutrition, breeding, health, and behavior.

Within this demand for knowledge is the desire to understand the

qualitative and quantitative aspects of learning in the horse. For it is
learning which is the very basis of man's relationship with the horse.
Without his ability to learn, to be trained and to retain in his memory what he has learned, the horse would probably be treated in the
same manner as cattle or sheep or swine—as a food producing
commodity.

This book has been organized into chapters to inform the novice
owner about basic learning principles and how they can be utilized
in training a horse. It is not my intent to write a horse training man-
ual per se, but to provide the tools and framework within which successful horse training can be accomplished. The examples used to
illustrate the principles involved in learning are those with which I
have been successful and which have a strong basis in learning
psychology.

The early chapters introduce the reader to learning concepts basic
to any species, including the horse. General behavioral patterns in
the horse and their influence on how an individual horse may learn
are investigated, establishing the working vocabulary for later chapters. A review of scientific literature dealing with learning ability in
the horse and a discussion of current training techniques in view of
these scientific findings are included. Much of the latter part of this
discussion deals with my own conclusions about the effectiveness
and efficiency of current training methods. Chapter V deals with the
individual trainer's ability to apply learning principles in horse
training. The remainder of the book deals with basic horse training
according to the principles of learning set forth in earlier chapters.
The examples given concern only basic schooling maneuvers, but
the underlying principles can be utilized to teach even the most difficult movements.

It is impossible to write a book such as this without feeling somewhat humbled by the task. There are so many excellent books available on all facets of equestrian lore—equitation, breeding, showing,
training, feeding and health care. But I hope this book provides new
understanding in the knowledge of the average horseman, enhancing
his relationships with his equine companions.

How Horses Learn

PART ONE

LEARNING BEHAVIOR IN THE HORSE

CHAPTER ONE

Horse Behavior Patterns and Their Influence on Learning

THE HORSE is a product of evolution. His physical characteristics, his mental capabilities, his natural instincts are all born out of millions of years of environmental pressures.

Prehistorically, the horse was the size of a small dog, running on padded toes through the marshy areas of what is now the western United States. He browsed on coarse vegetation such as small stems and leaves, was ever on the watch for the large flesh-eating animals who preyed upon him. His survival depended upon his keen senses, his ability to hide, and most importantly, his ability to run.

As the environment slowly changed from marshy swamp to forests and plains, the horse adapted and changed as well. He dropped the multiple digits in favor of a single toe; he became a grazer as the forests disappeared and the grasses developed and his legs grew in length and strength enabling him to travel farther and faster in his quest for survival. In his travels the horse crossed the land bridge that existed between the New World and Siberia and he populated Asia and Europe.

Then suddenly, the horse vanished from the New World. Perhaps the ecology of North America changed more rapidly than the horse could adapt to it, or perhaps some infectious, fatal disease swept through the bands of horses, decimating them so completely that the New World horse vanished as a breed. For whatever reasons, the horse did not return to the New World until much later, brought by the Spanish conquistadors.

The horse had been domesticated in Central Asia since 3000 B.C.

Later, the horse spread to Southern Europe and Egypt. From Egypt, to Greece, to Rome the domesticated horse moved as man became aware of the many uses for this splendid animal. Without the horse, the survivial and progress of the human race would have been far less dramatic.

Under domestication, the horse was again required to adapt. He had to overcome his natural fear of man and accept this demanding two-legged creature as his master. Fortunately, the horse willingly adapted to this partnership and man and horse ruled the world until the advent of mechanization.

What are the traits of the horse that made this partnership possible? His physical attributes are obvious—he is strong and swift and can carry a heavy load long distances much more quickly than a man can. But behavioral characteristics of the horse that make him so useful to man are much less obvious; only recently have researchers and knowledgeable horsemen been able to accurately describe and categorize basic behavioral patterns in the horse.

Behavior within an animal species is more easily understood when related behaviors are classified together under a general heading. For this reason, most animal psychologists place individual behavior within one of nine categories.

Contactual Behavior

Contactual behavior is exhibited by any animal seeking warmth and protection from members of his own species or, less frequently, from members of another species. Horses are gregarious creatures and exhibit numerous forms of contactual behavior. During bad weather, horses will huddle together, their backs to the wind in an attempt to gain warmth and protection from the elements. In herds of wild horses the animals instinctively move closer to each other when danger approaches.

In the modern horse this desire for contact with others of his species can cause training difficulties. It can be difficult when out riding, to make a horse leave a group of other horses and go on by himself. The horse may stubbornly resist cues to which he is nor-

Figure 1. Contactual behavior is exhibited most often between mare and foal.

mally obedient, simply because he doesn't want to leave his friends.

But a sensitive trainer utilizes this behavior characteristic to his advantage. He furnishes the reassurance normally provided by other horses to his mount and the horse learns to rely on the trainer for confidence and protection, in situations where he's unsure.

A dramatic example of the ability of a trainer to transfer confidence to his horse is recounted by Col. A. Podhajsky, former director of the Spanish Riding School in Vienna. In his book, *My Horses, My Teachers*, Podhajsky tells of the night he performed on one of the famous Lippizan stallions in a huge, brilliantly lighted outdoor amphitheater. At the end of the ride the lights in the arena suddenly were extinguished except for a single spotlight focused on the Colonel and his horse. Suddenly a helicopter dropped out of the night, settling within a few yards of the startled Colonel and his terrified stallion. Several children leapt from the helicopter with flowers to present to Podhajsky for his beautiful performance. Throughout this frightening episode the white stallion stood stock-still. Only Podhajsky knew, as the horse trembled beneath him, the true extent of his terror. But because the stallion had complete confidence in his rider, he remained still in the face of such terrifying sights and sounds.

Establishing a strong bond of confidence with his horse allows a trainer to predict behavior in strange situations more reliably. He can use both physical and emotional contact (seat, legs, hands, voice) to diminish the horse's fear. A horse unsure of his rider, as well as his surroundings, is much more likely to "misbehave" than his confident counterpart.

Ingestive Behavior

A second behavioral category is ingestive behavior, which is associated with the consumption of food or drink. Taking nourishment in some form is basic to all life and the ingestive urge is a strong one. Minutes after birth the young foal seeks nourishment at its dam's udder, and if given the opportunity will begin nibbling grass and grain within the first week after foaling.

Because horses are grazers, their digestive system is anatomically and physiologically adapted to accommodate small amounts of food eaten at frequent intervals. While grazing, horses cover large areas (if given ample space), taking small bites of grass while maintaining almost constant movement.

Because of this behavioral and physiological trait horses are unable to digest large amounts of feed at one time, and are prone to digestive upsets when fed only once or twice a day.

The unnatural habitats in which we keep our horses can also result in some abnormal ingestive behaviors. Chewing wood, either the planks in a stall or bark on a tree, and tail chewing, often seen in young animals and brood mares housed in close confinement, are both abnormal ingestive behaviors and are due to either one or a combination of causes including lack of roughage or nutrients, boredom, and/or lack of exercise.

Drinking is also an ingestive behavior. The average adult horse consumes about twelve gallons of water daily, depending upon his working condition, the weather, and the type of feed he consumes. In stables under modern management automatic waterers are becoming more and more popular. This relieves the manager of much labor and time but prevents accurate assessment of the amount of water a horse drinks. Changes in the frequency and/or quantity of water consumed may be an early indicator of illness.

Horses not only possess a keen ingestive urge, they also seem to have inner clocks which tell them when it's time to eat. Once a horse is established on a particular feeding schedule even a few minutes delay in the arrival of his meal may cause him to become irritable and impatient, and he may, when the feed does arrive, bolt it down nervously without much chewing. Most horsemen agree that a regular feeding schedule strictly adhered to is extremely important in good management, and can cite examples of horses who received excellent feed in sufficient quantities but failed to utilize it properly simply because of a haphazard feeding schedule.

Eliminative Behavior

Eliminative behavior includes urination and defecation. Horses have definite behavior patterns when it comes to urination and defecation, some of which must be overcome in training, especially for show horses.

Although a horse usually will stop whatever it is doing in order to urinate or defecate, it can be trained to continue to move forward when defecating. This training is necessary in performance horses.

"Toilet" areas are often established by horses for eliminative purposes in pastures or stalls if enough space is available. In pastures, horses will usually not graze these areas until all other available feed sources are gone. Although little research has been done, many horsemen feel the tendency to be a "clean" as opposed to "dirty" horse is a characteristic learned from the dam. Mares who restrict their elimination to certain areas of their stall or paddock often produce foals with similar tendencies.

Many horses develop the habit of urinating or defecating just prior to or during certain activities. Countless horsemen have been frustrated by the horse who defecates the minute he's put in a trailer or van! This behavior probably develops initially as a nervous reaction, and eventually becomes a conditioned reflex.

Not only do most horses establish discrete areas for elimination, there are different sex-related behavioral patterns regarding these areas. Stallions usually approach their "toilet," smell it, walk up on it or turn around and back up on it before eliminating. As a result, the stallion's elimination area usually doesn't expand too much. Mares and geldings, however, smell their toilet and simply eliminate where they stand, thereby increasing the size of the area.

Sexual Behavior

Sexual behavior includes all activities associated with courtship and breeding. These patterns are exhibited by geldings as well as by stallions and mares.

Sexual behavior is both neurally and hormonally controlled, and is naturally of most concern to the breeder and stud manager. But sexual behavior and the physiological and psychological activities that are associated with it strongly influence the ability of a horse to learn and accept training. The problems inherent in training a stud are well-known to horsemen. Unless a stallion is taught to restrict his sexual urges to the breeding shed, his preoccupation with mares may make handling and training him difficult and dangerous. While the effects of sexual awareness on learning and training in the filly and mare are less well known, recent research (see Chapter IV) indicates that the estrus periods in the cycling mare may negatively affect learning.

Epimeletic Behavior

Any nuturing behavior is categorized as epimeletic. The most common example of this behavior is exhibited between mare and foal, but there are other instances as well. It is quite common, on a sultry

Figure 2. Common head-to-tail position of two horses, an epimeletic behavior termed wither-nibbling.

summer day, to see two horses standing head-to-tail in their pasture or pen, whisking their tails over each other's faces and necks to fight off flies. "Wither-nibbling" is another example of epimeletic behavior. Horses kept together may often be seen scratching the neck, withers or backs of their partners with their teeth. The relaxed manner of this behavior differentiates it from biting which occurs in agonistic behavior (described later).

Et-epimeletic Behavior

Not only do horses perform epimeletic behavior with other horses, they often signal their *own* desires for care and attention. This is et-epimeletic behavior, and is usually announced through the horse's vocalizations or movements. Again, the more obvious example occurs with mares and foals when foals call excitedly for their dams when separated or weaned. But et-epimeletic behavior occurs between mature horses as well, and many horsemen have dealt with the horse who neighs nervously whenever separated from his stable or pasture mate. Horses may also exhibit et-epimeletic behavior toward humans: at feeding time horses often call for their owners.

Horses do not restrict these relationships only to other horses and people, however. Many horses, particularly high-strung racehorses, establish strong et-epimeletic relationships with a variety of mascots—chickens, goats, dogs, cats and other animals. These animals act as "security blankets," and the loss of a mascot can cause severe behavioral changes in the horse.

Allelomimetic Behavior

Allelomimetic behavior is that in which one animal imitates or mimics the behavior of another. In some animal species, notably birds, this type of behavior is common. It is seen to a lesser extent in horses. Many allelomimetic behavior in horses, particularly those of horses kept in close confinement, are the result of boredom. Wood chewing, cribbing and weaving are all examples of behavior that can spread through a barn contagiously, by imitation, when the horses are exercised too little to release pent-up energy.

Mimicry can also play a role in the horse's learning process and is often used, although perhaps not as a recognizable psychological tool, in handling and training horses. Young horses, when first ridden, are often accompanied by older, settled horses on their daily exercise. Although several types of behavior, including contactual behavior, are evident here, mimicry is still a working force. The young horse, seeing his older companion move along quietly, is much more likely to do so himself than if he were ridden alone.

Investigative Behavior

Investigative behavior is highly developed in the horse and involves the use of the sensory systems—sight, hearing, smell, taste, touch—to inspect and evaluate the environment.

Horses are extremely curious animals and find new objects and places very agitating until they have had a chance to look at, smell, touch, listen to, and sometimes taste them. During investigation, all the sensory systems are on "red alert" and slight sounds or movements can frighten and panic the horse. Horses have been severely injured running through fences after being badly frightened by a strange new object or environment. But the horse's investigative behavior isn't restricted to inanimate objects or surroundings. Heightened sensory awareness is evident when a horse is introduced into a paddock with a strange horse or group of horses, too. Some of this increased activity is due to the dominance hierarchy, which must be re-established on the introduction of a new individual into the group. For whatever reason, it may be several days before the horse calmly accepts new surroundings.

Horsemen often deal with the horse's investigatory urge and its sometimes unsettling aftermath. Any young horse (and many mature horses, too, for that matter) may shy at unfamiliar objects and places, and the best approach to these situations is simply to allow the horse to settle the matter for himself. Punishing a young horse for shying will simply reinforce his suspicion that there was an ogre lurking behind that rock or beneath that bridge! Calm, firm, sympathetic reassurance will normally result in the horse's accepting the situation as a harmless one.

The horse's urge to investigate is often misinterpreted as intelligence. A horse, out of curiosity, may begin sniffing and nibbling at a stall door latch and quite by accident cause it to open; this behavior is devoid of any real reasoning power on the part of the horse. The horse had no prior intention of opening the stall door—the door opened by accident as a result of his nibbling on the latch. But because the horse didn't start out with the intention of opening the door doesn't mean he won't quickly learn the association between nibbling the door latch and being able to get out of his stall! One or two successes are likely to make a confirmed latch-nibbler of any horse.

Agonistic Behavior

The final category of behavior patterns, agonistic behavior, causes many problems for horsemen and includes fighting, aggressive and submissive behavior (dominance hierarchy), and various escape mechanisms. By evolution horses are "flight" rather than "fight" animals. This means that under most conditions a horse would rather run from its enemies than stand and fight to protect itself. This flight reaction largely accounts for the survival of the horse as a species. But although the horse is primarily a flight animal, there are definite agonistic behavior patterns exhibited within the species (between horses). By far the largest percentage of these intraspecific conflicts are related to the dominance hierarchy.

Dominance hierarchies or "pecking orders" (so called because the phenomenon was first described in birds) are evident in many animal species including *Homo sapiens*, and are, in simplest terms, a social ranking of the individuals within a group according to their relative dominant and/or submissive tendencies. These dominance hierarchies are extremely important natural phenomena which channel many of the aggressive instincts of animals into non-lethal activites.

At first, it might seem that nature has drastically erred by introducing aggression into the physiological and psychological makeup of the animal world. But a closer inspection reveals that aggressiveness is often the basis for motivation, and an aggressive animal is normally a better provider and protector of his subordinates. Still, aggression must have limits. There has to be some means of maintaining social order within a group which does not lead to the death of large numbers of its population. This is the function of dominance hierarchies. Once a group rank is established the mere threat of aggression is sufficient to quell any arguments and maintain order. The degree of fighting that occurs during the establishment of these hierarchies varies somewhat depending upon the sex and age of the animals as well as upon the environment in which they are placed.

Among horses, the dominance hierarchy is quickly established when strange horses are placed together and there is ample room for the submissive horse to retreat. Some kicking and biting is usually evident but serious damage rarely results unless one or more of the horses is excessively aggressive or unless they are confined to a small area which forces the submissive animal to stand and fight. Naturally, stallions or very "bossy" mares can seriously injure or even kill their opponents if not separated. It's always wise to keep an eye on any newly established group of horses until the dominance hierarchy has been worked out. This is true not only when strange horses are brought together but also when a horse is removed from a group, since the remaining horses are likely to quarrel in re-establishing the order.

Not only are dominance and aggressiveness important to the horseman in terms of management, they may also affect training. A young horse that has established a high-ranking position among his peers may view training as another dominance struggle, and often requires a firmer, more demanding training program than a more submissive animal. But it follows that once this dominant individual accepts the supremacy of his trainer, he is likely to show more aptitude in learning and more "brilliance" in performance by virtue of his heightened aggressiveness and motivation. Aggressiveness or natural boldness is difficult to infuse into a more submissive horse even though the more submissive animal may appear less of a challenge to train.

All this is *not* to say that it is necessary to subdue the aggressive horse through cruel or harsh treatment; this results in a *loss* of natural boldness which is usually replaced by a sour outlook and a nasty disposition. It simply means that the trainer cannot afford to show any hesitation or uncertainty in his training regimen. He must be especially careful to establish and maintain a good working relationship with the horse.

Children or novice riders are rarely capable of training and handling dominant horses, and even many professional trainers lack the patience and resolve necessary to train these animals without destroying their dispositions. Crabby, cold-backed, "wring-tail" horses who move like machines are a sad commentary on a trainer's ability to work with animals.

Identifying Personality Types in Horses

Although identification and categorization provides a relatively easy and neat means of studying behavior patterns, the behavior we see results from a complex interaction of physiological, psychological and environmental factors. No two animals react in exactly the same manner to a given set of circumstances, and it follows that the behavior of a particular horse may not always follow the book.

Every trainer would like to be able to predict a horse's behavior—especially early in the horse's life. It's impossible to know irrefutably what a horse will be like when he's behaviorally mature simply because environmental influences have such impact on equine personality. But it is possible to identify basic personality types and thereby increase the likelihood of accurately forecasting mature behavior.

Much of a horse's behavior can be attributed to the degree of dominance or submissiveness in his personality. I like to rank horses on a scale of one (submissive) to 10 (dominant) recognizing that the majority of horses score around 4. Four is the average because horses, being flight animals are much more likely to submit to an opponent than to try to dominate him. This fundamental quirk in the equine personality allows man, a much slower and weaker animal, to control the horse.

A horse's rank within a group can be determined by observing his behavior with other horses. A dominant horse defends his territory and feed from other horses. When a new horse is introduced to the herd, the dominant horse is the first to inspect the addition and possibly pick a fight in order to establish his dominance over the newcomer. (The degree of fighting depends on the relative dominance or submissiveness of the newcomer). The submissive horse is easy to spot in a herd. He's the last one to eat if the horses are group-fed and the one frequently running to escape the wrath of his more dominant herds mates. He may keep to himself unless he is fortunate enough to have an equally submissive friend in the herd.

In the stable there are additional indicators which can be used to establish a horse's relative dominance or submissiveness. A dominant horse usually meets you at the stall door while a submissive horse may turn partially or completely away from you as you enter. During early training the submissive horse will usually be easier to work with while the dominant horse may be stubborn and willful until you've established your dominant position over him.

Overlaid on the dominant/submissive traits in the horse is emotionality. Some horses, like some people, are more emotional or nervous than others. An emotionally heightened animal responds to a greater number of stimuli within his environment than a less emotional animal even if the stimuli are unimportant. An emotional horse lacks the ability to weed out inappropriate stimuli and because of this is easily distracted and less able to concentrate on the task at hand. A *less* emotional horse ignores stimuli in his environment that do not immediately affect him; thus, he can concentrate better and is more likely to learn faster.

Just as with dominance and submissiveness a horse is not simply emotional or unemotional. There is a range of emotional levels. Again I use 1 (unemotional) to 10 (very emotional) which, combined with the relative dominance score, allows the trainer a good bit of insight into the trainability potential of a horse.

Emotionality scores are somewhat easier to assign than dominance scores. The highly emotional horse is skittish, spooky and rarely relaxed, even in the stall. Emotional horses are quite often finicky eaters, while less emotional horses are often considered lazy, and are almost invariably easy keepers requiring very little feed to maintain good flesh.

To determine the ideal horse by these parameters we must think in terms of the job we want the horse to perform. For example, a child's horse needs to be very unemotional and relatively submissive (say a score of 2 to 3 emotionality and 3 to 4 dominance). An event prospect needs to be bold and somewhat more emotional (7 to 9 dominance and 6 to 7 emotionality). An amateur hunter might best average 5 on each scale.

Not only the horse but the rider must be considered in this selection. While a bold horse is a good choice for an event prospect, he wouldn't be a good choice for a very timid rider *unless* he already has been well trained by someone who has been able to command his respect without destroying his natural spirit. A bold horse who has developed lots of self-confidence through good handling and training can be an excellent horse for the less aggressive rider. Conversely, a bold, confident rider is the choice for a horse that excels athletically but is submissive and unsure of himself psychologically.

Understanding basic equine behavioral categories and personality types requires continuous observation, assessment and reobservation and reassessment of each horse. Only through careful evaluation of each horse's behavioral makeup can we hope to achieve optimum effectiveness in our training and full enjoyment in our association with the horse.

CHAPTER TWO

Sensory Systems in
the Horse

THE SURVIVAL of an animal depends almost totally upon its ability to perceive and evaluate its environment. This is as true for the one-celled amoeba as it is for man, the differences being in the type of stimuli that must be interpreted, the complexity of the analytic systems, and the intricacies of the resulting responses. The horse, too, must perceive and analyze its environment in order to survive, and much of this perception and evaluation falls into the realm of learning.

So to have as full an understanding as possible of learning in the horse, we must know how the horse picks up the various types of information from his environment that provide the material for learning.

Information is transmitted to an animal's brain as electrical signals called *neural impulses*. These impulses may originate from within the body of the animal (internal organs, glands, skeletal muscles) or from environmental stimuli, but they always function in the body as *electrical* impulses. However, environmental stimuli come in many forms, not just as electrical energy. Where and how does the change from environmental stimuli to neural impulse take place?

The process of converting environmental stimuli into neural impulses is called *transduction*, and the sensory receptors—eyes, ears, nose, tongue, skin—are known as biological transducers. It is their function to take in the various forms of environmental stimuli (visible light, sound, odors, etc.) and transduce or change them into a single form of energy that can then be transmitted along neurons to

17

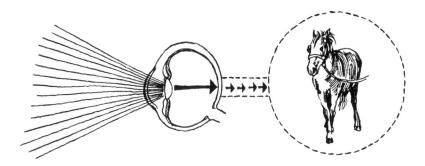

Figure 3. Schematic of the reception, transduction and transmission of neural impulse by the eye: light is received by the eye and transduced as an electrical impulse (small arrows) *to the visual centers in the brain for interpretation.*

the central nervous system. This transduction of energy forms is similar to what occurs when you walk through the automatic doors at a supermarket. As you enter, the pressure receptors in front of the door transduce the change in pressure from your weight into an electrical signal which, through a mechanism, opens the door.

As we talk about sensory systems in the horse, it should be kept in mind then that the eyes do not *see* or the ears *hear*, they simply receive and translate stimuli into neural impulses which travel to the brain. It's the brain which does the seeing and hearing.

All of the sensory systems function essentially in this way, but the different types of biological receptors are selectively sensitive to certain types of stimuli. Thus, the eye transduces light but not sound waves; the ear transduces sound waves and not light.

In looking at the incredible array of stimuli coded by an animal, we should remember that in order to learn, simply experiencing and transducing the stimuli isn't enough. The animal must analyze and utilize the transduced information to adapt his behavior to his environment. This can become very complicated when you consider that an animal is bombarded with continuous stimuli. The animal must learn which stimuli to give his attention to and which to ignore.

We will see in the chapters to follow how the horse learns to discriminate and respond to various stimuli. Needless to say, a good trainer is familiar with the horse's various sensory systems and how they affect his learning.

Taste

Although taste, as a sensory tool, does not have as critical a value for survival as hearing and sight, it is still an important means of experiencing and learning from the environment. This is particularly true in animals such as the horse which do not have the use of hands or paws to investigate strange objects.

Taste is a chemical sense. This means that the sensory receptors for taste must transduce chemicals into neural impulses. Taste receptors are known as *chemoreceptors*, and are sensitive to chemicals in either solid or liquid form. (Olfactory chemoreceptors are sensitive to gaseous chemicals.)

The chemoreceptors for taste are commonly called *taste buds* and are located in pits on the top and sides of the tongue and, to a lesser extent, in other parts of the mouth. These taste buds have a relatively short life-span as sensory receptors go, constantly dying and replacing themselves. Taste buds have microscopic hairlike projections—*microvilli*—where the actual transduction is thought to occur.

There are four basic taste sensations—sweet, sour, salty, and bitter. Researchers have found that certain receptors are particularly sensitive to certain tastes and that these receptors tend to be concentrated on certain areas of the tongue. For example, sweet and salty receptors are found in the front of the tongue, sour receptors on the sides, and bitter receptors at the back. It is currently thought that all taste sensations are a mix of the four basic tastes of sweet, salt, sour and bitter, much as the three primary colors produce all the intermediate ones.

In the horse, taste as a learning tool plays a major role primarily in early life. Horses, particularly young horses, are very curious animals. Much of their early curiosity is satisfied by smelling and tasting objects in their environment.

There is also great variation among horses concerning taste likes and dislikes. Some horses like carrots but spit out apples; others gobble apples and scorn carrots; and there are those "easy keepers" who demonstrate little preference, eating everything that's offered except, of course, the apple-flavored wormer that they're guaranteed to eat right out of your hand!

Some horses, like some people, develop particular fetishes for certain tastes. Ice cream, peanut butter cookies, soft drinks, beer, leather goods, and other unusual appetizers have claimed many horses as addicts, often to the detriment of their health! However, these taste preferences can sometimes be put to an advantage. Rubbing a bit with something sweet if the horse is a sweet lover offers a young horse immediate reward for accepting the bit. It's impractical to carry out this little ritual past the first few bitings—any beneficial effect will have been accomplished by this time anyway—but it can add to that foundation of trust and goodwill you are trying to establish with the young horse.

Taste is difficult to separate from smell, as we will see in talking about the olfactory senses. In working with horses, observant trainers note again and again how closely related these two senses are.

Smell

Horses are real sniffers! For them smell is a highly developed and well-used sensory system for investigation of the environment. Smell plays a particular role in dam/foal recognition and recognition of estrus in the mare by a stallion.

In order for an object to "smell," it must release molecules into the air, and in order for these molecules to be perceived and transduced by the chemoreceptors in the nostrils they must be water soluble. Thus, not everything has an odor, and some substances, due to the character and number of airborn molecules they give off, have much stronger smells than others.

Smells are transduced into neural impulses by chemoreceptors sensitive to gaseous molecules that are located in special nasal tissues known as *olfactory epithelium*. Like taste buds, smell receptors are constantly damaged by colds, dust, and other irritants. Because of this damage there is a continual loss of olfactory chemoreceptors, but unlike taste buds these smell receptors are not replaced. Thus, the sense of smell diminishes as an animal ages.

Researchers have not categorized basic smells as easily as they have basic taste sensations. Terms such as "musty," "floral," and "pungent" have been used but are not very exact in describing smells that humans perceive much less the odors noted by horses. Even labeling odors as either noxious or pleasant causes trouble because what smells like a rose to one individual may smell like a skunk to another! Personal preferences and experiences seem to play a particularly large role in distinguishing smells as pleasant or unpleasant.

Smell is the horse's primary tool for recognition. A mare initially recognizes her foal through smell before visual and auditory cues are established between them. Horses, when first placed together, immediately touch noses and smell each other. Depending upon whether they recognize each other's smell, a fight for dominance may ensue. A stallion sniffs a mare's urine to detect estrus, and he rarely shows further interest in a mare who does not smell to be either coming into or in heat.

Many horsemen subscribe to the notion that horses can "smell" fear. Numerous examples are cited of quiet, docile horses who become apprehensive when timorous persons handle them. Naturally, much of this fear may be transmitted through touch, particularly if the nervous person tries to ride the horse. But there is also evidence that humans and animals emit body odors known as *pheromones* which change according to the "state of mind" of the individual. Thus, an animal could give off a smell of fear, of anger, or of sexual readiness, and it is not too far-fetched to believe that the horse, with his excellent sense of smell, could detect these pheromones in man. This is an area of research that could be of great value and interest to horsemen.

A horse's sense of smell can be used as an investigatory tool in

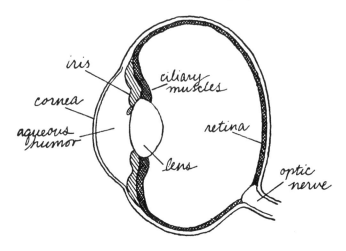

Figure 4. Basic anatomy of the horse's eye.

training. Allowing a horse time to smell strange objects or equipment can help to alleviate his anxiety and possibly prevent some real battles later on. For example, allowing a horse to explore and smell a trailer before asking him to enter it can often eliminate some, if not all, of the fear and resistance he may exhibit if the trainer simply tries to force him in. Likewise, taking the time to let a young horse smell the blanket and saddle before they're put on his back helps him realize that they're not going to hurt him.

There are times when a horse's keen sense of smell becomes a problem for the trainer. A notable example is when medication or other supplement must be added to the feed and the horse literally turns its nose up at it. Of course this is a combined effect, with both smell and taste playing the culprit. Sometimes a little Vaseline or similar substance spread around the nostrils to hamper smell can fool the horse long enough for him to eat the medicated feed.

Both smell and taste are important to the horse in investigating his environment, but they have little significance in training when compared to the three remaining senses of sight, hearing, and touch.

Vision

The sensory organ for sight, the eye, is a highly complex, specialized structure. It is, in fact, an extension of the brain because it not only transduces light waves into neural impulses but also processes certain types of environmental stimuli.

The anatomy of the eye is complex. An in-depth knowledge of the structure of the eye isn't necessary in order to understand how the eye functions, but it is important to be able to visualize certain features of the eye and how these features relate to one another in intercepting and transducing light.

A horse's eye is structurally similar to the human eye, but it has certain peculiarities which cause it to function differently from a human eye.

Light first enters the eye through the *cornea*, a transparent shield on the front of the eyeball. The cornea lacks blood vessels—thus it is transparent—and functions primarily in initiating the focusing process.

After passing through the cornea, light waves travel through the *aqueous humor*, a fluid substance located in the chamber between the cornea and the lens. The aqueous humor provides the needed nutrients for the bloodless cornea. The light waves next encounter the *iris*, a pigmented, contractile membrane partially covering the lens. The small opening in the center of the iris is the *pupil* and the size of the pupil determines the amount of light that reaches the retina in the back of the eye. In horses, small projections of iris hang over the opening of the pupil. These iris projections are called *corpora nigra* and have no adverse effects on a horse's vision.

In the young horse the pupil is round in shape, but as the horse matures it takes on a more rectangular or elliptical shape in a transverse direction (across the eye). This allows for a larger lateral field of vision than a round pupil does.

Dilation and narrowing of the pupil are controlled by two sets of smooth muscles which are influenced by the autonomic nervous system. (The autonomic nervous system influences such involuntary or unconscious functions as heart rate, blood pressure and sweating.) These muscles regulate the amount of light that enters the interior of the eye. In darkness, stress, or periods of intense concentration, the autonomic nervous system causes the pupil to dilate, thereby increasing the amount of light entering the eye. When an animal is relaxed or in bright light, the autonomic nervous system stimulates the pupil to contract, decreasing the amount of light entering the interior of the eye. Because the pupil dilates in excitement or stress, the size of the pupil can be used as an indicator of stress and an examination of the eye is often included in veterinary checkups during endurance and competitive trail rides.

The *lens* of the eye is a transparent sphere behind the pupil and iris. Light waves which have passed through the pupil must also pass through the lens before reaching the retina. (Light waves also pass through the *vitreous humor*, a fluid between the lens and retina which nourishes the lens just as the aqueous humor feeds the cornea.) The lens completes the job of focusing begun in the cornea.

Once through the lens and vitreous humor, light strikes the retina where it is transduced by neural receptors called *rods and cones*.

Before we can fully understand vision, particularly that of the horse, we must understand some of the properties of light. Vision is the ability to recognize light waves that radiate from the sun as they strike objects in our environment.

When light waves hit a solid object they may be totally absorbed by the object, or partly absorbed and partly reflected. It is the light reflected from an object which provides the visual image that we see. If the object is not perfectly smooth (as most objects in our environment are not) the light waves do not strike the surface evenly. The contrast between the areas of reflected light and un-lighted areas creates shadow. Reflected light and shadow produce the images that we interpret in our environment as specific, labeled objects: trees, houses, etc.

It is a property of light that it tends to scatter. The degree to which it scatters, and must then be bent by the cornea and lens in order to focus on the retina, depends on the distance between the eye and the object viewed. The greater the distance light travels, the less the angle or scatter of the light waves, and the less need for focusing in the eye.

The eye focuses light waves through refraction within the cornea and lens. *Refraction* is the bending of light waves that pass through transparent substances (such as the cornea and lens). Objects vary widely in the degree to which they can bend light.

Light waves that originate far from the eye require very little bending in order to be focused as a single point of light on the retina. But as the source of light approaches the eye more bending or focusing is required to get a sharp image. There must be some means of changing the eye's ability to focus relative to the distance of the object viewed. In humans this change in focusing abilities is accomplished through *accommodation*. The human lens changes shape—from flat to spherical—depending upon the degree of focusing required. This change in lens shape is accomplished through the contraction and relaxation of the ciliary muscles which are attached to the lens (see Figure 4).

When viewing a distant object, little focusing is necessary; the lens remains flat due to the contraction of the ciliary muscles. But a close object requires more focusing to create a clear image on the retina. This is accomplished by relaxation of the ciliary muscles, allowing the lens to bulge more to bend the light waves.

Research shows that the horse, however, has very poor ciliary accommodation. The horse's lens cannot change shape to the degree possible in the human eye. How, then, is it possible for a horse to focus clearly on objects at varying distances? Many researchers feel that, unlike the human eye, the equine eye has a "ramped retina." This means that the distance from the lens to the retina is not the same at all points. Focusing is accomplished by raising and lowering the head to direct the light waves onto the most suitable part of the retina. Some authors suggest that the horse raises his head to focus close objects and lowers his head to view distant objects. Others put forth the exact opposite position. There is still debate among researchers as to the validity of the ramped retina as a focusing tool, but there is practical evidence to support the theory that a horse does change head position when viewing various objects.

Horses also possess an exceptionally wide range of vision; they are able to see backward and forward at the same time. The total range of vision is thought to be about 350 degrees. The only blind spots a horse has are directly in front of his nose and directly behind his head. In prehistoric horses, this was a very convenient arrangement that allowed the horse to keep an eye out for danger in just about any direction, thus making it difficult for prey to stalk him. For the modern horse, this enlarged field of vision can pose training problems. Horses may spook at objects we do not see. Some race horses require blinkers to keep their minds off horses coming up from behind.

Another question that is subject to a lot of controversy is whether horses see colors. Very little research has been done in this area; it's open to a great deal of subjective speculation.

In order to understand color vision we must know a little about the structure of the retina, the site of neural transduction. The retina is composed of three layers of cells, but the cell layer we wish to draw attention to is that of the receptor cells—the *rods* and *cones.*

Receptor cells are named for their shape. Rods are slender cylinders with rather low thresholds of excitation. This means that relatively small amounts of light are required to trigger neural impulses in them. Because of this they are thought to operate more at night or in the dark. Although rods are very sensitive to light, they do not function chromatically: they do not distinguish color. Some animals, such as rats, have only rods in their retinas; they see the world in gray, black, and white.

Cones differ from rods both in shape and function. Cones are broad and bulb-shaped with a strong chromatic (color abstraction) capacity. Cones also have a much higher threshold of excitation than rods; they are triggered more by strong light such as sunshine. Cones also have a greater resolving capacity than rods: they show more detail in a visual image. Although it has been established that the horse's eye possesses cones, there is still disagreement as to whether horses see colors and, if so, to what extent.

Many questions remain to be solved about vision in the horse. The lack of information about how and what a horse sees makes it difficult to predict the impact of visual images on learning in the horse. How much of a role does vision play in the horse's learning mechanism? At present we can only guess, but certain relationships between vision and learning can be established.

The first and foremost point to remember is that the horse does not see the environment as we do. Because he has relatively little binocular vision, the horse cannot perceive distances between objects. In fact, research indicates that while a horse may clearly focus on one object, the remaining areas in his field of vision, occurring at different distances from the eye, are blurred.

In addition, the horse can receive two separate visual images (one right and one left) simultaneously because of the placement of the eyes on the sides of the head. Thus, in any training situation the horse may be more distracted than we think simply because he is exposed to so many visual stimuli. It's very difficult to secure, and rather unfair to expect, a horse's undivided attention in a training session if he's in a situation in which he's exposed to many visual distractions. It's much easier and much less frustrating to work with a horse, particularly a young horse, in an enclosed arena or a round pen where visual distractions are reduced to a minimum. This isn't to say that a horse shouldn't be taken outside to be ridden or worked, but the trainer must be aware that the level of distraction is apt to be much higher outside. If a good basic training vocabulary is established with the horse first, these excursions outside are usually much more pleasant and more likely to enhance the learning process in the horse.

Hearing

Just as the eye transduces light waves into neural impulses, the ear changes sound waves into neural impulses. The ear is not only an efficient biological transducer but shares with the eye tremendous powers of selectivity in transducing environmental stimuli.

Along with vision (and to a lesser extent smell), hearing enables an individual to gather information from environmental stimuli that may be far away. The ability to perceive distant changes in the environment helps to insure survival in the wild state. Until the horse was domesticated, natural selection necessitated acute hearing. Consequently, the modern horse has excellent sound perception.

The ear and the eye share one other characteristic—complexity. The ear is just as intricate as the eye. Before we delve into the anatomy of the ear, however, we must take another short side trip into physics to look at the phenomenon of sound.

We talk about sound in terms of waves, but what are these waves composed of and where do they originate? Basically, sound waves are made up of "disturbed molecules" (in the physical and not the psychological sense!) Vibrations (e.g. from a tuning fork, a guitar string, the larynx of an animal) disturb airborne molecules, causing them to oscillate. As the molecules move together they become compressed, and the air pressure around them increases. As this occurs, there is a corresponding decrease in air pressure in the areas vacated by the molecules which sucks the compressed molecules back into it. Thus, the molecules oscillate from compression to decompression; this phenomenon is known as *rarefaction*.

As an object vibrates, it radiates waves of molecules in all directions in various stages of rarefaction—sound waves. These waves travel at a uniform rate of speed—about 750 miles per hour—and are characterized by three basic traits: amplitude, frequency, and timbre.

Amplitude is the loudness of a sound. It is determined by the number of molecules compressed into a given area. The more molecules compressed, the greater the amplitude of the wave, and the louder the sound sensation received by the ear.

Frequency is the rate of vibration of the wave. It is usually measured by the Hertz (Hz), which is the duration of the sequence from compression to decompression to compression of oscillating molecules in sound waves. The faster the vibration, the higher the frequency, and the higher the pitch of the sound produced. Thus, a man singing bass produces sound waves which have a lower frequency than those produced by a woman singing soprano.

Timbre refers to the purity of sound. There are few *pure* sounds, because most sounds are a mixture of frequencies. If you watch a plucked guitar string as it vibrates you see that the vibrations of the string vary in *amplitude* (that is, the distance the string moves from its resting position when plucked). Large vibrations produce sounds known as fundamental tones, and small vibrations produce overtones. The fundamental tones of the large vibrations would

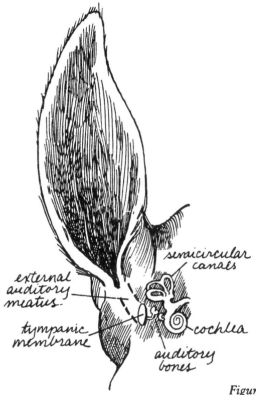

external
auditory
meatus.

tympanic
membrane

semicircular
canals

cochlea

auditory
bones

Figure 5. Basic anatomy
of the horse's ear.

have low frequencies, and the overtones, high frequencies. This is the reason why Middle C on a guitar sounds different from Middle C on a flute.

Sound waves are affected by two major factors: the environment in which they travel and the distance they must traverse. Objects in the environment absorb sound waves to varying degrees (a principle applying to light also). Consequently, sound can be affected both in amplitude and frequency by the environment in which it occurs. The sound of your voice is quite different in a carpeted, draped room from what it is in a room with bare windows and floors. The distance sound travels will affect the amplitude but not the frequency of the sound: the soprano's voice will have the same pitch whether you are seated in the front row or the last row, but the loudness will change accordingly.

Now that we understand what sound is and how it is generated, let's look at the anatomy of the horse's ear to learn how this sound is received and transduced into neural impulses.

The first physical structure sound encounters in the horse's auditory system is the *auricle*—the funnel-shaped flap we usually think of as the ear. The horse has considerable control over the position of the auricle or outer ear. With ten muscles to control the outer ear, he can turn it in a 180-degree arc to the front, side and rear (humans, by contrast, have only three vestigial ear muscles). The horse's two ears can be turned in different directions simultaneously, allowing the horse to hear sounds from different directions at the same time.

A small hole in the depths of the auricle marks the beginning of the *external auditory meatus*, a short passageway connecting the outer ear to the tympanic membrane (eardrum). The vibrating molecules of a sound wave travel into the ear and along the external auditory meatus to strike the eardrum, causing it to vibrate in turn. Thus, airborne sound is converted into a mechanical movement in the membrane, duplicating the incoming sound in frequency and amplitude.

The *middle ear*, situated just beyond the eardrum, is an air-filled space containing three auditory bones: the *malleus* (hammer), the *incus* (anvil), and the *stapes* (stirrup). These bones are arranged in chainlike fashion with the malleus adjacent to the eardrum. The incus occupies the center and the stapes, which rests next to an oval window separating the middle and inner ear, is last. The mechanical displacement of the eardrum by sound wave molecules is passed along these bones and results in a displacement of the oval window. Because of the anatomy of these bones, sound that penetrates the ear is greatly amplified by the time it reaches the oval window. Amplification—of approximately twenty-two times the sound's original volume—occurs because the sound is conducted through progressively smaller areas while maintaining the same force. You can appreciate the principle of amplification better if you think of driving a nail into a board with a hammer. As you hit the head of the nail the force of the blow spreads down to the tapered end and the nail penetrates the board's surface. But the same pressure exerted by hammering a square block of wood on the board doesn't increase through amplification. Consequently, the blunt end of a block of wood does not penetrate the surface.

Once sound passes through the middle ear and is amplified by the auditory bones, it reaches the inner ear through the oval window. The intricate inner ear is composed of the *semicircular canals*, the *vestibular sacs*, and the *cochlea*.

The semicircular canals and the vestibular sacs primarily maintain body position and balance. Although they are located in the ear they have little to do with hearing. So we'll restrict our discussion of the inner ear to the cochlea.

The cochlea is the retina of the ear. It is the site of the biological transduction of the mechanical pressure of sound waves into neural impulses. The cochlea is a short stubby cone with a central bony column encircled by three fluid-filled canals. On the floor of the middle canal lie the *hair cells of the Organ of Corti.* These correspond to the rods and cones of the retina of the eye. They are the receptor cells for sound. The vibrations of the oval window cause the fluid in the canals of the cochlea to move, stimulating the hair cells which produce neural impulses.

Now that we are familiar with the basic anatomy of the ear and have some notion of what happens to sound waves within the ear, we should focus our attention on the behavioral aspects of hearing in the horse, particularly with regard to learning and training.

As we have seen, the horse, because of his evolutionary status as a prey animal, has very acute hearing. He is able to perceive a much wider range of sounds than man. Because of his ability to orient his outer ear to the direction of various sounds he can also gather and interpret more auditory stimuli from his environment than man can.

Auditory stimuli are powerful and effective tools in horse training. We will see in later chapters how they can be incorporated into a training program, and how they can facilitate the learning of other cues. But, while a horse's hearing, like its vision, plays an important role in learning, it can also create problems because of its acuity. Horses have been demonstrated to hear frequencies up to 25 kilocycles per second (20 kilocycles per second is the upper limit of human hearing). A horse often hears sounds that we cannot perceive, and may be distracted by them in a training session.

While there has been little scientific research into hearing in the horse, relatively recent work suggests that auditory stimuli may be even more effective learning tools than currently recognized by most horsemen.

In talking about auditory cues in horse training we should keep in mind that it is frequency (pitch) and amplitude (loudness) by which a horse identifies various vocal cues used by the trainer. The horse does not understand the meanings of words used in training. He responds simply to the physical characteristics of the sound. Because of this, the horse trainer should be much more concerned with how he presents vocal cues than with the words themselves. It is just as easy to teach a horse to trot on the command "stop" as it is to use the appropriate word "trot." In fact, simple sounds such as clucking can teach the horse to respond as much as words, assuming that each command is distinguishable from the others and that the trainer is consistent in presenting these cues to the horse.

Although hearing in the horse can be a valuable training aid, it is only a means to an end. A finished horse must respond to subtle commands from the rider's legs and reins. The final sensory system that we'll discuss—touch—is perhaps, from a trainer's point of view, the most important.

Touch

The word *touch* is often used to describe the sensory system dealing with sensations received from contact between the skin and environmental stimuli. It is a poor choice of words, however, because it tends to restrict our understanding of the information this sensory system gives us about our environment. A more scientifically acceptable term to describe this system is *somesthetics.* Somesthetic sensations are divided into four categories: pressure, pain, warmth, and cold.

Although research has gathered a great deal of information about these sensations, there is still much that remains a mystery. Certain sensations—notably, tickle or itch—don't fall exactly into any of the four categories of somesthetics. While most researchers feel these two sensations are a lessened form of pain, arising from weak stimulation of pain nerve endings, we all agree to their realness as tactile sensations!

The value of touch, in terms of adaptive behavior, is obvious, particularly with regard to the sensation of pain. Pain is an early-warning system, a defense against injury or illness. Without pain receptors, an animal would have no means of detecting internal or external illness or injury. The likelihood of survival without these warnings would be remote.

But while touch is vitally important to an animal, it has certain disadvantages when compared with the other senses. Unlike sight, hearing or smell, touch is a contact sensory system. It gives little information about distant stimuli, requiring the stimuli to contact the skin before sensation occurs. Touch also requires many more times as much energy (approximately 100 million times more energy) to produce a sensation than do vision or hearing. Finally, touch suffers *fatigue.* This is an extremely important fact to remember in horse training. When we touch something with our finger, the somesthetic receptors in our fingertip quickly fatigue and grow less sensitive. This fatigue accounts for the fact that you are not consciously aware of the touch of your clothes or the pressure on your seat and legs from the chair on which you are sitting.

This phenomenon of tactile fatigue is the downfall of many would-be horse trainers. Either because they do not understand the effects of tactile stimulation, or because they ride poorly, or, in some cases, because of a quasi-sadistic concept of horse training as a means of physically dominating an animal, many people proceed on the principle that if a little bit of cueing is good, a whole lot must be even better. What they fail to realize is that, physiologically, the horse's skin receptors are overwhelmed after awhile. Any hope of response to light, subtle aids is, therefore, lost.

Just as with the other senses, there are discrete somesthetic receptors involved in the transduction of environmental stimuli into neural impulses. Several distinct types of receptors have been isolated: *Meissner's corpuscles* are sensitive to touch; *Pacinian corpuscles* are sensitive to deep pressure; *Krause end-bulbs*, to cold; *Ruffini corpuscles* are sensitive to warmth; and *free nerve endings* are sensitive to pain, and possibly touch and temperature as well. *Hair* can also be thought of as touch receptors. Even a slight movement of a hair will stimulate the nerve fiber at the base of the hair, initiating a neural impulse. In the horse, certain long hairs around the eyes and muzzle are called tactile hairs although they do not appear to be any more sensitive than the hairs of the horse's coat. Most of the research into somesthetic senses deals with the Pacinian corpuscles. Generally more is known about the coding process for pressure and touch than for temperature and pain.

There are two major types of touch receptors differentiated by how they produce a neural impulse. There are those stimulated by (1) a *momentary* physical change in the receptor and those stimulated by (2) a *continuous* change or deformation of the receptor. Hair is an example of the first type of touch receptor because displacing the hair stimulates a neural response that ends almost immediately after the displacement stops. The Meissner and Pacinian corpuscles also fall into this category. Other receptors (probably free nerve endings) transmit impulses continuously for long periods of time; they are the second type of receptors. These receptors are greatly outnumbered, however, by the first type of receptor. Thus, touch is more a sensation of changing body contact than continuous contact. You may be unaware of the touch of your clothes except at points of considerable pressure, but you feel the smallest insect crawling through the hairs on your arm immediately.

There is also a relationship between the tactile sensitivity of a particular area of the body and the corresponding cortical area in the brain that interprets impulses originating in this area. The more sensitive the area of the body the more densely packed are the sensory neurons in the appropriate part of the brain. Horses are particularly sensitive to touch in the areas of the mouth, lower leg, flank, neck and shoulders and, according to current theory, should have a corresponding density of sensory neurons in the areas of the brain receiving impulses from these spots.

As with any physiological phenomenon, there is tremendous variation among individuals regarding sensitivity to touch, pressure, pain, and thermal changes. What may be intensely painful to one individual is only mildly annoying to another. The somesthetic senses, perhaps even more than the other senses, appear to be particularly affected by the level of arousal of the animal. Touch or pressure or pain is much more acutely sensed by an excited individual than by a more docile, relaxed subject. Aggravated sensory perception may be due to a heightened response in the brain's arousal area, the *reticular formation*. The effect of stimuli in arousing the reticular formation and anatomical or physiological differences in this area of the brain may account for varied sensitivity to different tactile stimuli.

The Horse—A Sensory Animal

From our abbreviated review of the equine sensory systems, it should be obvious that training a horse entails a good deal of thought on the part of the trainer if he or she hopes to be successful. The horse is evolutionarily a prey animal; his senses are geared for protection and safety through flight. The trainer must overcome this flight tendency by instilling confidence and trust in the horse. He must investigate and understand *each* horse that he works with as an individual with unique behavioral traits that must be encouraged or discouraged to fit into a learning situation. He should be aware of the characteristics of the sensory systems of each horse and adapt his training techniques to take advantage of various, positive stimuli.

A good horse trainer is dynamic, knowledgeable, and understanding. He knows what he is doing, but, more importantly, he knows why he is doing it.

CHAPTER THREE

Basic Concepts in Learning

THE PSYCHOLOGY of learning is a relatively new science, having been recognized for only a little over sixty years. In studying the learning process, psychologists attempt to describe responses that animals are capable of learning and circumstances under which they learn these responses. From this information basic principles governing learning processes are formulated.

But what is learning? What constitutes the learning process? Is there only one way to learn or many ways? Is a rat's learning process different from that of a horse or a man?

Although it is easy to cite examples of learning, absolutely defining learning is not so easy. One might say that learning is any process which changes an animal's behavior. This seems to be a valid statement, but not all change in behavior is due to learning. Fatigue, growth, and other physiological factors may elicit changes in behavior unrelated to learning. A better definition of learning, and one generally accepted by psychologists, is that learning is a relatively permanent change in behavior resulting from experience.

Learning is, for the most part, an adaptive process. A child touches a hot stove and learns the danger of fire. A horse learns to press a metal bar in his automatic waterer to receive a drink. Both of these learning processes are adaptive; they increase the organism's chances of survival. Survival is the motivating force for all behavior, learned or instinctive.

But learning may also be maladaptive. This is observed when irrational behavior develops from a learned response. The fear characteristic of phobia is a learned response; it is also maladaptive because in extreme forms it can totally incapacitate an animal or produce behavior that can endanger the animal.

Learning can be divided into two general categories: classical conditioning and instrumental conditioning (for the purposes of this book conditioning is synonymous with learning). In both types of learning the animal predicts relationships between environmental and/or behavior factors.

In classical conditioning an individual learns relationships between two or more environmental effects. It may be thought of as passive learning because the animal is not required to respond actively in order to learn the relationship. A good example of classical conditioning is the sound of the dentist's drill, indicating forthcoming pain, and triggering a tightening of the stomach muscles. The "conditioned stimulus"—the sight of the dentist's drill—after repeated pairing with the "unconditioned stimulus"—the actual drilling—results in the ability to predict the relationship between the two events: a dentist's drill causes pain, therefore the stomach muscles tighten at the sight of it.

We are surrounded by conditioned stimuli. Television advertisements make extremely effective use of classical conditioning. But "passive" learning is only a small part of the learning process. The much more dynamic area of learning, known as instrumental conditioning, comprises the majority of learning experiences and is also the primary learning process used in training horses.

What is the difference between classical and instrumental conditioning? Suppose you are crossing a street and you hear the sound of a car horn. Classical conditioning has taught you to predict from this sound that a car is approaching, but instrumental conditioning has taught you what response to make—getting out of the street. Your "learned behavior" (moving to the sidewalk) is "instrumental" in your getting a positive reinforcement from the experience (not being hit by the car!) As we will see, reinforcement provides the feedback which tells us whether the consequences of a response are good or bad. It provides the impetus for learning.

Learning is not simply a change in behavior due to experience, but a relatively permanent one. Thus, the ability to retain and recall a learned response at a later time is necessary to satisfy our complete definition of learning. Not only must predictions about the relationship between events and the appropriate response be learned, but this information must be stored. This is memory.

Much research has been done to investigate the physiological factors involved in learning and memory. It is hypothesized that learning involves both neuroelectrical and neurochemical processes in the nervous system and that memory creates structural changes within the brain. Many questions remain unanswered concerning these processes.

We have talked about the fact that learning is divided into two general categories—classical and instrumental. But the reader should keep in mind that the variety of behavior exhibited by most higher animals, especially humans, involves complex interactions between these two types of learning.

In order to learn an animal must have the tools to do so. The tools for learning are the senses—sight, smell, hearing, touch and taste—which feed information about the environment to the brain for analysis. Naturally, to complete the learning process an individual must also have the capacity to respond physically or mentally to the given information.

Differences in sensory capabilities partially explain the variation in learning ability among animal species and among individuals within a species. Impairment or loss of one or more of the basic senses critically hampers an animal's effort to learn. Learning is also affected by numerous other physical and environmental factors. For this reason no two individuals learn in exactly the same manner or to the same degree, but the final result—a learned response to a specific stimulus—can be acquired in almost all animal forms.

In order to understand learning as the dynamic process that it is and to apply learning principles in training animals, a basic working vocabulary is vital.

Various stimuli have already been mentioned. What constitutes a stimulus? Broadly speaking, a stimulus is anything which elicits a response in an animal. A pin prick is a stimulus because it causes a withdrawal response. Leg pressure applied to a horse's sides is a stimulus because it elicits a response—forward movement. There are literally millions of stimuli which will result in certain responses.

Stimuli are both unconditioned and conditioned. An unconditioned stimulus causes a response without any prior association. A pinprick is an unconditioned stimulus because withdrawal is a reflexive response; you don't have to be taught to remove your finger from the pin.

A conditioned stimulus must be learned, usually by repeated association with an unconditioned stimulus which elicits the desired response.

In training horses, most stimuli or cues that are used are conditioned. Very few unconditioned cues are used simply because the finesse and subtly desired by most riders cannot be obtained using conditioned stimuli.

If few of the cues used in training are unconditioned or natural where does the trainer start? He or she starts with basic cues that are closest to natural stimuli and then builds upon these. For example, a leading rein is an unconditioned stimulus since it shows the horse the direction in which he is to go; all that is required is that the horse follow his nose. Most horses learn this rein effect quickly. But the trainer desires more subtle cues in teaching the horse to change directions so he introduces a new "conditioned" stimulus. He could, for example, pair the neck rein with the old stimulus until the pressure of the rein on the horse's neck alone causes the animal to change directions. It is often easier to understand this sequence of events step by step, with the help of a "table," as on the following page.

Naturally, the association between the conditioned stimulus of the neck rein and the unconditioned response of the leading rein won't be established with just one pairing. It is necessary to repeat these paired cues until the conditioned stimulus alone results in the desired response.

One way to enhance or speed up learning in this example is to present the neck rein slightly before presenting the leading rein and then allow them to overlap. This results in a specificity of cues, enabling the horse to distinguish the two rein effects as separate cues, each of which demands the same response.

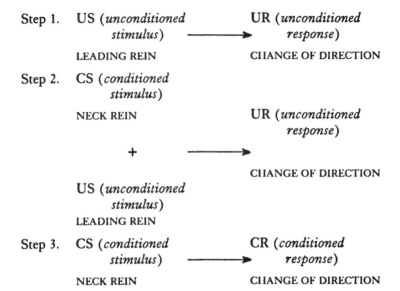

Step 1.	US (*unconditioned stimulus*)	→	UR (*unconditioned response*)
	LEADING REIN		CHANGE OF DIRECTION
Step 2.	CS (*conditioned stimulus*)		
	NECK REIN		UR (*unconditioned response*)
	+	→	
			CHANGE OF DIRECTION
	US (*unconditioned stimulus*)		
	LEADING REIN		
Step 3.	CS (*conditioned stimulus*)	→	CR (*conditioned response*)
	NECK REIN		CHANGE OF DIRECTION

Table showing steps in teaching a horse to perform a change of direction as a "conditioned response."

In describing stimuli we talked about responses without first defining what constitutes a response. An overt response, such as the change in direction a horse makes because of rein effects is obvious: it's a physical movement. Responses do not have to be overt movements, however. Much of man's learning involves mental responses; but in training a horse, the desired responses are largely physical movements that we ask the horse to perform. We may define a response for our purposes as a specific act or movement which an animal makes consequent upon a stimulus. And horse training is, therefore, teaching a horse to make desired responses on cue.

In the elementary stages of training, most responses asked of the horse are individual, discrete movements. Giving to the pressure of a halter, picking up a foot for cleaning, trotting on voice command are all examples of relatively singular responses that result from learning the appropriate cues. But in later training, especially in training for performance events, we may ask a horse to perform a maneuver composed of many smaller responses linked together. A spin, a rollback, an extended trot, a properly jumped fence all appear as a single fluid movement in the finished horse, but, in reality, are comprised of many discrete responses each of which had to be learned individually before being combined in the movement that we see. It is vitally important that a trainer recognize the discrete responses within a larger movement in order to give the horse a solid foundation upon which to build more complex movements.

Training a horse is not simply a matter of stimulus and response. There has to be some means of showing the horse whether or not the response he gives to a particular cue is the correct one. We do this by reinforcing the response either positively or negatively depending upon whether the response is correct.

Reinforcement, much like the two types of stimuli, can be divided into primary and secondary categories. *Primary reinforcers*, like unconditioned stimuli, do not have to be learned; they are naturally reinforcing to an animal. Feed is the best example of a primary reinforcer: it is an obvious reward. A primary reinforcer satisfies a basic need—hunger (the reinforcer is food), thirst (water), fatigue (rest), boredom (exercise), sexual drive (breeding). Very few primary reinforcers are used directly in horse training but their importance in establishing secondary reinforcers is tremendous.

Secondary reinforcers, like conditioned stimuli, must be learned by the animal. They are learned in a similar manner to the conditioned stimuli. A secondary reinforcer, after repeated pairing with a primary reinforcer, reinforces on its own. An excellent example of a secondary reinforcer is the pat on the neck that is so much a part of horse training. Many people assume the horse "knows" that a pat on the neck means we are pleased with him, but this isn't the case. To be truly effective as a reinforcer for good work, the pat on the neck should be learned by pairing it with a primary reinforcer. An easy and effective way to accomplish this is to pair the pat on the neck (and perhaps some kind words) with the end of a training session—rest—which is naturally reinforcing to the horse. After awhile the pat on the neck develops its own reinforcing quality even when not associated directly with the end of the training session. In this way it becomes an effective tool to let the horse know we are pleased with a response he has made to a particular cue.

Reinforcers, regardless of whether they are primary or secondary, can be divided further into two general types. These types are positive reinforcers and negative reinforcers. Positive reinforcers are those things an animal desires. Again, feed is an excellent example. But in actually training a horse, most positive reinforcers are secondary ones such as the pat on the neck and kind words.

There can be no doubt that positive reinforcement, or reward, is a powerful means of altering an animal's behavior. There is ample scientific data to support reward as an effective reinforcement for learning. But many people are confused about the proper utilization of positive reinforcers. Most problems arise when the reward is given indiscriminately to the horse rather than as a specific consequence of a desired response. This happens more often with young people and their horses perhaps because they tend to think of their horses a bit too much like pets. They often fail to realize a cardinal principle of training: whatever behavior occurs in the horse just prior to his receiving a reward is the behavior that will be reinforced—even if the behavior is undesirable.

Negative reinforcement is anything an animal tries to avoid or get rid of if given the chance. There are two major methods of training horses with negative reinforcement.

Escape conditioning is a type of learning in which a punishing, or *aversive* stimulus is applied with little or no cue and independently of what the horse is doing. A specific response by the horse is necessary for termination of this annoying stimulus. An example of this would be a horse who refuses to jump a fence except on being spurred. He jumps the fence to escape or get rid of the discomfort of his rider's spurs.

A second type of negative reinforcement training, and the one which is used most often with horses, is *avoidance conditioning*. The horse is first presented with a cue. If the response is correct no aversive stimulus is applied. However, if the response is incorrect or latent (that is, slow to appear), a negative reinforcer is applied to

Figure 6. The use of escape and avoidance conditioning in horse training. During the first few halter sessions with a foal, a come-along rope is used to urge the foal forward. The foal moves forward to "escape" the pressure of the rope. Pairing the pressure of the come-along rope with a neutral cue like a voice command will lead the foal eventually to respond to the cue alone, thereby avoiding the rope pressure.

create an escape conditioning situation. The working hunter who refuses the fence demonstrates how this works. As he approaches the fence, his rider, through leg, rein, seat and perhaps voice aids, cues the horse to jump the approaching fence. If for some reason the horse refuses, the rider resorts to escape conditioning by applying spurs to the horse. The horse escapes this discomfort by jumping the fence.

Punishment is used in horse training when the horse responds inappropriately, in the *absence* of a cue, and is then punished for it. The aim is not to acquire a new response but to get rid of an undesirable one that the horse already exhibits. We punish a horse that kicks, that bites, that rears. The difference between negative reinforcement and punishment can be confusing but it is an important concept to understand. Strictly speaking, a negative reinforcer precedes a response and punishment follows a response. Using this criterion, it is obvious that aversive stimuli can act simultaneously to punish disobedience while reinforcing a correct response. For example, when a rider applies his spurs because a horse refuses to jump a fence he is punishing that response since it was made in the absence of any cue to make that particular response (we have to assume that the rider did not inadvertently cue the horse to run out or stop by being out of balance or hanging on the reins; in this case punishment is unfair and will only serve to frighten the horse). When the horse responds to the spurs and jumps the fence, the rider removes the spurs, thus reinforcing the correct response.

For any reinforcement to be effective it must be given almost immediately after the response it aims to encourage or discourage. The term *contingent reinforcement* describes this principle. That reinforcement be swift is particularly important in negative reinforcement because of the dual roles (punishing and reinforcing) of aversive stimuli. Contingent application of an aversive stimulus (crop, spurs, strong leg pressure) lets a horse know which response is undesirable, and provides for immediate reinforcement of the correct response by removing the stimulus when the horse has done what he was asked to do. But indiscriminate use of aversive stimuli has no value in an equine training program.

Another important aspect in effectively using negative reinforcement as a training tool is the availability of alternative responses. This means that when an aversive stimulus is applied to punish a wrong response the trainer must be sure that the desired response is known to the horse. Getting back to our balky hunter as an example: it does very little good in terms of reinforcing the jumping response to have the horse facing away from the fence when the spurs are applied after a refusal. The refusal is inadvertently reinforced if we remove the aversive stimulus while the horse is facing away from the fence. The removal of the stimulus then reinforces turning away from the fence. Unfortunately, this very thing occurs more often than it should at horse shows and in training sessions because riders become frustrated and impatiently act without considering the consequences of their actions.

We're now familiar with reinforcement in its various forms, but when and how often should reinforcement be applied? Schedules of reinforcement have a direct effect on how any animal learns, and affect the rate of learning in the horse as well. There are three general schedules of reinforcement used in learning psychology. *Continuous reinforcement* means that every response is reinforced, negatively or positively, depending upon whether it is a desired response. At the other extreme is *extinction:* no reinforcement at all, regardless of the response. Between the two extremes are an infinite variety of intermittent schedules of reinforcement which rely upon either the number of responses made or a time interval as criteria for reinforcement.

The early learning stage for any animal, when behavior is first acquired is called the *acquisition phase.* Research has demonstrated that during the acquisition phase, learning is enhanced if *all* responses to cues are reinforced on a continuous schedule. In other words, the horse is praised for every correct response to a cue to encourage its recurrence and punished for undesirable responses to discourage repeated mistakes. In this early learning period, when a horse may make several responses simultaneously to one cue, it may be necessary to inadvertently reinforce some bad behavior in order to encourage the response desired at the particular time. But after repeated exposure to the cue, the desirable response will be strengthened and the undesirable responses eliminated. For example, when a horse is first asked to canter on cue he may not strike off on the preferred lead, but he definitely should be praised for responding to the cue to canter. We can worry about confirming leads later when the horse is responding well to basic canter aids.

Once an animal has learned a particular response to a stimulus, research shows that he will continue to perform more readily if switched from a continuous to an *intermittent* schedule of reinforcement. And a horse that is performing on an intermittent schedule of reinforcement will continue to perform longer on an extinction schedule (that is, in the absence of all reinforcement) than a horse that is performing on a continuous reinforcement schedule. Psychologists aren't all agreed as to why this is, but the phenomenon is seen in many different species, including man. This simply means that people and horses retain what they've learned longer if they are only occasionally reinforced for making correct responses. This is of paramount importance in the effective use of positive reinforcement in training. If your horse has learned to perform a rollback, for example, as a part of a reining pattern, occasionally reinforce that behavior with a strong reward. Once or twice a week when your horse performs a particularly good rollback for his level of training get off your horse immediately after the rollback is completed, strip off your tack and let the horse loose in a paddock for an hour or so (the ultimate reinforcement!) Give the horse a reward to work for, not simply negative reinforcement to avoid or escape.

It should be remembered that each cue-response-reinforcement relationship that we ask a horse to learn is a separate entity and therefore, a horse can be in the acquisition phase of learning and on continuous reinforcement for one relationship and already into an intermittent schedule of reinforcement for a relationship he has already learned.

We have outlined the mechanisms for learning and have looked rather closely at how the three components—cue, response, reinforcement—relate to each other, but putting theory into practice doesn't always follow the book. Theory has to be interpreted and applied to suit the individual animal. One way to do this while taking into account individual variation in learning is a technique called *shaping*. In the acquisition phase of learning, the initial response to a particular cue may only vaguely resemble the ultimate desired response, but successive approximations of the desired response must be positively reinforced in order for the animal to understand what the final response should be. For example, when a rider applies leg pressure to a horse's sides he wants the horse to move forward and to continue to move forward until the rider introduces another cue to alter or terminate this response. But a young horse at an elementary level of training may simply move a few steps only to stop when presented with this leg pressure. For the horse to learn the meaning of leg pressure, we must reinforce positively even this semblance of the response that we want. Further training in which we demand a little more at each response before positive reinforcement, eventually teaches the horse that the leg cue means to move forward until told otherwise.

Another factor that affects learning in an individual is the effort required to accomplish the response desired. It's much easier to teach a horse a response that requires little physical and/or mental effort than a difficult maneuver that requires a great deal of both. Thus, it is easier to teach a horse to stop than it is to teach him to do a proper shoulder-in. It also means that the more difficult the response the faster it disappears on an extinction schedule of reinforcement. The trainer must be aware of the difficulty of the task he is asking and the individual horse's physical and mental capabilities to perform the task.

A trainer must also realize the ineffectiveness of massing trials. This means that one three-hour training session, particularly in the acquisition phase of learning, is not nearly as effective as six half-hour sessions. In this case you could almost say the sum of the parts is greater than the whole. A horse does not have the concentration span that a human has, and can only assimilate small amounts of information at one time. Forcing a horse to perform beyond his mental capacity usually results in frustration and sourness on the horse's part.

We've discussed the horse's ability to learn and how he goes about doing it, but what about intelligence? Are intelligence and learning ability synonymous terms? No, they're not. Intelligence is associated with reasoning power, and the horse doesn't make a very good showing in so-called "intelligence tests" for domestic animals (the pig always seems to win). But because the horse is lacking in reasoning power does not mean that he is not capable of learning. When presented with a logical learning procedure involving the appropriate use of cues and reinforcement, horses can learn incredible feats. At the heart of this learning is the simple formula of stimulus-response-reinforcement, with a sprinkling of good horse sense thrown in!

CHAPTER FOUR

A Scientific Review of Learning in the Horse

THE SUBJECT of learning ability and intelligence in horses has always kindled heated discussion among horsemen. Great wisdom and, conversely, boundless stupidity have been attributed to the horse. It all depends on who happens to be talking. Opinions about the horse's capacity for learning are usually based not on evidence of learning but on how a particular animal has adjusted to the demands of its owner or trainer. Thus, what most horsepeople mean when they say how "smart" their horse is has more to do with temperament and trainability than with true intelligence.

Since most horsemen are interested in their horse's ability to be trained, we should try to see how relative learning ability fits into the framework of horse training.

The final test of any animal's trainability is his performance. How does this animal perform the tasks for which he was trained compared with other animals similarly trained? And, more importantly, how difficult a task was it to bring the animal to this level of performance?

Naturally, the final performance of any trained animal is based upon an almost infinite number of ingredients including genetics, physical ability and conformation, environmental effects, and motivation. Genetics includes the physical and emotional factors which determine a horse's potential for performance. This is the framework upon which all other factors are built. Conformation is important in relation to the tasks demanded of the horse during training. In other words, physical conformation is more likely to influence the training and eventual performance of an open jumper than a pleasure horse.

It is primarily environmental factors—nutrition, health, handling, training—which the trainer manipulates. All affect a horse's learning ability and final performance. Motivation or desire, on the other hand, is the most nebulous factor affecting final performance. Strong motivation can make a physically inferior animal perform beyond realistic expectations. It is also the factor we know the least about: why one horse will perform tremendous feats, even in pain, while another continually tries to "cheat," is still a mystery.

Learning ability, as with all behavior, is rooted in genetics. Each horse has a genetic potential for learning based upon its individual neurophysiological and anatomical makeup. However, learning abil ity is not a static quality. Many factors affect this genetic base, positively or negatively altering the basic learning potential of the horse. Nutrition, health, age, handling and other environmental effects can greatly alter a horse's learning ability.

Research into equine learning ability has only scratched the surface in attempting to define learning mechanisms in horses, as well as in investigating individual learning differences among horses. Much of the research with horses has been conducted by psychologists interested chiefly in human applications of their discoveries in horses. Therefore results have often not been interpreted and presented to the horse-owning public. Recently, animal scientists have taken a much greater interest in studying the behavioral patterns of horses, particularly learning behavior. Within the next few years many of our questions about how horses learn and what effect various environmental factors have on learning may be answered. In the interim, a review of current scientific literature on learning in the horse provides some insight into the mind of the horse.

Early scientific research into learning in animals attempted to rank domestic animals according to relative intelligence. One of the earliest such studies was G. V. Hamilton's "A Study of Trial and Error Reactions in Mammals" published in the *Journal of Animal Science* in 1911. In this study, several species of domestic animals were tested in an escape conditioning situation and then ranked according to their performances on the test. Hamilton ranked horses very low in this study, implying extremely poor learning ability. But these early attempts to compare species in terms of relative learning ability failed to account for such factors as sensory dominance and preparedness to associate particular stimuli and responses. Thus, the testing procedures were so biased that the results were essentially unreliable.

In 1933 the *Journal of Comparative Psychology* published a paper entitled "The Responses of Horses to the Situation of a Closed Feed Box," by L. P. Gardner of Cornell University. This was the first of several papers published by Gardner on learning in horses. In this first paper, Gardner was interested in observing how horses responded when the feed box in which they were normally fed was fitted with a hinged cover. The results indicated that the horse had been maligned by previous assessments of its relatively low learning ability. Gardner conducted several more studies in an effort to obtain a more realistic understanding of the learning ability of horses.

The second of Gardner's studies "The Responses of Horses in a Discriminating Problem" was published in 1937 in the *Journal of Comparative and Physiological Psychology*. Gardner tested forty-five horses to determine if they could learn to discriminate between a grain-filled feed box covered with a black cloth and, empty regular feed boxes. The horses were given two trials each morning; all the horses learned to discriminate between the two types of feed boxes. This led Gardner to conduct a more complicated discrimination problem, the results of which were published in the same journal as "The Responses of Horses to the Same Signal in Different Positions." Forty-four horses, ranging in age from seven months to sixteen years, were used in this study. Twenty-one were mares or fillies, five were stallions or colts and eighteen were geldings. In this study three feed boxes were used and the black cloth, instead of lying over the feed box containing the feed, was positioned above the box or directly below the box. Again, each horse was given two trials each morning. The correct feed box (the feed box with the black cloth to indicate feed) was alternated randomly during the test period. Again data showed that the horses could learn to discriminate a "signal" to tell them which feed box contained the feed. The results also showed that younger horses of less than four years made fewer errors than older horses. Gardner concluded that younger horses learn more readily than older horses, possibly because of the younger animals' curiosity.

With the coming of World War II, the days of the horse as a vital component in food production, military defense and transportation in America were numbered. The sharp decline in the utilization of the horse in agriculture and other areas dramatically reduced the horse population. Interest in horse research, particularly behavioral research, waned.

But while Americans were enjoying the fruits of mechanization and modern living, many other countries continued to rely heavily on the horse. Russia, trying to rebuild itself after the tremendous losses of World War II, put heavy emphasis on research into agricultural fields. Many studies in animal behavior resulted.

In 1956, N. F. Popov published his paper "Characteristics of Higher Nervous Activity of Horses" in a Soviet journal. This treatise examined the physiological psychology of the horse and resulted in some rather elaborate and elegant studies. Popov found horses to be acutely sensitive animals in terms of their sight and hearing. The horses he tested could differentiate between 96 and 100 beats of a metronome, between a frequency of 1,000 and 1,025 cycles per second, and between 69 and 70 decibels. Visually, they could differentiate between light stimuli of eighty-seven and ninety watts. All of these experiments were conducted in a conditioning situation in which reward was based on the animals' ability to discriminate between appropriate cues. The horses were also able to establish a conditioned response to an auditory stimulus at 20,000 cycles per second, the limit of most humans' hearing. One of the most interesting and revealing aspects of Popov's data was his success in teaching horses to perform "third-order" conditioned responses. This meant that the horse, in order to receive a reward, had to respond to three separate conditioned stimuli (sound, sight, touch) with three different conditioned responses, each response depending upon the correct completion of the previous response in the cycle. Popov's horses readily differentiated between the sequences of the conditioned stimuli.

In 1960, results of another Russian study—"Typological Features in the Higher Nervous Activity of Race Horses"—appeared in the Soviet journal *Konevodstvo in Konnyi Sport.* The researcher, I. Bobylev, demonstrated individual differences in exploratory and orienting behavior among thirty-nine horses in a test situation, and was then able to correlate this behavior with the relative ease or difficulty of later racing training. This was one of the first attempts to define and relate "emotionality" to training in horses.

By the 1960's, a new horse culture, based on riding as a leisure activity began to gain popularity in the United States. The horse population that had decreased so dramatically during and after the war suddenly took a turn upward as more and more people discovered the pleasures, challenges, and pride of horse ownership. In addition, behaviorists and psychologists, who traditionally restricted their learning research to laboratory rats, began to investigate other species, including the horse. This produced several new studies in equine learning behavior.

In 1960, a paper entitled "Operant Responding in a Horse under Several Schedules of Reinforcement" appeared in the *Journal of Experimental and Analytical Behavior.* R. D. Myers and D. C. Mesker from Colgate University examined the effect of different reinforcement schedules on a conditioned response in the horse. The subject, a ten-year-old gelding, was required to nudge a lever to activate a dispenser that would drop grain into his feed box as a reward. The researchers initially shaped the horse's behavior by rewarding him every time he approached the lever, then every time he touched it, until he finally learned to press the lever for the reward. Then, instead of rewarding the horse every time he nudged the lever, the researchers put the horse on an intermittent schedule of reinforcement, with only every third response rewarded. The ratio of response to reward was then lengthened to every fifth response then to every eighth response. Finally the horse was rewarded only after eleven correct responses. With each increase in the number of responses required for a reward, there was a significant increase in the rate of responding by the horse. He became very adept at rapidly flicking the lever with his lips. At this point, the researchers switched the horse to a fixed-interval reinforcement schedule. Regardless of how many times the horse responded correctly, he was rewarded only at three-minute intervals. A marked change in his response behavior was evident after five days on this fixed-interval schedule. Instead of responding rapidly and continuously, the horse anticipated when reinforcement was due and increased his rate of responding only toward the end of the three-minute interval. Immediately after the reward, the horse virtually stopped responding, but his rate of responding increased again toward the end of the next three minute interval. This behavior is termed "scalloping," because of the pattern it creates when shown graphically. Scalloping is common among animals rewarded on a fixed-interval schedule. Although the research by Mesker and Myers involved only one subject, it illustrated some of the basic learning characteristics in the horse, and also provided practical information about how various schedules of reinforcement affect learned behavior in horses.

In 1962 J. M. Warren and H. B. Warren published "Reversal Learning by Horse and Raccoon" in the *Journal of Genetic Psychology.* They questioned whether differences in learning among various animal species were due to newly evolved capacities for solving complex problems or to increases in the rate of simple learning. Psychologists have debated for years whether the difference in learning capacities between humans and higher mammals and the lower vertebrates and invertebrates was a qualitative or quantitative one. The question has yet to be settled. The major thrust of this type of research is to discover phylogenetic differences in learning among animals. The Warrens' research was aimed at such differences. Nevertheless it also provided additional basic information on learning behavior in the horse.

The Warrens used two horses from a riding stable for their research, testing the horses in a large paddock at the stable. The horses were required to choose between two feed boxes placed twenty feet apart, forty feet from the entrance to the paddock. The box on the right was black and the one on the left was white. This combination of brightness and spatial cues gave the horses more visual information with which to make their choices. On the first training trial both feed boxes were empty, so that the researchers could determine if the horses had any position preferences (right or left). On the second series of trials, the non-preferred box was the correct choice and each horse was asked to choose between the feed boxes until he had made eleven correct choices out of twelve attempts. The last eight responses had to be made without error. This satisfied the learning criterion established before the research began. When the horses met this criterion the researchers were convinced that they had learned which box held the food reward. The reward was now switched to the previously non-rewarded feed box and testing resumed. Again, both horses were tested until they satisfied the learning criterion and were consistent in choosing the newly rewarded box. Then the reward was switched back to the initially correct feed box. Alternating the reward between boxes continued as the criterion for learning was satisfied in each set of trials. One horse was tested through six reversals and the other through nine reversals of reward. The results showed a rapid reduction in the number of errors made in learning the successive reversals. One horse solved all the reversals more quickly than he had the original discrimination and averaged fewer than two errors per reversal over the series of nine trials on which he was tested. The other horse made the same number of errors on the first reversal as on the original discrimination and averaged two errors in six reversals.

These results indicated that horses were able to "learn to learn," or, in other words, apply previously learned information to solve a new problem. In order to show a successive reduction in errors throughout several reversals, the horses had to learn the general principle of reversal of reward and then apply this principle to each new problem. The practical significance of this type of learning behavior in terms of training horses is particularly interesting because it suggests that a horse's ability to learn advanced responses may be affected by how well he learned the initial ones. For example, a horse who has learned thoroughly the general principle of moving away from the pressure of the rider's leg will learn an advanced maneuver, such as shoulder-in, more readily than a horse who has not grasped this association between stimulus (leg pressure) and appropriate response (moving away).

In 1966, the Midwest Psychological Association Convention in Chicago heard Jane Dixon speak on "Pattern Discrimination, Learning Set, and Memory in a Pony." The research was part of Ms. Dixon's graduate studies in psychology, and the results appeared later as a popular article in the *Thoroughbred Record* (1970). In her study, Dixon asked a seven-year-old gelding named Pecos to learn twenty pairs of patterns drawn on eight-by-ten-inch pieces of wood. There were fifteen black-and-white patterns and five color patterns of varying complexity. Only one of each pair of patterns was the correct (rewarded) pattern. The pony was tested in a large paddock where he was separated from the testing apparatus by a chest-high bar. The pairs of patterns were presented in wooden frames laid flat on a bench just beyond the restraining bar. Each pair was presented simultaneously with the correct pattern randomly displayed in the left or right position. If Pecos chose the correct pattern by nudging it he was rewarded with a piece of carrot. If an error was made the patterns were removed immediately and no reward was given.

Pecos was taught to differentiate the twenty pairs of patterns in eighty-seven consecutive sessions of one hundred trials per day. Each daily session lasted about fifteen to twenty minutes. The learning criterion was based on errors. Pecos had to make fewer than eight errors in fifty trials (15 percent error rate) before it was felt he had learned to differentiate the correct pattern in a pair. Periodic reviews of previously learned pairs were given throughout the eighty-seven days of testing.

In a final test, Pecos was presented with all twenty pairs of patterns in succession. He scored 92.5 percent correct choices, an excellent score considering the number and complexity of the patterns. Dixon then retested Pecos at intervals of one, three and six months on all twenty pattern pairs to determine the degree of memory loss over various time periods. After one month, Pecos scored 81 percent correct choices when tested with the twenty pairs; at three months he scored 78 percent correct; and at six months 77.5 percent correct. There was a total memory loss of only 15 percent for the entire six month period and only a 3.5-percent loss for the five-month period between the one-month and six-month re-tests. It was obvious from Dixon's work that while horses might not score well on intelligence tests that require relatively complex reasoning abilities, they nonetheless are able to learn complex associations between stimuli and reward. Furthermore, they can retain and recall these learned associations over a long period of time.

In the early 1970's, several studies were conducted under the guidance of D. D. Kratzer of the University of Kentucky on learning in horses. One study dealt with avoidance conditioning in twenty-one ponies. In this study, the ponies were trained to respond to a buzzer as a conditioned stimulus to avoid an electrical shock. The conditioning chamber was a ten-by-ten–foot stall divided by a one-foot barrier which the ponies had to jump in order to avoid a shock administered through a heart/girth belt attached to a retractable cord from the ceiling. The testing was divided into three sets of ten trials each.

Only one pony failed to make an avoidance response (jump the barrier) during the first set of ten trials. One pony had a 70-percent avoidance response rate on the first set of trials. The mean response rate for all the ponies on the first set of trials was 36.6 percent. On the second set of ten trials the following day, three ponies had a 100-percent response rate and the average response rate for all ponies had increased to 78 percent. On the third day of trials, over half the ponies responded to the buzzer and avoided the shock on all ten trials. The group as a whole averaged a 91-percent response rate. The researchers reported that on each successive day the ponies appeared calmer and more sure of themselves in responding. They would stand fairly still until the sound of the buzzer, at which they would jump the barrier to avoid the shock.

In another study at the University of Kentucky, Kratzer and his associates tested thirty-seven yearling Quarter Horse geldings in a learning experiment using a maze. The maze was built with a single entry where the horses were required to turn right or left in order to reach the outside pens where water, which had been withheld during the night, was available. The horses were given one maze learning trial per day. Both the left and right sides could be made into blind compartments with a movable partition.

Three different observations were made for each horse at each trial. Errors were recorded each time a horse looked into a blind compartment. How long the horse took to select one compartment (that is, the *latency* of the response) was recorded as the total time the horse spent in the maze. And a side choice indicated whether the horse chose the left or right compartment as its first choice.

In the first five trials where one compartment was "blind," the horses had to turn right in order to escape and get the water. There was an average decrease in the number of errors the horses made on successive days of testing. Accompanying this decrease in error was a significant decrease in the time it took the horses to escape from the maze—from about seventeen seconds on the first trial to about eight seconds on the fifth trial. There was also an increase in the number of initial right-side choices, indicating that the horses chose the right side because they knew it led to water. It was not simply a random choice.

In a second series of five trials, the horses were required to choose the former blind compartment—the left side—in order to escape. On the first day of this new series of trials the average error rate increased sharply because of the previous conditioning the horses had received. However, over the next five trials with left-side choice as the correct one, there was a significant decrease in errors. The time the horses spent in the maze also decreased from about twenty-six seconds to about fifteen seconds. But, interestingly, the horses' initial choice was still to the right.

At this point the researchers added an aversive stimulus to the right side of the maze as punishment for a wrong choice. They expected to see a further decrease in error and time spent in the maze as well as a tendency to start using the left side as the first choice. There was a further decrease in the error rate, but the time spent in the maze, instead of decreasing, increased! The horses were making fewer errors but were spending more time making their choices.

They did show a tendency for more initial left-side choices, however. Kratzer's data suggest several things about learning in horses. First, horses can learn an escape choice response. Many people doubted this was possible because of numerous instances in which horses, separated from their mates, try to jump or go through fences to rejoin them, ignoring open gates that allow them easy access. Secondly, punishment of an incorrect response does facilitate learning in horses, at least in terms of error rate. But there was an undesirable side effect of punishment manifested in Kratzer's study as an increase in the horse's response time.

In the last few years, several new investigations into learning in horses have been undertaken at Texas A&M University. The first of these was done by B. F. Yeates and involved various sensory cues and their relative effectiveness in equine learning. The senses tested were hearing, sight, and touch. Three horses were used in this experiment and each horse was tested with each sensory cue.

The horses were tested in a twelve-by-twelve–foot stall. On the wall was a feed box. Next to the feed box was a flap that the horses could push with their noses causing food to fall into their feed tubs. Of course the catch was that the feed reward was released only when the flap was pushed as a response to a cue, either an auditory one signified by a buzzer, a visual one from a light in the stall, or a tactile stimulation received from a specially equipped girth strapped onto the horse.

The final data showed that the horses evidenced learning from the auditory and visual cues, but not from the tactile cue. However, much of the lack of learning from tactile cues was attributed to the researchers' inability to produce a cue, rather than a shock, with the electrical apparatus used for tactile stimulation. The auditory cue was the most satisfactory stimulus for obtaining a correct response from the horses. It was also noted from these data that horses learned more easily with each successive problem. Essentially this means that these horses were applying what they had learned in previous discriminations (when the cue is presented, the feeder works) to new tests, even when the cue was changed.

In the spring of 1976, I conducted a second study of learning in horses at Texas A&M. This study dealt with differences in learning ability among horses in a herd. A main objective of the study was to develop a practical technique for investigating learning ability in horses. I was also interested in studying the effects of emotionality on learning ability in horses, and variations in learning ability, if any, between the sexes in horses. Most importantly I wanted to attempt ranking a herd of horses according to relative learning ability and then see if this ranking correlated with trainability scores given by an independent trainer.

Twenty-six Quarter Horse and Thoroughbred yearlings were used in the study. I divided them into three groups according to sex—nine colts, nine fillies, and eight geldings. The testing appara tus consisted of a modified maze using standing stalls located across the aisle from each other in a barn. A large feed bucket was placed against the back wall of each test stall. The bucket in the left stall was white and the one in the right stall was black providing a combination of cues similar to what the Warrens had used in their 1962 study.

On the first day of testing each horse was brought into the test area and placed in the "start box," a standing stall located directly across the aisle from the two stalls with the buckets. The horse was positioned in the start box facing the test stalls and then released to choose between the two test stalls across the aisle in order to receive the food reward placed in one of the feed buckets. If an incorrect choice was made, the horse was returned to the start box and the next trial begun. If a correct choice was made the horse was allowed about thirty seconds to eat before being returned to the start box for the next trial. The first day the rewarded stimuli combination was the black bucket in the right stall. The next day, the reward was switched to the white bucket in the left stall and trials were run with each horse as on the first day. Each horse was tested until he chose the correct stall/bucket combination eleven out of twelve times with eight consecutive correct trials. On the third day of testing, the reward was returned to the black bucket in the right stall. These daily reward reversals continued for a total of twenty-one days.

The data derived from this study provided a good deal of information not only about basic learning mechanisms in the horse, but also about individual differences in learning ability. Tentative conclusions drawn from this study suggest that learning ability in horses can be measured quantitatively at a relatively young age. The study also indicated that the mechanism of a horse's learning a reversal discrimination (that is, learning to select correctly when the reward position was reversed daily) had a pattern similar to that reported for other species. In addition, a distinction in learning ability was evident (probably in interaction with other factors such as age and temperament) between the three horse sexes—colts, fillies and geldings. Colts and geldings scored better than fillies; however, much more research is needed before we can make any real assessment of the effect of sex on learning in horses.

"Emotionality" also affected learning performance in these tested yearlings. The more nervous horses had poorer scores. And finally, an analysis of the test data showed a correlation between learning scores derived from the test and scores determined by relative trainability. This suggests that it may be possible to predict a young horse's relative trainability based on his capacity to learn.

Hoping to find out even more about the learning behavior of horses, a third study utilizing my study in 1976 was undertaken in the spring of 1977 by Kathy Baer and Sue Pearson. Six horses chosen randomly from those I had tested the previous year were re-tested with a shorter learning test similar to the one I had used. We wanted to see whether their relative learning ability scores had changed in one year.

The group of six horses we re-tested included the two best performers from the previous test, three that had scored previously in the mid-range and one that had performed poorly on the first test.

The results of the second test were startling and provided fuel for many lengthy discussions among us in an effort to explain them. All six horses showed much less variation in performance than we had previously observed. The two superior performers from the earlier test achieved only average scores on the second test, not significantly different from the other four horses. Even more baffling, however, was that while these two good learners dropped in their performance, the poorer learner from the previous test improved dramatically. In an attempt to explain these results in light of the previous year's conclusions, we turned to human educational psychology research for some ideas and answers.

Psychologists now recognize that a child's learning capacity is greatly influenced by the environment in which the child is raised. This is especially true in the classroom situation, where educational stimulation and the demands placed on the student must be suited to individual needs in order for the full learning capacity of the child to be realized. Environment is especially important for the superior learner who becomes bored and frustrated when presented with educational materials and techniques that do not challenge his mind and maintain his interest. This new understanding of learning behavior in humans accounts for the increased emphasis on individual programming and enrichment studies in our school systems.

The data from our second test suggests that a similar phenomenon exists in horses. The learning capacity of the horse is greatly affected by the type of training regimen in which the horse is taught. All six of our horses had since our initial tests, been involved in a training program at the university which was part of an undergraduate course in horse management and training. Because of the nature of the course, the training techniques which the students used were somewhat rigidly controlled. There was very little opportunity to design individual training programs for each horse. It appears, then, that the differences in relative learning ability scores for the six retested horses were due to training effects. The two superior performers, because they had not been challenged to work at their optimal capacity, had lost some of their superior learning abilities. This was evidenced by their lower relative scores on re-test. In the case of the poorer performer, who increased in relative learning ability, the reverse was true. The training he had received had stimulated his learning capacity and enabled him to make up the deficit in learning ability he had exhibited the year before. The three middle-range horses, who evidently received enough stimulation in their second year of training to maintain their relative learning capacity, had similar scores on both tests. To paraphrase *Goldilocks*, the superior horse's learning motivation was too cold, the poor performer's learning motivation was too hot, and the middle range performer's learning motivation was just about right. Naturally, much more research is needed in the area of learning motivation in horses before we can fully understand the effects of training on relative learning ability in horses. The conclusions drawn to date are only speculative, but there is certainly sufficient evidence to suggest that drastic changes can occur in a horse's learning capabilities depending upon the type of training he receives.

A study conducted by Suzanne Taylor Cottongim at Georgia State University in 1977 illustrates how environmental manipulation can alter performance in the horse. She was interested in observing the effects, if any, of positive reinforcement on a previously learned behavior. In this experiment, a horse was taught to halt from the walk, trot, and canter using conventional aids. Baseline measurements of the time required for the horse to come to a complete halt were made from all three gaits (tracking both to the left and right). The same horse and rider were used for all experiments. The average time to halt was 4.25 seconds from the walk; 4.08 seconds from the trot; and 4.75 seconds from the canter. Then positive reinforcement, in the form of bits of carrots, was introduced by the rider immediately after each halt. The average time to halt during this experimental phase was 2.58 seconds from the walk (1.67 seconds faster than baseline), 2.25 seconds from the trot (1.83 seconds faster then baseline) and 2.58 seconds at a canter (2.17 seconds faster than baseline). The researchers also noted a marked improvement in the quality and willingness of the horse's performance once positive reinforcement was introduced. The dramatic effect of positive reinforcement on performance has been recognized and utilized for many years in other animal species but only recently have horsemen recognized its value.

Today several other behavioral studies into learning in horses are being conducted in this country and abroad. The results from these studies should be made available to the horse-owning public and many of the questions which still remain concerning learning in the horse will be answered.

But while much remains unanswered, the knowledgeable horseman must realize that a horse cannot be well trained with an overly structured, narrow-minded approach. Regardless of whether the trainer deals with horses as a business venture only, or approaches horses with a good deal more emotion and sentimentality, the basic principles of learning psychology cannot be denied if the trainer hopes to be successful. The trainer who refuses to understand the horse as a living entity, who approaches each training session with false notions about the "utter stupidity" or, conversely, the anthropomorphic "intelligence" of the horse is doomed to failure. The horse is neither an utterly stupid creature who must be beaten into submission or a wise and reasoning animal who can anticipate your every wish. He is an animal with varied learning capabilities who can be taught to perform a large number of complex maneuvers when trained through the use of basic learning principles. To attribute characteristics to the horse which he does not possess does the animal a great injustice and can only hinder the trainer's efforts to understand and communicate with his horse.

PART TWO

APPLYING LEARNING PRINCIPLES IN TRAINING

CHAPTER FIVE

The Trainer

IT IS IMPOSSIBLE practically to separate learning ability in the horse from teaching ability in the trainer. The ability of a trainer to present his desires to a horse in a clear, concise and understandable fashion has a tremendous influence on how quickly and how thoroughly a horse learns his lessons. Learning principles incorrectly applied can only hamper the learning process, creating confusion and often fear for the horse and frustration for the trainer.

Therefore, a complete examination of learning in the horse and how it is best achieved must include a rudimentary look at the attributes, both physical and mental, necessary to be a successful trainer. Naturally, no two individuals are likely to have these ingredients in equal amounts, and often an abundance of one attribute can make up for the relative lack of another (such as in the case of an exceptionally athletic rider who unfortunately also has a short temper). But for the most part, a person who hopes to be at least marginally successful at horse training should have some of the basic characteristics outlined below.

Riding Ability

Unless your goals in training horses point toward liberty acts in the circus or driving four-in-hand coaches (both of which, by the way, are exceedingly precise and challenging training processes), a good basic riding technique is necessary for you to train your horse properly. Very few well-trained horses (if any at all) are finished by sloppy riders.

Perhaps before we go any further, it should be pointed out that the type of riding ability we're concerned with is not the "equitation" necessary to compete successfully in a Medal class at Madison

Square Garden or a horsemanship class at the Quarter Horse Congress. We are concerned with functional horsemanship, and we will look at equitation not so much from the rider's standpoint as from the standpoint of its effect on the horse's learning process. Many people who narrow-mindedly claim that there's English riding and Western riding and "never the twain shall meet" may be in for a bit of an eye-opener. Good horsemanship is effective horsemanship, whether the rider is in an English saddle clearing a four-and-a-half–foot fence or on a stock saddle putting his horse through an intricate reining pattern.

With these thoughts in mind and with the hope that the reader will approach horsemanship with an open mind let's look at some of the physical characteristics of effective riding.

Many people, after learning what a good riding position looks like and then attempting, with varying degrees of success, to duplicate it on a horse, are overwhelmed by the physical effort required to really sit properly on a horse. We all know that most people can "sit" on a horse without too much help; but to do so as an effective, active partner rather than simply as a load for the horse to bear requires some effort and practice.

One of the first principles a new rider must learn is to disassociate one part of his body from another. In other words, what your seat and legs are doing shouldn't affect what your hands are doing. Because of this "separate but equal" approach to various parts of the rider's body, it's usually best to view riding position and technique from three general areas—seat and legs, upper body, and hands.

The seat and legs must perform a twofold job. They are not only a major source of the cues or aids used in riding but they must also perform the important function of keeping the rider on the horse. In the preliminary stages of riding, most people are content to let their seat and legs perform only the latter task. It's only after a good deal of practice and experience that a rider begins to take full advantage of the use of his seat and legs.

What is a good functional position for the seat and legs while riding a horse? Many manuals on equitation (excellent for the truly serious rider) are extremely specific, diagramming positions with mathematical angles and lines drawn through various parts of the rider's body. Many of these perfect positions are impossible for some riders to copy simply because of the particular rider's individual conformation. Good riders and trainers come in a variety of shapes and sizes, so there can always be some tailoring done to meet an individual's needs as long as the fundamental position is adhered to as closely as possible.

The motive for positioning our seat and legs according to certain specifications is to get into and stay in balance with the horse, regardless of the gait that he is moving at or the maneuver he's executing. Our center of gravity should be directly over his, if possible, and it should stay there, unless deliberately changed to elicit a particular response from the horse. Even in these cases, the rider is still in balance with his horse because his position helps rather than hinders the horse's performance.

A "deep" seat is usually recommended for most riding styles, with the possible exception of hunting and jumping; and even there a deep seat provides the reassurance necessary to steady a horse approaching a fence. In order to sit deeply in a saddle, the rider should place his weight as directly as possible over his pelvic bones, not allowing his buttocks to provide the soft cushion which seems so desirable. He should sit as far forward (toward the pommel of the saddle) as possible and allow his legs to hang freely, with the inside of his thighs (rather than the back of his thighs) against the saddle. If a rider has the opportunity to ride in several styles of saddles (English or Western), he quickly discovers that certain saddles greatly aid him in attaining this balanced seat, while others make him work overtime simply to maintain a correct position.

Once the seat is secured correctly and the legs are hanging with the inside of the thigh resting against the saddle flap or fender, the next consideration is the position of the lower leg and the proper length of the stirrups. There's a lot of disagreement about lower leg position and stirrup length, and many criteria have been proposed which a rider can use to test whether his lower leg is correctly positioned. But again, we want to look at the rider's overall functional position, so the basic premise that we work under is that the position

Figure 7. Correct seat for most riding styles.

which allows the rider the security, control and finesse necessary to properly communicate with his horse *is* the correct one.

Ideally, the lower leg should rest comfortably against the sides of the horse and the knee should be bent only enough to rest the ball of the foot on the stirrup. Proper stirrup length can be determined by allowing the leg to hang naturally and then adjusting the stirrups until they hit just at or slightly below the ankle joint. Stirrup length shouldn't be rigidly measured, however. Variations in rider's builds and the riding task at hand must be considered in determining proper length. A rider wanting to practice dressage or cutting cattle is more concerned with control and security and wants a longer stirrup to achieve a deeper seat. On the other hand, a rider schooling a horse over fences or developing a horse for the race track is more concerned with allowing the horse the necessary freedom of movement to jump and gallop; the stirrups must be shorter in order to lighten his seat and, consequently, the horse's load.

Placing the ball of the foot on the stirrup allows the greatest flexibility of the lower leg while simultaneously providing the desired support. Placing the toes on the stirrup tends to destroy a rider's secure seat; he is much less able to allow his weight to sink into his heels. Placing the stirrup "home"—as far as the heel of the boot—may provide more security for the rider but it lessens the sensitivity and flexibility of the heel and lower leg. However, in certain competitions, notably with cutting horses, the stirrup is often placed home to strengthen the rider's seat during the hard stops and pivots characteristic of a good working cowhorse.

Many riding styles emphasize the position or angle of the toes in relation to the horse. Some call for the toes to be out, some say the toes should be perfectly parallel to the horse's side, and others feel the rider should sit pigeon-toed. Functionally, if the rider's thighs, knees, and lower legs are properly positioned the toes fall naturally into line with the rest of the leg. For most people this means they turn out just a shade. Exaggerated attempts to turn the toes one direction or another often cause the rider to destroy the good basic position he's developed in his seat and legs, which is much more important than his toes.

Once the proper stirrup length has been determined and the rider has positioned his leg correctly according to his conformation, the next step is to lower the heels so that they hang below the level of the stirrup. This not only allows for a deeper, more secure seat but the lowering of the heel causes a tightening of the calf muscle which is used as an aid in riding. If the heels are allowed to rise above the toes, the rider has a tendency to push off his foot, thereby undermining his security. Raising the heels also relaxes the calf muscle and prevents it from being a truly effective driving force.

Once leg position has been achieved some thought must be given to how the leg should hang in relation to the upper body. A functional way to do this is to place the legs under the body so that if the horse suddenly disappeared from underneath the rider, the rider would land standing, rather than sitting. In other words, a rider should straddle his horse actively instead of sitting on him like an old easy chair! This is usually accomplished when the leg is directly under the seat and when the heels rest in a line descending through the hips and shoulders (assuming correct upper body position). If the lower leg swings too far back it causes the rider's upper body to fall forward, and if placed too far to the front it causes the rider to be "behind his horse," leaning to the rear.

Once the seat and lower leg positions are mastered the next step is to align the upper body. Naturally, without a strong foundation of seat and legs it's practically impossible for the upper body to function properly. The body should be carried erect but in a relaxed manner. Care should be taken to keep the lower back straight, not allowing it to round over. This usually happens when a rider becomes lazy and settles on his comfortable posterior instead of sitting on his seat bones. Controlled relaxation is the goal that should be acheived in positioning the upper body. A tense rider never is able to follow and absorb his horse's movements and is likely to transmit his tension to the horse. At the same time, an overly relaxed rider is a sloppy one who sacrifices effectiveness in horsemanship for his own comfort.

The final elements in achieving a functional riding position are the arms and hands. Good hands are usually the last riding attributes that a horseman develops, simply because the rider must have a totally secure and independent seat, leg and upper body position before he can hope to use his hands meaningfully to transmit aids and reassurances to his horse. Ideally, the upper arm should hang naturally from the shoulder with the elbows close but not clamped to the rider's sides. The position of the hands may vary depending upon the stage of the horse's training and the activity in which the horse and rider are engaged but they should be held somewhere between the lower portion of the rider's rib cage and the point of contact between his hips and legs.

Now that we have a basic idea of what a balanced rider looks like, we must see why this position is used when training a horse.

When talking about seat and leg positions, we offered evidence for the correctness of these positions in terms of the rider's security. Some riders, however, might feel more secure with their arms draped around the horse's neck! We need to have even more evidence of the value of this basic position for functional training.

When we watch a young horse (or any horse, for that matter) running and playing in a pasture we marvel at the speed, agility, strength, and balance of such a large animal. At times he appears to float over the ground instead of running over it, and he has little trouble performing what are considered difficult maneuvers under saddle naturally. If these same horses are then asked to carry riders while performing much simpler movements, those that haven't learned to carry a rider's weight properly appear clumsy and stiff and a far cry from the graceful creatures of a few minutes before. Many riders simply aren't aware of the effect that a rider's weight has on a horse's balance, equilibrium, and muscle control. Perhaps this is why so few riders take the time and trouble to learn first what it means to be in balance with a horse and secondly, to practice this balanced position. But a simple test often illustrates this effect. Take a backpack weighing approximately 15 percent of your body weight and adjust it so that it hangs further down on your back than it should to be carried comfortably. Try to move normally—take a few jogging steps. Only by leaning forward and trying to move your center of gravity under the misplaced backpack can you hope to carry it with some semblance of a normal gait!

This is the basic problem the horse faces. A rider who desires to work with rather than against his horse should make every effort to bring his center of gravity as closely as possible into line with that of the horse. To accomplish this the rider must place himself in the saddle as close to the withers of the horse as possible without being directly over them. As noted before, a well-made saddle greatly facilitates accomplishing this weight distribution.

Assuming the rider is sitting in a balanced position in the saddle, what value other than the security we spoke of earlier does having the lower leg directly under him offer? It places the rider's leg in the most effective position for cueing the horse and developing impulsion from the hindquarters without substantially affecting the horse's balance and rhythm. Any superfluous movements on the part of the rider that can be eliminated should be. Only those stimuli or cues necessary to achieve a desired response should be evident to the horse. Any unnecessary shifting around on the rider's part is only going to interfere with the horse's perception and understanding of the aids that are applied.

We talked about the importance of controlled relaxation in terms of upper body position and the detrimental effects rider tension has because it is so quickly transmitted to the horse. Tension in the upper body, particularly in the shoulders, quickly carries down through the arms to the rider's hands. They become rigid and fixed, lacking the elasticity and softness necessary for them to communicate to the horse's mouth properly. Instead the horse is punished, albeit inadvertently, at every stride and soon tries to evade the bit altogether. After too much of this treatment, the rider might as well throw away the reins completely for they have lost any real value as a means of controlling and communicating with the horse.

Trainer Psychology

We're familiar now with the basic riding position and some of the reasons for its effectiveness both in terms of rider security and efficiency in training. We'll be returning to this, in specific contexts, in the chapters to follow. But what about the intangible qualities that separate the passenger on horseback from the horse trainer?

In the writings of the "great" horse trainers, both English and Western, one factor is evident throughout their teachings: in order to be a truly good trainer an individual must possess a basic love and respect for horses. It is human nature to work best at those things which we enjoy. We are most likely to use our skills, talents and minds effectively in pursuing something that has great value to us— not necessarily monetary value.

Horses are big business for many people today and, unfortunately, greed for the almighty dollar has led to some inefficient, crude, and often cruel training methods. Trainers pride themselves on turning out "ninety-day wonders" that are supposedly polished, finished horses. But in reality, these horses are only a shell of what they might have been. For every one that is presented as a trained horse several have been cast aside as vicious or stubborn simply because they would not buckle under the extreme, unyielding demands of these so-called trainers.

Even good trainers who have a proper perspective on the goals desired in training horses, are placed in the precarious position of having to show instantaneous success with a horse if they expect to appease the horse owner. The public simply refuses to wait, and in its desire for instant gratification scorns a trainer who proceeds slowly in a systematic and sensible manner.

It is obvious then that love and respect for the horse are not the only ingredients necessary for the successful trainer; an abundance of patience and an inquisitive and systematic mind are of tremendous importance as well.

The motto YOU HAVE TIME should be posted in every trainer's tack room as a reminder that nothing is so important that it justifies rushing a horse's training. A ribbon, a gold belt buckle, or a silver platter are little compensation for the real damage that can be done by pushing a horse beyond either his physical or mental capabilities. In the long run, too, the material rewards for successful training will come in much greater abundance and with much more regularity to trainers who stick to a well-thought-out and properly executed training plan that takes into consideration the individual animal's own characteristic strengths and weaknesses.

People with short tempers often find horse training a frustrating and unrewarding occupation. Horses trained through force and punishment rarely exhibit any ability beyond a mechanical obedience from fear. This obedience is quickly extinguished or forgotten if the horse is not continually reinforced with harsher and harsher methods. Most of these horses, except for the very timid, become sour, unruly and dangerous animals.

The three major psychological ingredients, then, upon which good training ability are founded are an affection for horses, patience and a large measure of self-control. Assuming an individual has these basic traits, how does he proceed to apply learning principles in horse training?

First, it is necessary to approach horse training with specific goals in mind—not simply in terms of what the finished product should look like, but also in terms of the daily progression needed to produce the finished horse. It may even be helpful to formulate a written training schedule for the horse, keeping in mind that it may vary according to the particular horse's ability and the ability of the trainer to communicate his ideas to the horse. But by writing out a training schedule, the trainer is forced to think about what goes into the making of a well-trained horse and how best to accomplish the task. Thinking before acting should be practiced as much as possible by horse trainers and can help to eliminate many training problems before they occur.

Once the trainer knows what his goals are in training a particular horse, and how he intends to reach these goals his primary effort must be toward establishing communication with the horse. His vocabulary consists of aids—stimuli—and various forms of reinforcement that let the horse know whether he is responding correctly to these aids.

What are the aids or stimuli available to the trainer? Technically there's no limit to them, but years of horsemen's experience have produced certain aids that are particularly adapted for horse training. These aids include the trainer's voice, leg pressure, weight distribution through the rider's seat, and rein effects. These are commonly known as *natural aids*. In addition, there are certain *artificial aids* used to reinforce the natural ones. Artificial aids include the whip, spurs, side reins, check reins, martingales and other equipment.

It's obvious to the reader who fully understands learning principles that all of the aids play a dual role, acting either as stimuli or negative reinforcers depending upon the degree or severity with which they're used. It's the manipulation of this dual role that finally separates great trainers from mediocre ones. And it's the appropriate use of the aids that makes the "born horseman." It is difficult to teach someone to sense when an aid is a cue and not a negative reinforcer. Some riders, because of their keen observation and sensitivity naturally know when to apply aids and to what degree. Other riders must work long and hard and ride many different horses before experience begins to teach them to be truly effective riders and trainers. Many riders don't possess the ability, patience or desire to perfect their communication skills with the horse. For them the horse is a vehicle. While the rider may gain pleasure from being carried around by his horse, it is doubtful whether the horse gains much pleasure from being abused by his insensitive and ignorant rider.

CHAPTER SIX

Influencing Learning Patterns Through Early Experiences

EARLY EXPERIENCES have a tremendous influence on the behavioral development of a horse, as well as laying the psychological foundation for subsequent training.

From the moment a foal is born, his sensory systems pick up information from the environment, interpret the data received, and store it, in an as yet unknown fashion, as memory. Most horsemen attest that the equine memory is phenomenal. Actually, this memory is probably more a result of the habit-forming behavior of the horse and his general shyness, than of any extraordinary psychological capability. Once a particular response or group of responses to a situation is reinforced a similar situation at another time most likely will produce a similar reaction. The horse has little reasoning power and learns dynamically. He doesn't premeditate his behavior, but reacts to stimuli as they occur, utilizing responses that have proven successful in similar situations. This type of behavior is the result of evolution's selective process and can be anthropomorphically translated as "Why take a chance on a new response to this situation when I know the old one works!"

The horse's ability to form and retain habits enables humans to successfully train him, but it's also the cause of a great deal of frustration during training, for the habits or responses formed in a particular situation are often not the ones the trainer desires. Bad habits are formed as readily—if not more readily—than good ones in the horse, because bad habits usually result from the horse responding out of fear. Reducing fear is a highly motivating force in learning. If the horse's response to an aid decreases his fear or eliminates the object that frightens him, this reduction in fear strongly reinforces the response in his mind. Thus, the probability of a similar response occurring the next time the situation arises is very high.

For example, many people have problems teaching their horses to load into trailers. The problem isn't always restricted to loading the horse into the trailer, but may involve the way he exits as well. If, in an early experience with trailering, a horse is injured or badly frightened when backing out of a trailer he may develop one or more of several undesirable responses. He may refuse to get back into the trailer at all, but more often in this case he loads normally but refuses to back out when asked, or he comes out like a bolt of lightning. In both of these responses the horse attempts to reduce his fear of being injured or badly frightened again while coming out of the trailer. People often spend hours teaching their horses to load and ride quietly but forget that unloading is just as important a part of a safe trip.

What this example points out is that the first few experiences a horse has in any phase of handling or training will greatly influence the eventual behavior exhibited by the horse in that situation. This is true not only for specific responses such as loading or unloading from a trailer, but for general attitudes toward training, and trainers, as well. Good trainers try to develop a horse's confidence because this confidence (both in the trainer and in his own abilities) reduces a horse's fear, and a reduction of fear always strongly reinforces a response.

Confidence building or reducing should begin as soon as possible after the foal is born. Quiet, deliberate, gentle handling at birth is a good beginning for any foal and should be practiced throughout his early life.

There's a good deal of debate as to whether it is best to turn a foal out with his mother until weaning or to keep him closer at hand in order to allow daily human contact. There are arguments, pro and con, for both sides. Turning a foal out until weaning allows him to get plenty of exercise, and if he's with other mares and foals it allows him to develop normal social relations with other horses. Young horses turned out with their dams seem to develop more competitive personalities than those kept in more confined, controlled environments (depending upon their genetic predisposition), because of the continual interaction with other foals. Foals out on pasture also appear to be more acutely attuned to their senses because of the more varied environmental stimuli they encounter.

But the disadvantages of the lack of daily human contact on the part of the foal kept on pasture will become obvious at weaning. The young horse undergoes the trauma of being separated from its dam as well as the sudden intrusion into its environment of a strange two-legged creature who begins all kinds of painful and frightening maneuvers—worming, immunizations and halter breaking. Not a very confident beginning for a young animal used to freedom and the security of its mother.

What are the advantages of maintaining human contact with a young horse during this early period, rather than turning him out? Primarily, it allows the trainer to instill confidence and respect for humans at the only stage in the horse's development when the trainer has a real physical advantage in the event of a fight. Nothing can do more damage to a training program than getting into, and *then losing*, a physical battle with a horse. Once a horse is assured of his physical superiority to the trainer there is no basis for respect and the very foundation of the relationship between horse and man crumbles. First and foremost the horse must obey. True, unquestioning obedience comes through a respect for and confidence in the trainer.

One of the most dramatic and important lessons a young horse can learn is the supremacy of man. A very effective way to teach this lesson early is simply to place your arms around a young foal and hold him firmly for a few minutes. He'll struggle to get loose, but if the trainer has one arm around his hips and the other around his chest he can maintain the physical advantage and keep the foal from getting away—imperative if the lesson is to work. After a few minutes of struggling, the foal, realizing that he's getting nowhere, stops. The foal has learned his first major lesson—that man is physically superior—but also that he wasn't hurt by the whole affair.

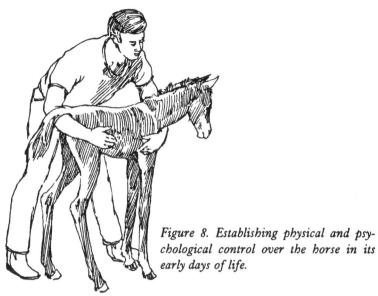

Figure 8. Establishing physical and psychological control over the horse in its early days of life.

This approach provides a good foundation for the respect and confidence we hope to build.

Halter Breaking

Halter breaking can be one of the most traumatic experiences in a horse's life if left until weaning or later. It usually ends as a battle between horse and man and requires a good deal of physical effort on the part of the trainer involved. A much better approach, from a physical as well as psychological viewpoint, is to begin halter breaking shortly after foaling. Put a proper size halter on the foal a few days after birth and let him wear it while in a stall or paddock where he can be watched. It's dangerous to turn a foal loose in a large area with a halter on because of his chance of injuring himself on a fence or some other object in the pasture. Haltering lessons should be repeated daily with lots of taking the halter off and putting it on again. Always halter the foal in the same manner—remember, we're trying to teach him the respect and confidence that come through thoroughly repeating each lesson. Approach the foal from the near (left) side; place your right hand on his croup and slide it up toward the neck on the off (right) side. Hold the halter in your left hand by the unbuckled crown piece. As you move your right hand up along the neck talk reassuringly to the horse until you're standing just behind his throatlatch with your right arm over his neck. Pass the halter under his throatlatch and grab the crown piece with your right hand, holding the buckle of the left cheek piece in your left hand. Move both hands slowly forward until you can slip the nose piece over the foal's nose and pull the halter up into place to buckle it.

Remember to use the same procedure for haltering the foal every time. Not only is he learning to wear the halter without fear, he's also learning that every time the trainer follows this routine a halter is put on. Don't ever begin to halter a foal (or any horse, for that matter) and then not finish the job. This lets the foal know that you're not consistent in your behavior. Consequently, the foal may begin to experiment to see what responses he can make to keep you from haltering him again. Most horses that are hard to catch and halter simply weren't taught properly in the first place. Horses may not have great reasoning powers but they are keenly observant and take advantage of any inconsistencies on the trainer's part to make things easier on themselves.

Once the trainer is able to halter the foal without problems and the foal wears the halter quietly, it's time to teach the foal to respond to pressure on the halter. If the foal is halter broken while still suckling, these lessons can begin by having someone lead the haltered foal behind its mother. Usually the desire to follow its mother is enough impetus to keep the foal moving, but if not, a rump rope or come-a-long can be used. This is simply a loop of rope placed behind the foal's hindquarters with which the handler applies pressure, in addition to the halter pressure, to encourage the foal to move forword.

This is the young horse's first serious introduction to escape and avoidance conditioning. Attitudes formed at this time influence subsequent training. If the foal learns to resist the trainer's demands successfully at this stage, he's well on the way to becoming a problem horse.

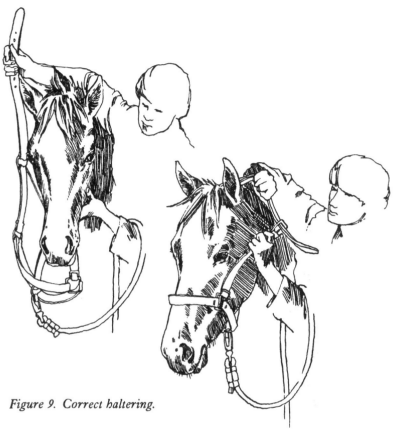

Figure 9. Correct haltering.

In considering halter training from the viewpoint of learning psychology, we see that halter pressure represents a stimulus and the degree to which pressure is applied determines whether the particular training situation is one of escape conditioning or avoidance conditioning. The initial presentation of any of the standard cues (halter pressure, leg pressure, rein pressure, etc.) usually results in an escape conditioning situation. The cue startles the horse and he responds in order to escape it. His reinforcement comes as a reduction in fear when the cue stops. After several presentations, especially if the desired responses have been reinforced positively, the horse no longer is startled or frightened by the cue. This is where escape conditioning should be replaced by avoidance learning and where serious horse training begins. The halter lesson with the foal demonstrates the transition.

The first time the handler applies pressure on the halter to get the foal to move forward, the foal usually struggles to get away from the new sensation. He may be frightened and pull backward or jump sideways to escape the pressure. When this fails, he moves forward, perhaps only slightly. It's imperative that *any* indication of forward movement be instantly rewarded by releasing the pressure on the halter. This release reinforces the response; and it must be contingent on the response for effective learning to occur. Repeating the procedure a few times normally results in the foal moving forward when halter pressure is applied, provided the pressure is released and not re-applied as long as the foal moves forward satisfactorily. Don't be impatient or expect too much too soon. Reward correct responses with petting and kind words in addition to releasing the pressure.

At this point the foal has learned an escape response. He moves to get away from the pressure of the halter. Some people go no further than this in halter-breaking foals, perhaps because they don't realize they can. But the problem with stopping here is that the adverse property of the stimulus decreases with time and habituation. The slight halter pressure which once startled and motivated the foal won't cause much of a stir as the horse matures, and stronger and stronger pressure is needed to effect the desired response. To avoid this, the trainer can switch to avoidance conditioning as soon as the escape response is learned. This involves the introduction of a neutral cue just prior to the old pressure stimulus. This neutral cue can be a vocal one such as the command to "walk" or a visual one such as the trainer moving forward slightly just before applying halter pressure. If the same new cue is presented every time, just prior to the old adverse stimulus, the horse eventually learns to respond to it in order to avoid the old stimulus. Thus we have a horse that moves off on command without any pressure applied to the halter, a much easier situation for both trainer and horse. Once the avoidance response has been learned, the old adverse stimulus of halter pressure

Longeing

One of the best means of teaching obedience as well as developing confidence and suppleness in the young horse is through longeing. A longe is simply a line about thirty feet in length, made of soft cotton rope, webbing, or nylon which the trainer attaches to the horse's halter or longe cavesson (a type of reinforced halter with noseband rings especially designed for longeing). The trainer plays out the longe line as the horse moves in a circle around him.

A great deal can be taught to a horse on the end of a longe line. Not simply basic exercises such as trotting or stopping on command, but more advanced training such as basic dressage and jumping. But perhaps the greatest benefit of longeing is that it allows the horse's training to progress even when he is still too young physically and mentally to carry a rider.

If we remember the basic principles of learning, it is easy to teach a young horse to longe properly. Training on the longe line can begin somewhere around nine months of age, assuming the foal is well halter-broken. It's important to remember at this stage, however, that the foal is an immature animal who cannot accept too much physical or mental stress without some ill effects. Early lessons on the longe line should be limited to fifteen minutes at the very most and the horse's gait should be restricted to a walk.

Having two people available to teach the longe lessons speeds up the learning process, but one person can teach a horse to longe effectively, although a bit more time and patience may be required for a really good performance. It's best to conduct the lessons in an enclosed area such as a round pen, small paddock or large box stall, especially if the trainer has no assistant.

If two people are available for the job, one should be at the horse's head and the other should be in the center of the circle holding the end of the longe line. Initially, the circle should be small, both to control the young horse and to make sure he focuses his attention on the trainer's commands. The horse is led by the assistant walking on the outside of the circle with the horse between himself and the trainer.

Some attention should be given to proper longeing techniques before we explain this procedure further. In riding we utilize several types of aids, both natural (legs, hands, weight) and artificial (spurs, whip, martingale) to shape the performance of the horse. In longeing, however, we lose this physical closeness, and consequently most of these aids. We must develop other means of acquiring the responses we want. If we look at these aids as learning stimuli, we realize that most riding aids rely on tactile stimulation. But in teaching the horse to longe we must introduce different types of stimuli to replace those we use in riding. From a psychological viewpoint, just about any stimulus is effective, as long as the horse perceives it and as long as it is consistently applied and properly reinforced. But experience has proved certain stimuli to be particularly effective in teaching the horse to longe. These include visual cues such as the trainer's body position and the sight of a longe whip held at various angles, and auditory cues such as the trainer's voice and the sound of the whip being snapped. Tactile cues are used also in the initial stages of learning to longe when an assistant is available to lead the horse.

As we said earlier, longeing is an excellent means of teaching obedience in the young horse, but unfortunately many people don't understand that the methods and procedures used to teach the horse to longe must stress consistency and contingency, just as any other training must. Trainers often allow a horse to perform poorly when longeing—making irregular circles and failing to respond to commands—without realizing that each time a trainer demands a response and the horse, by whatever means, gets away *without* responding, the basis for respect and obedience in all phases of training is undermined. This doesn't imply that there is always a battle of wills between trainer and horse, however! If properly taught from the beginning, longeing is a rewarding and relaxing experience for both horse and trainer because the horse knows exactly what is expected of him and has confidence in the consistency and fairness of the trainer. As long as he responds to the trainer's demands as best he can he is never unjustly punished and often receives positive encouragement in the form of a soothing voice, petting, a favorite tidbit, or a rest period. Only when he refuses to obey or responds half-heartedly does the trainer reprimand him. The punishment is always in keeping with the crime and is never inflicted out of anger or frustration on the trainer's part.

The reader should realize immediately that if this kind of solid, intelligent longe training foundation is laid before any attempt is made to ride the horse, the breaking and training period go much more smoothly, and learning on the horse's part is fairly rapid. Naturally, trainers are only human and all of us make mistakes in judgment when working with horses, particularly if the horse is very high-strung or very stubborn. It's easy to become frustrated and irritable when the same training procedure has been repeated thirty times and the horse still hasn't a glimmer of what is being asked. But it's at this point that the qualities of an exceptional trainer come forth. The exceptional trainer tries one more time, maybe in a different way, to communicate to the horse what he wants. He continues to experiment with different stimuli and reinforcement until the horse is performing at his peak.

Now that we have some idea of the immediate benefits of teaching a young horse to longe, and of the beneficial effects of longeing on later learning and training, let's get back to our discussion of the procedure to use in teaching longeing.

Naturally, as with most aspects of horse training, there are several ways to teach a horse to longe. The method described here has been very effective for a large number of trainers (the author included) and, more importantly, seems to be effective with the majority of horses.

In the first longeing lesson the horse makes a small circle at a walk around the trainer who pivots in one spot in the center of the circle. If an assistant is available, he leads the horse from the outside of the circle. If the trainer is alone, he must lead the horse around by himself in a small circle, playing out the line slowly as the horse begins to understand what is expected of him.

The position of the trainer's body in relation to the horse is very important in these longeing lessons. The trainer's body position along with the voice and whip provides the driving force to keep the

Figure 11. Correct position of trainer in longeing.

horse moving. The trainer should keep his eyes on the horse's hip while longeing. By doing this his body automatically assumes a driving position in relation to the horse. Once the horse is moving on the circle without being led, the trainer should take up this driving position and stay there unless he moves to specifically ask for a different response from the horse. The trainer's body position becomes a stimulus or cue and its presentation to the horse must be consistent if the trainer wants consistent responses. The trainer should never try to pull the horse around him with the longe line. If it's necessary to pull on the halter or cavesson to get the horse to move forward, the trainer hasn't done his work well enough in halter breaking the horse. He should forget about longeing and go back to the basics of halter breaking. This brings up an important point—don't ever try to teach a horse something new if he hasn't thoroughly learned the preceding lesson. Proper longeing depends upon the horse being properly halter-broken. A horse can't be expected to respond well in an advanced procedure if he hasn't learned the elementary one yet.

Secondly, longeing is an elementary lesson in itself, a step towards more advanced work. One of the basic lessons of longeing is to teach the horse to respond to driving aids by moving forward in a balanced, relaxed manner. Until the horse does this, we cannot hope to teach him long-reining or driving, preliminary lessons to mounted work. Without this, the initial mounted lessons are much more frustrating and difficult for both horse and rider.

Once the horse has learned to move quietly on a circle around the trainer, it's time to teach the horse to stop on the circle on command. Again, if the early lessons in halter breaking were thorough this shouldn't be difficult. If a voice cue such as "whoa" was used to stop the horse during halter breaking the same cue can be used effectively in longeing. It may also be combined with a visual cue such as the trainer moving out of the driving position toward the horse's head. The cue or cues used are not so important as the consistency of their application.

At this point it's probably a good idea to talk about some of the problems that may arise during these early lessons, because training rarely goes exactly according to the book. One common problem is the horse's failure to make round circles. He may cut corners or try to pull away from the circle if he's not in an enclosed area. Teaching the initial lessons in a fenced ring greatly lessens these problems, but if no ring is available, the corner of a paddock at least offers some boundary. Using a longe whip helps prevent the horse from cutting corners. As he comes in on the circle the whip should be flicked at his shoulder until he moves back into a proper circle. If he tries to pull out of the circle, the trainer should brace himself against the longe line, increasing the pressure on the halter or cavesson until the horse moves back onto the circle, at which time the line should go somewhat slack again.

The other major problem encountered in these early lessons is caused by faulty position of the trainer. If he gets out of his driving position (eyes focused on the horse's hip) and turns toward the horse's head, the horse will almost invariably stop and face the trainer. This is simply another example of the horse's basic nature: he won't do more than is asked—a trait certainly not restricted to equines. He moves forward in response to the cue presented by the trainer's position; if that changes, the response usually ceases, especially in the early acquisition phase of learning to longe.

Assuming the horse is longeing quietly at a walk in both directions, starting and stopping on command, and that any problems up to this point have been overcome, we're ready to ask for a trot. Sound judgment must be used to decide whether a young horse is physically up to longeing at a trot. Your best advice here comes from your veterinarian, who can examine the horse for structural soundness and evaluate how much physical stress the horse can tolerate at this stage without ill effect.

If your vet gives you the go-ahead, you can introduce a few circles at a trot at the end of a regular longeing session. Use some neutral cue (voice cues such as "Trot" are especially effective) to signal to the horse that a new response is desired. Reinforce the cue with the whip, either pointing it at the horse's hip, or, if necessary, popping it in the direction of his lower hind legs. Only in rare cases is it necessary to actually strike the horse with the whip. The cues cease as soon as the horse begins trotting and are re-applied only if he slows to a walk again. Two or three circles at a trot are sufficient for the first lesson, after which the horse is allowed to relax and return to its stall or paddock.

These lessons are repeated until the average fifteen-minute longe session includes ten minutes of work at a walk and five minutes at a trot, with trotting and walking sequences alternated to avoid the stress of a long trotting period. Numerous stops, both from a walk and a trot are interspersed throughout the lesson and several changes of direction at both gaits are demanded.

Longeing at a canter or lope shouldn't be taught at this time. The physical stress is too much to ask the young horse to bear right now, and there is little that can be taught at a canter that can't be taught at a walk or trot. In addition, the faster gaits are naturally more exciting to the young horse, and may only foster new problems if speed is introduced too early in the training program. Longeing at a lope or canter is introduced at a later stage in the breaking period when our control over the young horse is more complete.

By this point the young horse is probably into his second year and approaching the breaking period which includes saddling, bridling, bitting, ground driving and the initial mounted work. A solid physical and mental foundation for further training has been laid in our young horse. He is obedient but good-natured and approaches his training sessions as matter-of-factly as his own disposition allows. He has confidence in and respect for his trainer and is developing the boldness and eagerness which comes from having confidence in his own ability to do what the trainer asks.

CHAPTER SEVEN

The Breaking Period

THE BREAKING PERIOD is the most difficult, frustrating, and ideally the most rewarding period in the horse's training. This time might be more appropriately called the "making" period, because it's during the months of bridling, saddling, ground driving, and initial riding that the full behavioral personality of the horse is developed.

Naturally, it's every trainer's desire to make breaking as painless a learning process as possible, both for himself and for the horse. There will undoubtedly be disagreements between horse and rider, but if the trainer is skillful and tactful, he'll overcome this resistance through patience, firmness and many hours of thought.

As we'll see in a later chapter, no two horses react in exactly the same way to breaking and training. Some seem to train themselves while others resist every attempt to communicate with them. Most learning behavior in horses falls somewhere in between. Because of personality differences among horses, training techniques and timetables need to be adjusted to meet the needs of individual horses. The following training techniques and approximate ages at which various procedures are introduced are guidelines, not dogma. Certain horses proceed rapidly through some stages and have difficulty in others. The cardinal rule to follow is not to advance to a more difficult stage until the horse has learned and accepted training in the preceding stage. Remember—*you have time.*

It's a good idea at this point in the young horse's development to sit back and critically evaluate his initial training. The trainer has to make every effort to put his ego aside and be as truthful as possible about the horse's progress. If there are areas where the horse's performance isn't what it should be the trainer must ask why. Is the horse physically unable to do the work required? Was too little time spent on basic halter breaking and gentling? Was the trainer too heavy-handed in his negative reinforcement, causing the horse to be nervous and frightened? Or perhaps not enough firmness was shown with a particularly rambunctious foal; did the horse get the upper hand during training sessions? All of these questions and more must be asked before beginning more advanced work. If the trainer is honest and discovers and corrects any faults in the horse's training at this stage, he's ahead of the game when the breaking period begins. Ignoring serious training problems doesn't make them disappear; in all likelihood they'll be compounded during further training. This is simply an indication that the trainer is too ignorant, too egotistical, or too lazy to accurately assess the result of his training.

If after assessing his progress the trainer believes the horse has assimilated as much of the early training as possible, he can turn his attention to breaking the horse to ride. This is not to say that the early lessons in halter-breaking and longeing are forgotten. They are a permanent part of the horse's training program and will be used frequently to reinforce responses already learned as well as to assist in learning new ones.

Equipment

During the breaking period the trainer introduces a number of new pieces of equipment to the horse, including bits, bridles, saddle pads, saddles, driving reins and side reins to name the more common items. Before describing the application of this equipment in the training program, however, we need a working knowledge of each piece, and how it affects the horse's performance.

Bits. There are three general categories of bits: snaffles, pelhams and curbs. In addition, there is the combination of a curb bit and thin snaffle used in a double bridle.

The snaffle is a bit, regardless of the material of which it is made, that has the reins attached directly to rings on each side of the mouthpiece. The headstall buckles onto these rings as well. There is a seemingly endless variety of snaffles, including jointed snaffles, full and half-cheek snaffles, mullen-mouth snaffles, twisted-wire snaffles and gag bits. They vary widely in severity and many should be used only by expert horsemen, if at all. Snaffle bits put pressure on the outside of the bars of the horse's mouth, the lips, the tongue, and the corners of the mouth depending on the type of bit and how it is used. The thinner and straighter the mouthpiece, the more severe the action of the bit. A smooth, thick, curved jointed snaffle, with or without cheekpieces, is the best bit to introduce to the young horse. If it does not have cheekpieces, it should have large enough rings on each side to prevent the bit from being pulled through the horse's mouth.

Curb bits differ from snaffles in that the reins are not attached to a ring at the mouthpiece but to rings at the ends of shanks extending down various lengths from the mouthpiece. Curb bits vary widely in severity depending upon the shape of the mouthpiece and the length and shape of the shanks. Curb bits may have jointed mouthpieces. These bits are often sold as "western snaffles," but they are curb bits all the same and should be treated accordingly. Never start a young horse out in one of these bits thinking it is a snaffle; it's much too severe for this purpose.

Curb bits also have a chin strap or chain which runs under the chin groove of the horse, attaching to each side of the bit. Curbs exert their pressure on the tongue, bars, chin groove, poll (through the headstall) and, in some cases, the corners of the mouth. Again, the severity of the bit is dictated by the shape and size of the mouthpiece, as with snaffles, and the length and shape of the shanks to which the reins are attached.

The value of the curb, when properly used, is that it allows the rider to give more refined and imperceptible aids to maintain correct head position and a relaxed jaw. Used incorrectly or roughly, these bits are worthless. Many people believe that the more severe the bit the better the control. What they don't realize is that control of a horse comes through communication and understanding, not through force.

A pelham bit is a combination of a curb and snaffle on one

mouthpiece, with the snaffle reins attached to rings at the corners of the mouth and the curb reins attached to the shanks of the mouthpiece. The idea is to make one bit do the work of two. Some horses and riders do exceptionally well in this bit, but a pelham cannot approach the finesse and control afforded by a true double bridle with separate snaffle and curb mouthpieces.

Another piece of equipment that should be mentioned here is the bosal or true hackamore (not to be confused with the mechanical hackamore, a real work of the devil's art!). The bosal is composed of a braided rawhide nosepiece with a heel knot to which rope reins (mecate) are attached. The bosal is held in place by a conventional headstall or simple leather strap over the horse's poll. The bosal is particularly favored in the Western states where it is used to start young reining and working cow horses prior to introducing them to a spade bit. The "California" bitting process is beautiful when accomplished by a true expert and there is nothing more exhilarating than watching a reining horse perform that has been trained under these classical methods. But most of the true California reinsmen admit that a minimum of five years is necessary to train a horse properly in these methods and that great skill and tact are necessary to achieve good results. Consequently, most trainers who use bosals in their early training do so with the same goals as trainers who use the snaffle bit first—simply as a means of establishing basic communication with the horse. For this reason, the selection of a snaffle bridle or a bosal for the horse's initial bridling experience is really a matter of trainer preference.

Saddles. The two major categories of saddles are English and Western. The term English is used to describe any flat saddle such as a forward seat (hunt) saddle, dressage saddle, or cutback show saddle. Western refers to stock saddles such as those used for roping, barrel racing, cutting and reining. There are many different styles of saddles within these two categories, as well as degrees of quality in materials and workmanship.

Many trainers use both English and Western saddles in their training program, accustoming the horse to each type early in the breaking period. This is particularly true if the trainer plans to advertise the horse for sale as an "all-around horse." Many of the breed association horse shows now offer classes in both English and Western events and more and more riders are realizing the challenge and benefits of training and competing in both styles of riding.

In introducing the young horse to a saddle, the type of saddle used is unimportant compared to how it fits the horse. The tree of the saddle should be sound, and the leather soft and pliable. The saddle should sit properly on the horse's back without pressing down heavily on the sensitive withers or loin area. Even a thick saddle pad won't prevent a sore back if the saddle doesn't fit. The saddle should be checked regularly for worn spots and loose stitching and the girth for frayed or worn spots that might break under use. Many trainers have one or two saddles they reserve strictly for breaking purposes. These are usually light-weight saddles that are easy to work with when saddling and unsaddling young horses.

Side Reins and Driving Lines. Side reins are an artificial aid used in longeing to accustom the horse to bit pressure, as well as to teach him correct head carriage.

Side reins are attached to the saddle (to the front rigging on Western saddles or to the girth at the billets on English saddles) and run to the bridle where they attach to the rings of the snaffle bit. The reins can also be used with a longeing surcingle and crupper specifically designed for longeing.

Side reins can be purchased, or a homemade pair can be fashioned from an old innertube. It's important that the side reins have some elasticity to them to allow the horse normal head movement.

Driving lines are used in ground driving (long reining) a horse and should be about twenty feet long. They can be made from soft cotton rope, leather or nylon webbing and should have good heavy-duty snaps on one end. These snaps attach the reins to the snaffle bit rings during ground driving. Long reins serve a similar function as standard reins used when riding.

Bridling

With this brief introduction to the common equipment used in breaking and training we're ready to tackle the first major job in the breaking period—bridling.

If the trainer decides to start the horse in a bosal, he shouldn't encounter much difficulty in getting the horse to accept it, assuming the horse is well halter broken. The only time problems are likely to occur is when the trainer wants to slip the headstall into position by pulling it over the horse's ears. Many horses violently object to having their ears touched, probably because of the area's natural sensitivity. If the trainer has done a good job up to now, the horse has a basic respect and confidence in the trainer which makes matters much easier. Also, he's used to having the halter buckled behind his ears. The trainer should take every opportunity to rub the horse's ears during his early training. A bit of patient rubbing and scratching around the poll area and ears soon helps the horse to overcome his natural dislike of having his ears touched. Learning psychology speeds things up a bit, too. Each time the horse allows his ears to be worked with he should be positively reinforced by petting or even a favorite tidbit. If he pulls away from the trainer's hand touching his ears he may be reprimanded with a sharp "No," after which the process is repeated. Usually this combination of appropriate reinforcement teaches the horse to accept the procedure. Sometimes it may be necessary to use a different psychological technique called "flooding." A good stock or stall in which the horse can be closely confined without having to be tied is helpful for this. The trainer confines the horse and then rubs and scratches his poll and ears for thirty to forty-five minutes or how ever long it takes for the horse finally to submit. This process can be repeated on a daily or even twice daily basis until the horse accepts having his ears worked with as a matter of routine. If a stock is not available, this flooding technique can also be done with the horse tied to something solid. It's very important, since there's a good chance of a struggle, that the horse be tied properly with strong equipment. If, in the initial stages of the process, the horse pulls back to avoid having his ears touched

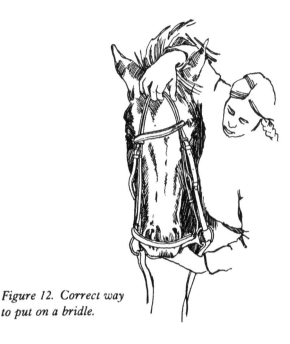

*Figure 12. Correct way
to put on a bridle.*

and manages to get loose, he's likely to develop halter pulling tendencies every time he's tied since he was successful once in getting loose.

Some thought needs to be given to the best method for putting on the bosal or bridle. Approach the horse from the near side with the headstall held in the left hand. Reach between the horse's ears with the right hand and grasp the crownpiece of the headstall. If a snaffle bit is used, cradle the bit in the left hand and slip it into the horse's mouth, using the thumb or ring finger to put slight pressure on the bars to get him to open his mouth. As you slip the bit in, pull the headstall up and slide the crownpiece over his ears. Adjust the bridle so that only one small wrinkle can be seen at the corners of the mouth where the bit lies. Many trainers like to rub the bit with something sweet the first few times they bridle the young horse. This gives him an instant reward for taking the bit.

Once the horse is bridled, remove the reins from the headstall and allow him to wear the bit in his mouth for several hours at a time. He can even be fed while wearing it. This will help to accustom him to the feel of the bit. Longe the horse with the bridle on by putting the halter or longe cavesson on over it and proceeding in the normal way. In essence, do as much as possible with the horse wearing the bit and bridle.

Remain in the bridling phase until the horse quietly accepts being bridled and wears the bit without a lot of fussing or head-tossing. Don't be too concerned if the horse chews on the bit. In fact, this is an encouraging sign because it means his jaw is relaxed. Watch that the horse doesn't get his tongue over the bit, however. The bridle may need to be adjusted to raise the bit in his mouth if this happens.

The bridling period may require only a few days or several weeks, depending upon the horse and trainer. There is no need to rush, however, because the horse is still immature and must not be asked to accept too much training too soon.

Saddling

Once the horse is accustomed to the bosal or bit and bridle, it's time to acquaint him with a saddle. Before the actual saddling process, several days of "sacking out" greatly benefit the horse in calmly accepting saddling.

Sacking out should be done in an enclosed area, preferably a large box stall or small paddock. A soft burlap sack or saddle blanket is used. The horse can be tied or held by an assistant. Initially, the trainer simply rubs the horse all over with the sack, talking soothingly during the process. Special care is taken to rub the horse under the belly, up and down the legs and over the croup. If the horse stands quietly for this, the trainer gently flaps the sack against the horse's side, repeating the process over his entire body. As the sacking out progresses, the trainer stands further back swinging the sack with a bit more force (although never to the point where it would inflict pain, which would produce results exactly the opposite of what we want). The trainer works from both sides and flaps the sack against the horse from all angles. As soon as the horse stands quietly for this he's rewarded with a good bit of petting and praise and the lesson ends. Sacking out is repeated for several days until the horse takes little notice of it; some trainers repeat the process until the horse appears to doze off during the sessions. At this point, the saddle is introduced. It's a good idea to give the horse a few minutes to smell and investigate the saddle. If it already has the smell of horses on it, this helps overcome some of his natural apprehension. Once he's had a chance to look and sniff at it, walk around to his near side and gently place the saddle on his back. Be sure to have a good saddle pad or blanket already on him. In fact, it's a good idea to use the same pad for saddling that was used for sacking out that day. Don't let the stirrups swing when you put on the saddle. If an English saddle is used the stirrups and leathers can be removed before saddling begins. If a stock saddle is used the stirrup on the off (right) side can be tied to the saddle horn to prevent it from flapping against the horse's side when the saddle is in place. Once the saddle is on, reach under the horse and grab the girth or have an assistant pass it to you from the other side. Gently tighten the girth or cinch, making sure that it's snug enough to keep the saddle in place in case the horse does some violent objecting. Don't make the mistake of leaving the cinch loose with the idea of getting him used to it slowly. If he does buck or jump and the saddle slips underneath his belly he'll be badly frightened. If he manages to buck the saddle off he'll be reinforced for his bucking. Neither set of circumstances is desirable.

If a stock saddle is used the trainer may want to take off the back cinch for the first few saddlings to allow the horse to become accustomed to the front girth first. Some trainers feel both cinches should be used from the start. In either case, when the back cinch is used make sure it's tight enough to prevent the horse from getting caught in it if he tries to kick up at it with his hind legs. Also, make sure the back girth is hobbled to the front girth so it cannot shift backward as the horse moves.

In many cases, if the horse has been thoroughly accustomed to sacking out he won't express much concern over the saddle while standing still. But as soon as he is asked to move and feels the girth tighten somewhat and the saddle shift on his back, he's liable to explode. The trainer should be prepared. Every effort should be made to keep the horse moving quietly. Talk soothingly and reassuringly to him. Longe him at a walk in both directions, stopping him frequently, petting and praising him as long as he remains calm. If he does get rambunctious, he should be urged into a strong trot on the longe line and kept at a trot until the bucking stops. As soon as he makes a complete circle without bucking or playing up, ask him to walk and praise him with a reassuring voice. As long as he's quiet, allow him to walk; if he starts bucking, push him into a trot again. He'll quickly figure out that all his bucking gets him is harder work; it does nothing to get rid of the saddle. Once he accepts the saddle and longes quietly at a walk, it's time to call it quits for the day. Remove the saddle as carefully as it was put on, walk the horse to cool him and put him away.

Some trainers like to leave the horse saddled for several hours, turning him loose in a small enclosed area. They feel this thoroughly indoctrinates the young horse into being saddled. However, there are several disadvantages to this procedure, the major one being that the horse almost invariably lies down and tries to roll or rub off the saddle. This is dangerous for the horse because he might tangle a leg in the stirrup or cinch, not to mention the wear and tear on the saddle. If a trainer chooses to do this, he should make sure that he or an experienced observer keeps an eye on the horse in case any problems arise.

During the second saddling, the trainer repeats the same procedure, including a thorough sacking out before saddling. After the horse is working quietly at a walk on the longe line he should be asked to trot. Ten minutes of longe work at the walk and trot should take any edges off the horse. At this point the horse should be stopped and praised. Then the trainer should take a few minutes to move the saddle back and forth on the horse's back, pull the stirrups down on each side and flap the stirrup leathers against the horse's sides. He should talk reassuringly to the horse during this process to help the horse understand that he won't be hurt. If the horse is used to being sacked out, there shouldn't be much problem.

This saddling process should be repeated three or four times a week. It isn't necessary or particularly advisable to work the young horse every day. He should be exercised every day, however, but this can be a good romp in the pasture, a light, unsaddled longe session, or simply a walk around the farm on a lead rope.

Longeing with Side Reins

At this point, the young horse is probably between fifteen and twenty months of age, depending upon how he has progressed in training and the age at which he was started; still too young to safely carry the average rider's weight. But we can begin now to teach him the basic vocabulary of aids used in mounted work. We begin this by teaching him something about bit pressure.

As has been mentioned several times already, control of a horse must come through understanding, not through force. Anyone who argues this point has only to ride a few "runaways" to be educated to the fact. When we analyze basic horse behavior, we find that the horse's innate reaction to pain is flight. If the pain increases so does the speed with which he tries to flee! This explains the utter uselessness of trying to stop a runaway horse by hauling back on the reins. It only increases his sense of panic and, consequently, his speed. The ignorance of some riders in this respect is really sad. High-headed, jigging, head-tossing horses with barbed-wire martingales are all too common in the horse world. It's difficult to understand how man, supposedly the most intelligent and gifted animal in nature, can at times be so ignorant and crude.

In developing an understanding with the horse, we first must strive to eliminate any fear or apprehension on his part. In terms of bit pressure we begin this by introducing side reins into the longeing program. Now that the horse is accustomed to longeing with saddle and bridle, we simply attach the side reins as previously described, leaving them relatively slack for the first few sessions. As the horse becomes used to wearing the side reins we gradually shorten them until a slight pressure is exerted on the bit when the horse's head is carried naturally. This gradual shortening of the side reins should occur over several days. If the horse becomes nervous or begins to fuss with the bit, the side reins should be returned to the previous, longer length. Once the horse is longeing quietly at a walk and trot with the side reins stretching slightly as he reaches for the bit, he is said to be "on the bit." His mouth should be closed and he should move without tossing his head or dropping behind the bit in an attempt to evade the pressure.

Trainers who start their horses in a bosal can help the horse understand noseband pressure by tying the reins of the hackamore to the saddle in a fashion similar to that described for side reins used with a bit. The horse should quietly accept the slight pressure of the bosal, yielding to it as the reins are shortened over a period of days.

Many trainers leave their horses saddled in a stall with the side reins or hackamore reins tied back for time periods ranging from thirty minutes to several hours. In principle, the horse learns to give to the pressure of the bit or bosal because only by tucking his chin and lowering his head somewhat can he relieve the pressure of the reins. The release in pressure reinforces the tucking response. This works to varying degrees, but the major drawback is that the horse may drop completely behind the bit or bosal, hindering later communication between horse and rider. Horses may also be tied back slightly to one side or the other with only one side rein. This teaches them to give to lateral pressure which is important in later work in ground driving and riding.

Once the horse longes quietly with side reins and accepts the pressure of the bit or bosal, it's time to teach him to canter or lope on the longe line. At this point he's both physically and mentally up to it.

In teaching the horse to canter on the longe we must be concerned with more than simply increasing his speed. We want the horse to strike off into a canter from both a trot and a walk on command, with a smooth, quiet transition into the gait and on the correct lead. A description of the footfall pattern of the canter helps to explain leads.

The canter or lope is a three-beat gait which begins in the hind

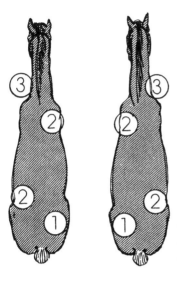

Figure 13. Footfall patterns for left and right canter (at left and right, respectively). *Note that the lead is initiated by the outside hind leg.*

legs. The horse pushes off with one hind leg then rolls forward onto the other hind leg and the diagonal foreleg. He finally catches his weight on the remaining foreleg. The lead is determined by which hind leg initiates the gait, but is classified by which foreleg provides the final step in the three-beat pattern. For example, a right lead is begun by the horse pushing off with his left hind leg, followed by the right hind leg and left foreleg striking the ground together and finally the total weight being supported by the right foreleg which appears to lead or move further ahead than the other legs. The left lead would be right hind leg, left hind leg and right foreleg, left foreleg.

A horse's willingness to strike off into a canter or lope on the particular lead demanded by the rider is important in several contexts. It displays the horse's willing obedience to its rider and demonstrates muscular suppleness on both sides. Horses are judged in this context in a dressage test. Secondly, having two leads for cantering affords a rider the means to distribute evenly the strain of a long ride. If the horse knew only one lead he would fatigue after traveling on that lead for several miles. Finally, it's important for a horse to understand thoroughly and be able to comply with the rider's demands for cantering on distinct leads because this lays the foundation for more advanced work.

In teaching the horse to pick up the correct lead while longeing we have to rely on trial and error. Usually the horse favors one lead and direction over another, but the months of longeing at a walk and trot in both directions should have done a great deal to alleviate any muscle stiffness on one side or the other.

A neutral cue, most appropriately a voice cue such as "canter" or a clucking sound, alerts the horse to a new demand. Reinforce the neutral cue with the longe whip only as much as is necessary to get the desired response. Try to determine as quickly as possible which lead the particular horse appears to favor. Work him in that direction only, until he has a good idea of the neutral cue and the correct response. The reason for this is to eliminate the confusion of teaching him to canter on command while simultaneously trying to keep him on the correct lead for that direction. Until he has developed a strong association between the cue and the canter response any attempts to correct his lead after he's cantering only confuse him. Therefore, until he's mastered cantering on command he should be worked only in the direction in which he is more likely to pick up the correct lead naturally. Once he canters quietly on command from a trot and walk, he should be worked in both directions until he picks up both leads equally well. Anytime he responds to a canter demand on the wrong lead he should be brought back to a strong trot and asked to canter again. Don't allow the horse to longe on the wrong lead once he has learned the canter response.

The time required to teach the horse to work properly in side reins, in addition to cantering on command on the proper lead, varies greatly depending on the physical and emotional characteristics of the horse and the skill of the trainer. Some horses perform quite well after two weeks, others require two months of work before they've accomplished the job satisfactorily. But again, it's very important that the training be judged by performance and not by time elapsed. Only when the horse is working well should the next step be attempted.

Ground Driving (Basic Long Reining)

Ground driving is a highly effective means of teaching basic cues and maneuvers to a young horse without the physical stress of a rider's weight. It's also a breaking process all too often skipped by hurry-up trainers. Any horse, young or old, can benefit from even a short course in ground driving.

With ground driving, as with all other training stages, it's imperative that the horse be properly prepared to learn the new task. In this case it means he should be completely halter broken, longeing quietly at all three gaits in both directions and have some notion about giving to the pressure of a bit or bosal. Assuming the horse passes this test we're ready for our first lesson in ground driving.

Initially we must be concerned with introducing new equipment to the horse and eliminating any fear or apprehension he may have about it. The first few lessons in ground driving are devoted entirely to getting the horse used to the sight and feel of the driving lines.

Saddle the horse as usual and put on a good nylon web or leather halter or cavesson. Hobble the stirrups by tying them together with a short piece of rope running under the horse's belly. If you're using a stock saddle with a horn, loop one end of each driving rein securely around the horn then pass the rest of the rein down through the stirrup, one rein on each side. If an English saddle is used snap the two lines together and with the snaps on top of the saddle loop each rein around the stirrup leather then through the stirrup to the ground. Allow the reins to drag loosely behind the horse. It's best to do this in a paddock or round pen where the horse can't pick up too much speed if the feeling of the reins brushing his legs spooks him. Depending upon how well the horse took to sacking out, the feel of the lines dragging against his sides and legs may not bother him at all, but this introductory lesson should be repeated until the horse walks and trots quietly with the lines attached. This may require only one lesson or several, but don't proceed further until the horse shows no concern for the lines.

Now we can get to the driving itself. Attach the two lines to the side rings on the halter or longe cavesson, or snap them onto the bosal on either side of the heel knot. Plan to work the horse in a large circle to the left or right. Assuming we decide to work to the right, run the line attached to the outside left ring through the stirrup on that side and then bring it up over the saddle to you. Run the other, inside, line on the right directly to you just as though it were a regular longe line. Longe him at a walk for a few circles to the right. Now slowly lift the outside left rein up and allow it to slide back over the horse's croup and down his hip until it rests around his hindquarters just above the hock. There should be only enough tension on the line to keep the rein in position above the hock. This rearranging of the line may cause the horse to spook slightly or break into a trot. Ignore it and keep the horse moving forward as calmly as possible until he is quiet and takes no notice of the line around his hindquarters. This may take ten or fifteen minutes, but don't let him stop and don't remove the line until he's quietly walking on the circle. When he's going well in one direction, stop him with a "whoa" and a gentle pull and release on the reins. Rearrange the lines and repeat the procedure in the other direction. Again, the total time involved in teaching this step varies among horses, but as soon as he goes quietly in both directions stop for the day.

In the next lesson, thread both lines through the stirrups and drive the horse from directly behind him. Use enough line to keep from being in striking distance of his hooves if he decides to kick out at the rope (he shouldn't if properly prepared, but it's always a possibility). Keep as gentle a feel of the reins as possible even though they're not attached to a bit yet. Developing good hands requires constant diligence.

When he is going quietly forward on command, change directions by pulling and releasing gently on the rein in the direction you want to turn. Do several figure eights to practice direction changes, keeping the cues as light as possible. Now try a 180-degree turn. Walk the horse along a wall or fence. Turn the horse into the fence by giving a firm, smooth pull on the rein in the direction you want him to turn. Remember to give what you take and release somewhat on the other rein to allow him to complete the turn. Keep your body as directly behind him as possible during the whole maneuver. Try a similar turn in the opposite direction. It's important to cue the horse to turn when he's in the most advantageous position to turn properly. This means he would pivot on the hind leg on the inside of the 180-degree arc he's making with his body. For a left turn this would be his left hind leg. Time your cue on the rein to coincide with the positioning of his inside hind leg. Pull when this leg hits the ground well under the horse's body. This will make for a smooth turn on the haunches.

When the horse is responding well to ground driving, both straight and in turns, it's time to teach the rein back. Have the horse standing quietly and well balanced. By alternating gentle pulls on the reins ask him to back. A voice cue may also be introduced; this facilitates later mounted work. Don't ask for more than one step at a time initially. When he takes the step backwards, immediately release any pressure on the reins, praise him, then urge him forward several paces before asking him to back again. Try to keep his backing straight and in cadence, not rushed. Speed in backing can be added later.

When the horse responds well to all of these maneuvers in a longe cavesson, halter or bosal it's time to try ground driving in a snaffle bit. Use the same bit the horse was introduced to in initial bridling. Naturally, those trainers who've chosen the bosal for their initial breaking and training may want to skip this procedure now, saving it for a later introduction of the bridle and bit. The procedure for driving should be the same but the importance of soft, communicative hands is vital. Give and take on the reins, do not give long, steady pulls. In order for the horse to become a "puller" he has to have something to pull against—don't give it to him. Always use only enough cue to get the desired response and no more.

Teaching ground driving normally takes several weeks from the first introduction until the horse responds smoothly and quietly to all the maneuvers in a bit. Again, have the ground driving lessons down well before any mounted work is attempted. It might save you a few headaches, not to mention a few broken bones.

Initial Mounted Work

Now we come to what everyone views as the fireworks. In reality, it should be the quietly triumphant climax to a well-thought-out and patiently executed breaking program. There is no good reason why the first time a horse is mounted should be rodeo time. Bronc busting really has little place in a modern training routine, except in cases of rank, spoiled, older horses or badly started young ones; and even in these cases it should be viewed as a last resort. Most young horses, properly started, and intelligently and patiently brought along, offer little resistance to being mounted.

Again a small paddock or round pen is helpful during the first few mounted sessions. It's particularly important to keep the horse's mind on the trainer and away from distractions that might be available in a large pasture or arena. However, with the help of an assistant, a young horse properly prepared can be mounted just about anywhere for the first time.

Saddle and bridle the horse as usual and put him through a fifteen to twenty minute longe session working at all three gaits in both directions with several stops. Then hook up the driving lines and drive the horse for another fifteen or twenty minutes practicing figure eights, turns and rein backs. The horse by this time should be quiet and working smoothly and calmly. Put the horse in an enclosed area or have an assistant stand at his head holding a lead rope attached to a halter fitted over the bridle. Remove the driving reins and replace them with regular reins. Unhobble the stirrups. Spend a few minutes flapping the stirrup leathers against the horse's sides. Place some weight in each stirrup by pressing down on them with your hand. Talk soothingly to the horse all the time. Now grasp the reins in your left hand and the saddle horn in your right hand. Place your left foot in the stirrup. If riding an English saddle, take the reins in the left hand and face the rear of the horse. Hold the stirrup with your right hand and put your left foot into it. Stand up slightly in the stirrup, talking continually to the horse. Step down again and pet and praise him. Step up into the stirrup again. This time lean over the saddle and pet him on the off side. If he offers no resistance slowly and quietly swing your right leg over his croup and sit gently in the saddle. Pet and praise the horse profusely. Dismount and mount several times from both sides. If the horse stands quietly for two or three mountings from both sides give him a favorite tidbit and put him away for the day.

In the second mounted session proceed as for the first. After several mountings from both sides, sit in the saddle and rock gently from side to side. Make sure the horse is aware of you in the saddle. Then ask the horse to move forward using your command for walk on the longe line. Don't use any leg pressure at this stage. If the horse moves off properly praise him generously; if not, urge more with your voice and squeeze slightly with your leg. Once the horse is moving, ask for two or three gentle changes of direction and several stops. If all goes well, call it quits for the day.

At the third mounted lesson, be prepared for more action from the horse. It may not come, but often a relatively complacent horse becomes unglued after one or two riding sessions and acts spooky and frightened at the slightest movement or noise. Be prepared for it and work around it, but do not punish this spookiness. It's only a temporary reaction.

With the fourth ride serious work can begin. The horse should be ridden several minutes in both directions at a walk with numerous stops and turns. Work on subtle communication, developing the slightest aid possible to effect a response. Ask for a few trotting steps. Again use vocal cues established in longeing, such as "Whoa," and work on changes of direction and transitions from trotting to walking and vice versa. Ride the horse, preferably in the company of an unflappable older horse, around strange sights and places in order to build his confidence. Begin working on the rein back while mounted, utilizing voice and rein cues learned in ground driving.

When the horse, after several sessions, is working calmly at a walk and trot, stopping and turning on cue, ask for a short canter. Be sure to watch that the horse picks up the correct lead. It's best to ask for the canter as the horse rounds a corner since the turning effect helps to guide him onto the correct lead. Work in both directions. Don't be too surprised if the horse feels terribly rough at the trot and canter early in mounted work. It requires some time and work before he re-establishes his natural balance while carrying the rider's weight.

When the horse stands quietly to be mounted, walks, trots and canters at the rider's command, stops quietly and squarely and backs several steps in a straight line, he can be classified as "green broke." From this point he leaves the breaking period and goes into basic training, where he is taught more complex maneuvers and refines maneuvers he already knows. He is still obedient, but good-natured and his sense of confidence and respect in his trainer has increased dramatically during the breaking period. His personality is taking final form and at this stage the trainer can begin to assess the relative merit of the horse for various types of equine endeavors. Knowing that he has done the best job possible with this particular horse, the trainer approaches basic training with a great deal of optimism for the future and a clear sense of satisfaction in the past.

CHAPTER EIGHT

Basic Training

A TRAINER'S understanding of basic learning principles and their proper application becomes vital during the basic training of a horse. In working with horses on a daily basis it's easy to get mired down in the sheer routine of it. Often a full appreciation of the learning and teaching processes that are taking place escapes even the most conscientious trainer.

As with so many of the phenomena around him, man often takes for granted the ability to learn not only among members of his own species, but within other species as well. Learning is not an automatic consequence of physical maturity. In order to learn an animal must be taught either through responses and reinforcement, imitation or reasoning. Thus, trainers are teachers. Good trainers utilize techniques in their work with horses similar to those elementary school teachers use in their work with children.

In basic training we're concerned with refining what we have taught the horse up to this point, as well as teaching several new cues and responses. Our goal is to produce an obedient, willing horse who has a thorough understanding of the basic maneuvers upon which more advanced work is built.

In the breaking period we concentrated on accustoming the horse to carrying a rider as well as introducing the horse to the pressure of a bit or bosal. He has some understanding of giving to this pressure and has no fear of the various pieces of equipment introduced up to now. He's got a firm grasp on the voice commands for walk, trot, canter, stop and back, and responds without resistance to each voice aid.

It's time to step back from the scene a bit and look at the overall performance of the horse in perspective. How does the horse's performance compare with the goals initially set when he was first halter broken? If the comparison isn't a favorable one, what are the reasons for the disparity? Was the trainer at fault or were the reasons for the horse not achieving his potential beyond the trainer's control? The only way to improve as a trainer is to evaluate past performances honestly and learn from mistakes. Self-evaluation is very difficult, but a sure road to true success as a trainer.

If the trainer is satisfied with the horse's performance at this stage, he'll want to use the initial weeks of basic training to strengthen and refine cues and responses the horse learned during breaking. He'll also utilize this time for introducing the horse to as many new and strange environments as possible in order to accustom the horse to working under varied conditions.

In the breaking period we spent a great deal of time in enclosed areas—round pens, paddocks, stalls. Now we should expose the horse to as many environmental stimuli as possible so he learns to obey under the stress of numerous distractions. New environments also help keep him interested in his work and help develop the boldness we desire in his personality. As much of the basic training period as possible should be spent in large pastures and on wooded trails. A large outdoor ring or arena is good for work although not nearly as preferable as the wide open spaces.

Gymnastics

One of the major concerns in basic training should be the development of suppleness and balance in the young horse. The methods by which this is accomplished fall under the heading of dressage. Many horsepeople have a restricted view of dressage and associate it only with the popularized stories and films of the white stallions of the Spanish Riding School in Vienna. However, dressage simply means schooling and by this definition anyone training a horse is engaged in dressage.

Dressage training actually began during the breaking period with frequent transitions from one gait to another as well as halts. Now these gymnastics need to be further developed to increase the horse's balance, suppleness and responsiveness. Not only are changes of gait required but transitions within gaits should be asked for such as normal trot to extended trot to slow trot to normal trot; halt to slow trot to extended trot to normal trot. It is important to maintain prompt forward movement in all transitions. After these transitions are mastered, similar transitions at a canter can be used, such as moving from canter or lope to extended canter to gallop and then back to a canter; from trot to canter to extended canter to trot to halt to canter. Numerous combinations of these transitions can be made to increase the responsiveness, obedience and balance of the horse. He'll learn to carry himself with his hind legs well underneath him which will lighten his forehand. It is important for the trainer to strive for calmness as well as responsiveness. If the horse becomes nervous, slower less abrupt changes should be sought. Later, these same sorts of gymnastics can be performed on circles, serpentines or broken lines.

At this point the trainer should begin asking for halts from different speeds and gaits, making sure that each stop is performed correctly. The horse's head should be raised only slightly, if at all, with mouth closed and hind legs well underneath him. This is a far cry from many stops seen where the horse's head is pulled into the air by the rider, the mouth gapes open in an attempt to avoid the pain of the bit and the hocks are pushed out behind a hollowed-out back. As with every other maneuver, the only way the horse will stop correctly is if he is taught correctly. He can't be forced to do something if he doesn't know how to do it. Another mistake that is often made is not securing a stop every time it's asked for. Don't use the vocal cue for stop ("whoa") and don't ask for a stop when riding or longeing without getting the response. Nothing teaches a horse disrespect more quickly than an inconsistent trainer who continually asks for responses and then doesn't insist that he get them. Once the horse knows how to stop correctly and stops obediently on demand, the trainer may want to increase the speed from which the halt is performed, asking for a "sliding stop." This type of stop should be asked for only occasionally, however, and the horse should be fitted with skid boots to protect the hind legs from burns.

Rein Effects

During breaking we relied almost exclusively on the leading rein effect and the rein of direct opposition to obtain directional changes from the horse. Now we want to teach the horse three additional rein effects to increase our training tools (see Figure 14, overleaf).

Bearing or neck rein. Next to the rein of direct opposition this is probably the most frequently used rein effect in finished horses, particularly stock horses and polo ponies. In order to teach it properly, we utilize our basic learning principles, particularly the principles of classical conditioning.

Response to the rein of direct opposition is already conditioned in the horse so we pair our new cue, the neck rein, with it until the neck rein alone achieves the desired response. It's important to remember the proper sequence of cue presentation for maximum learning efficiency—new cue then old cue somewhat overlapping new cue. Remember also, if you want the horse to respond to a light cue, teach him with a light cue; simply lay the rein against his neck.

Begin teaching the neck rein at a walk, then progress to the other gaits after the horse is performing correctly and consistently. Don't ask for sharp turns yet; keep to circles, figure-eights, and serpentines. The young horse isn't ready for rollbacks, spins or pivots.

Rein of indirect opposition in front of the withers. If we use the right rein as an example, this rein effect is applied as follows: the right rein is carried across the neck to the left in front of the withers and then pressure is applied to the left rear. This causes the horse's nose to turn to the right rear and places the horse's weight on the left shoulder. If the horse is standing still, the effect is to push the shoulders toward the left rear. With a corresponding movement of the hindquarters to the right front, the horse essentially turns in place around his central axis. If the horse is moving he turns to the left, the degree and sharpness of the turn depending on the length of time the rein effect is applied and the pressure used. This rein effect is used in teaching the turn on the haunches or rollback.

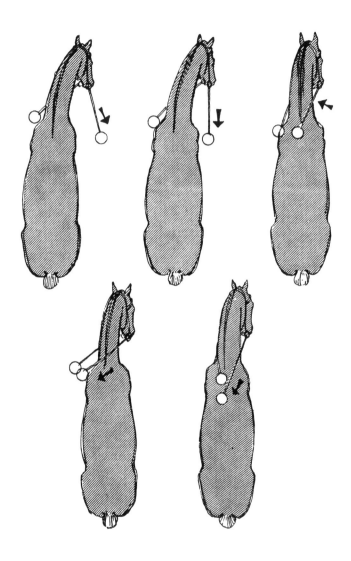

Figure 14. Five Basic Rein Effects. Clockwise from top left: *leading rein; direct rein; bearing or neck rein; indirect rein of opposition in front of withers; indirect rein of opposition behind withers.*

Rein of indirect opposition behind the withers. Again using the right rein as an example, this rein effect is applied as follows: the right rein is kept on the right side of the withers and drawn toward the left rear behind them. This again forces the horse's weight onto his left shoulder, but also forces his equilibrium to the left in the rear legs as well, particularly if the rider's right leg is used to drive the horse's hindquarters to the left in combination with the right rein effect. This rein effect is relied upon later in teaching the side pass and shoulder-in movements.

Turn on the Haunches

Now that the horse responds correctly to the five basic rein effects, we can use these cues, in combination with other cues, to teach the horse some basic maneuvers.

The turn on the haunches is the basic response to a number of more complex movements, including the rollback, spin, pivot and pirouette as well as being an important basic maneuver in itself. To teach the turn on the haunches we use the rein of indirect opposition in front of the withers in combination with a leg cue.

If we want to teach the horse a left turn on the haunches the sequence of cues would be as follows: just prior to beginning your turn, apply the right leg behind the girth. This prevents the hindquarters from swinging out to the right as the horse turns, as well as signaling to the horse that you're about to ask him for a response. Apply a right indirect rein of opposition in front of the withers, maintaining the rein effect until the turn is complete. When first teaching this movement work at a walk and try to plan your cues so that they are applied when the horse is in the most advantageous condition to respond, i.e. when the hind leg on the inside of the turn strikes the ground. This is similar to what we did when teaching the horse to turn when ground driving and makes for a smooth, clean turn on the haunches. Initially, only require a change in direction of 90 degrees. This is a quarter-turn or pivot. When the horse turns correctly at 90 degrees, pivoting around his inside hind leg, ask for a half-turn or rollback, a 180-degree change in direction. Always make

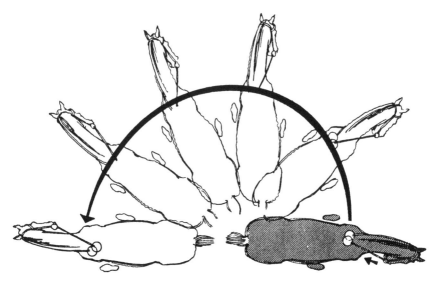

Figure 15. Turn on the haunches maneuver.

sure the horse is turning off his hindquarters and not simply turning around his center axis, sometimes termed "wagon-wheeling." Turning the horse toward a fence may help to prevent him from moving forward out of the turn in an attempt to avoid turning on his haunches. However, the fence shouldn't be used any more than necessary to obtain a correct turn.

Once the horse can do a proper turn on the haunches in both directions (for a right turn on the haunches the aids are the reverse of the above) the trainer can attempt them at a lope, again making every effort to cue the horse when the hind leg on the inside of the turn is on the ground.

Full turns on the haunches in place (pirouette) shouldn't be attempted until the horse correctly and consistently performs single half-turns at the lope or canter. This is because the turn on the haunches is a forward movement; the horse must maintain normal impulsion and remain lightened on the forehand with his hind legs well underneath him during the turn. Before he can do this he must fully understand and respond correctly to a turn of lesser degree. Once the horse is performing a correct complete turn on the haunches at a canter or lope, the trainer may ask for several consecutive full turns (spin), always striving to make sure forward impulsion and correct position are maintained.

Turn on the Forehand

The turn on the forehand is a valuable movement for the horse that is used as a working horse, a trail horse or a show horse in trail classes, as well as being an additional means of teaching obedience to the aids. It is essentially the reverse of the turn on the haunches in that the horse moves his hindquarters around the pivot provided by the foreleg on the inside of the turn. The advantages of being able to move the horse's hindquarters while holding the forehand still or vice versa, as with the turn on the haunches, is of real value in numerous situations both in and out of the show ring. Opening and closing gates while remaining mounted and maneuvering among ground obstacles are just two examples where the ability to move forehand and hindquarters independently is useful.

The aids for a turn on the forehand with hindquarters moving to the right are as follows: 1) the left direct rein is applied to indicate the change of direction; 2) the right direct rein is used passively to prevent further forward movement and then as a bearing rein to the left to assist the left direct rein of opposition; 3) the left leg, applied behind the girth, pushes the hindquarters to the right causing the hind legs to describe an arc around the pivot point provided by the left foreleg. A quarter-turn on the forehand should be taught first, followed by turns of one hundred eighty degrees and three hundred sixty degrees.

Appuyer and Shoulder-in

The shoulder-in is considered by many horsemen to be one of the finest gymnastic exercises available for the horse. If properly taught, it generates suppleness, relaxation and obedience in the horse. A

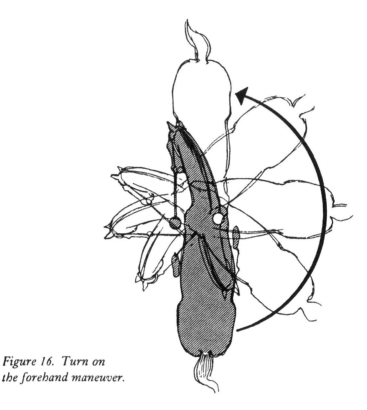

*Figure 16. Turn on
the forehand maneuver.*

mild form of shoulder-in (appuyer in French) should be taught
first.

In the appuyer the horse is walked along a fence or imaginary line
and then turned into a half-circle. After completing the half-circle
the horse is returned to the fence on an oblique line and reaches the
fence headed in the opposite direction from the start of the circle.
Appuyer is performed during the return to the fence on the oblique
line. For a half-turn and appuyer to the right the aids would be as
follows: 1) at the start of the oblique return to the fence a left indirect rein of opposition behind the withers is applied in combina-

Figure 17. Appuyer maneuver.

tion with a left leg aid pushing the hindquarters obliquely to the right. The combined effect is to cause the horse to cross his left hind and forelegs across the respective right legs in moving back to the wall. His body is bent slightly around the rider's left leg and his head is turned outward, away from the direction of movement. An appuyer to the left would require the opposite (i.e. right indirect rein of opposition behind the withers and right leg behind the girth). Once the horse has mastered the appuyer in both directions at a walk, he should be asked to perform the movement at a free, long-strided trot. It is at this gait that most benefit is gained from the exercise.

If the horse performs the appuyer well, little difficulty should be encountered in teaching the shoulder-in. Again, ride the horse along a fence or imaginary line. Using the right shoulder-in as an example, a turn to the right would be started with a right leading rein or direct rein of opposition. Just as the horse's forehand moves off the straight line the right indirect rein of opposition behind the withers is applied. In addition, the rider's right leg is applied behind the girth and the left leg at the girth to keep the hindquarters moving forward. The right fore and hind legs cross over in front of the left fore and hind legs and the horse's body bends around the rider's right leg. For a shoulder-in to the left, the corresponding aids would be left indirect rein of opposition behind the withers, left leg behind the girth, right leg at the girth. The horse would then bend around the rider's left leg.

The shoulder-in is a tremendous aid in suppling a horse, in teaching obedience to the aids, in developing balance and muscular coordination and in relieving the stiffness to one side or the other which seems to be a problem for many young horses.

Half-Pass (Two Tracks)

Although many people confuse shoulder-in and half-pass, close observation reveals one major difference. In shoulder-in the horse is bent away from the direction of movement. In the half-pass he is bent (if at all) toward the direction of movement. There should be no bending of the horse's spine itself, but a slight turning of the head in the direction of movement is acceptable.

The aids for the half-pass are diagonal ones. For example, a half-pass to the right requires a right direct rein and left leg predominating, with support from the left rein and right leg in maintaining impulsion on an oblique line. The horse's left fore and hind legs should cross over in front of the corresponding right legs.

As a gymnastic exercise the half pass doesn't have as much value as the shoulder-in and it is more difficult to perform correctly. If done properly, however, it indicates a high degree of obedience in the horse and great skill on the part of the rider.

Full Pass (Side Pass)

The side pass is a "must" for anyone wanting to compete and win in trail classes, as well as a further means of developing obedience in the horse. It is fairly easy to teach once the horse has mastered the shoulder-in. The full pass is simply two-tracking without forward motion and is performed at a walk. Begin by performing a half-pass first to the right and then to the left. Repeat the movement to the right, but adopt a more fixed position of the hands and try to prevent forward movement as much as possible while maintaining lateral movement to the right with the left leg. Use the right leg at the girth to prevent movement backward in response to the increased rein pressure. Ask for only a few side pass steps at first, then allow the horse to continue obliquely in the half-pass as a reward for performing correctly. Make sure the horse continues to cross the left legs in front of the right legs when side passing to the right (the reverse for a side pass to the left).

With each new lesson increase the number of side pass steps asked for until the horse can negotiate as many as the rider desires. However, don't bore the horse with numerous repetitions of the side pass. Intersperse them with other maneuvers, and be sure to practice two-tracking in both directions.

Simple Lead Changes at a Canter

Every horse should be able to execute a simple lead change smoothly and without resistance. If the horse has been brought along in a systematic manner there shouldn't be much difficulty involved in making him execute a fluid simple lead change either in a figure-eight or on a straight line.

Simple lead changes in a figure eight should be taught first. Work the horse at a strong trot in a large figure eight being sure to round off each loop of the eight before going into the other loop. The loops of the eight should be round, not egg shaped. As the horse nears the tangent point between the two loops pick up the correct lead for the loop you are entering, using the appropriate rein and leg aids. When the first loop is nearly complete bring the horse back to a trot for two or three strides and then pick up the correct lead for the second loop. With each successive figure eight reduce the number of intervening trotting steps until the horse completes a figure eight with only one trotting stride between lead changes.

Now the same work should be repeated on straight lines alternating cantering strides on one lead with a few trotting strides and then cantering strides on the opposite lead. When this is accomplished, practice similar figure eights and straight line lead changes going from a walk to a canter. This is where the gait transitions worked on earlier come in handy.

When the horse changes leads smoothly and without resistance from either an intervening trotting or walking stride, both on a figure eight and a straight line, it is time to ask for a flying lead change. But don't rush into a flying lead change if the horse shows any hesitancy, resistance or imbalance in simple lead changes. Any problems are simply compounded in attempting to do flying changes.

Flying Lead Changes

In executing flying lead changes, the rider must remember that a lead is determined in the hind legs and therefore the hind leg lead change should occur before or simultaneously with the change in the front legs. If this doesn't happen, the horse may change leads in front and not behind, a situation called cross-cantering. A proper flying lead change requires that the horse be collected with his hind legs well underneath him. Again, we can make good use of the figure eight in teaching the flying change. As the horse completes one loop of the eight on the right lead and reaches the tangent point between the two loops where the left lead is required, the rider should gently carry the right rein in direct opposition and the left rein in indirect opposition in front of the withers in order to impede the right shoulder and release the left. In addition, the right leg is applied just behind the girth during the suspension phase of the canter to signal the lead change for the hind legs. If a correct change is made the horse should be rewarded with a rest period during which he's allowed to relax on a long rein. The exercise should be repeated until the horse switches from right to left lead and vice versa with a smooth flying change. However, don't overdo this type of work in any one training session because fatigue or boredom may cause the horse to cross-canter or resist the aids completely.

When flying lead changes have been mastered in figure eights they should be done on straight lines as well, with a variable number of canter strides between each lead change.

Review of Training

If all has gone well up to this point, the horse is well prepared for any type of advanced training or just simple enjoyment as a pleasure horse. Naturally, the trainer probably encountered problems during the course of breaking and training which required a good deal of thought and patience to be solved. But if the trainer did think and was patient in attempts to discover and eliminate problems, they undoubtedly were no more than minor setbacks—not major obstacles. Many training problems are man-made because we compound initial troubles with our own lack of understanding, patience and willingness to evaluate a situation from the horse's point of view. If trainers could only learn to apply more psychology and less brute force to horse training, they could make their efforts much more enjoyable and efficient.

CHAPTER NINE

Individualism in Horse Behavior and Learning

THROUGHOUT THIS BOOK learning and training processes in the horse have been presented with the average horse in mind. But averages are derived from extremes, and this is certainly true in terms of learning in the horse. There really is no such animal as the average horse. As with physical characteristics, the emotional and mental traits exhibited by an individual differ from those of any other individual. This variation is due to several factors including genetic potential, age, sex, environmental influences, emotionality and motivation. Naturally, the uniqueness of an individual results from the interrelatedness of these six traits.

Genetic Potential

The genetic potential for learning in any organism (man, horse, dog, etc.) is impossible to measure empirically. About all that can be established is the individual's normalcy with respect to nervous system development and the sensory capacity to gather information from the environment. These two factors—sensory capacity and the ability to interpret sensory data—are basic to learning. But beyond this, raw intelligence really can't be measured because any measurement of intelligence is actually a determination of performance. For example, a child attending first grade is given an I.Q. test which supposedly assesses the child's intelligence. But the criteria used for making that assessment are performance on the test or the number of correct responses, and this performance is the result of numerous factors working on the basic genetic potential for learning. So what should be of primary concern to horse trainers is learning ability and performance, not intelligence per se.

Genetic potential is only one factor to be considered in assessing learning ability in a particular horse and, according to some authorities, not the limiting factor. But while genetic potential may not necessarily be the limiting factor in a horse's learning ability, it does significantly influence it. And it is a factor that can be improved through selective breeding. We have to consider that most breeders simply do not select for learning ability in their breeding programs. The Thoroughbred, Standardbred and other racing breeds are bred for racing ability almost to the exclusion of any other trait. This is certainly understandable and not necessarily detrimental to the learning ability required of a horse trained for racing. Any racehorse trainer knows that speed alone does not win races. Regardless of his ability to run, the horse must have the ability to learn to use his running capabilities to greatest advantage in a race. Thus, animals that have proven themselves on the track and have then been retired to stud transmit to varying degrees not only their genetic ability to run but also their ability to learn the mechanics of racing. But the primary selection pressure in Thoroughbred breeding (with the possible exception of Thoroughbreds selectively bred as hunters, jumpers and/or dressage prospects) has been for speed, not learning ability.

The other breeds are normally bred with a high selection pressure for conformation or color or both. Again, little consideration is given to genetic potential for learning or temperament, both of which affect the animal's ability to learn. This is not necessarily bad for the breed or species, but as we demand greater performance of our horses, we should be aware that we can increase the raw material with which we work by emphasizing selection pressure for learning ability and temperament in our breeding programs.

Age

Research conducted on many species, including man, indicates that learning is more rapid in young animals within a species (this is not meant to include newborns, whose sensory systems are not mature).

Most likely this is because the young of any species are more curious, less inhibited and more aware of their environment than their older counterparts, and consequently, there is a greater degree of sensory input. In addition, there are probably physiological factors which account for increased learning capacity in young animals.

In the horse and other animals which lack the ability to reason, this age differential apparent in learning ability is probably a function of prior learning experiences as well. Older horses, having formed responses in association with certain stimuli, are reluctant to learn new responses. It's a case of "You can't teach an old horse new tricks," except that we ought to substitute "it's difficult to" for "you can't." Anyone who has attempted to retrain a spoiled horse over eight years old is fully aware of the resistance to learning these horses can exhibit. Drastic measures are usually required to re-establish the horse's sensitivity to the environment and the trainer! These measures aren't necessarily limited to negative reinforcement but depending upon the horse may include an abrupt change in living conditions (stall to pasture), or a change in rider, tack, feed or stablemates. Any environmental change which forces the horse to deal with a novel situation may help unsettle old habits. The old adage that it's easier to train a horse right the first time than retrain him later is based on more than just casual observation.

Sex

Implying that individual variations in learning ability are partially sex linked is like walking into a beehive! But, with some clarification of the statement, I think most people agree that sex certainly has an influence on learning ability. First we must keep in mind that learning ability is not static, it is dynamic. We've all experienced days when solutions to problems were quite clear to us and, on the other hand, we've all experienced times when even simple solutions were beyond our grasp. There's every reason to believe that horses have similar "good and bad" days. What causes the good and bad days? Probably many factors, but certainly the physiological and emotional status of the animal is one of them.

Hormone levels in the blood are one physiological factor which influences behavior. During puberty the hormone levels of all animals undergo drastic changes. In horses, puberty usually occurs between twelve and eighteen months of age, just about the time most trainers are getting down to serious work. The physiological changes taking place in the young horse can influence the learning ability that the animal exhibits during this period. I don't think the change in colts is quite so traumatic in terms of learning, as it is for fillies, primarily because fillies begin to undergo cyclic hormonal changes. On the other hand, once colts reach puberty they are under the influence of a relatively constant hormone level (until castration, at which time the hormone level drops and remains constant). When the filly or mare is in heat, she may exhibit a lessened learning ability. This is probably a function of distraction and, perhaps, irritability and is not directly related to any inherent learning ability. Naturally, there are many fillies and mares that go through heat without any changes in their learning behavior, but anyone involved with training a filly during puberty should understand the tremendous physiological changes that are taking place as well as the cyclical nature of these changes, and gauge training progress accordingly.

Environmental Influences

Man's influence on equine learning ability is evident in environmental effects such as nutrition, health care, housing, early handling and training. Horse people often forget that every time they are in contact with their horse they're in a training situation, regardless of the stated purpose of the contact. This is where many trainers miss the boat because they fail to practice consistently what they preach in their structured training sessions. For example, simply because Saturday is a pleasure-riding day and not a training day for the rider, doesn't mean the horse is necessarily aware of the same priorities. If the trainer is sloppy in his cue presentation or slow in reinforcing responses on his day off the horse translates this as inconsistency. This wreaks havoc with training schedules. Although the horse is most often blamed for the poor performance that results from this inconsistent training approach, there is really no one to blame but the trainer. In addition to training effects there are numerous other environmental factors that influence a particular horse's learning ability. Enough research hasn't been done in the horse to tell us specifically to what degree and how factors such as nutrition, health and early handling affect learning, but if research on rats is extrapolated to humans and further extended to include horses, it would appear that all these factors affect how well a horse learns. Poor nutrition, particularly extremely low protein levels, has a detrimental effect on learning. Obviously, a sick or injured animal has a reduced learning capacity. And early handling appears to affect learning ability primarily through socialization and the reduction of emotional stress. A great deal of research is necessary before we can fully define the specific environmental factors that affect learning in horses and to what degree they affect individual horses.

Emotionality

The temperament, nervousness or distractability of a horse disrupts learning primarily by affecting his sensory mechanisms. In other words, a highly emotional or temperamental animal has a more difficult time sorting out important stimuli. Therefore, he tends to react more than a less temperamental or emotional animal simply because more stimuli attract his attention. Why some horses are more emotional than others can be explained by both genetic and environmental influences. The emotional horse, either because of prior experience or more likely because of some combination of factors judges as important and therefore reacts to stimuli that elicit only brief notice from a less emotional animal. The inherent emotionality of a particular horse can be affected to some degree by training in early life, but the degree to which emotionality can be influenced decreases as the animal ages.

Motivation

Of all the traits affecting learning ability in the horse, motivation is the least understood. Why will some horses perform brilliantly under adverse conditions (and in some cases, even pain) while other horses perform poorly or refuse to perform at all when only minor problems arise? Some trainers feel motivation can be instilled in a horse (usually through a sizeable dose of the spur or whip), but is this really motivation or simply fear of punishment? Is motivation a negative or positive trait? Do we work to gain something or avoid something? If motivation is instilled only through negative reinforcement or punishment, how do we explain performance in those instances where the physical or emotional stress on the horse would almost preclude performance? Is it simply that the horse's *fear* of us is greater than his fear of pain or stress? It would seem that motivation involves a good deal more than just a liberal application of aversive stimuli. There are many questions that haven't been answered accurately about motivation in horses and until they are answered we can only estimate the causes and effects of this trait on learning ability and resulting performance in the horse.

From this discussion of the factors affecting learning in the horse, we can readily see that successful training must be individually oriented. The same procedures and equipment won't necessarily have the same effect on any two horses. That is why an understanding of the principles basic to learning is so important. There is no secret to horse training—no special bit or certain martingale or other expensive equipment can make up for not understanding how an animal learns. The majority of equipment used by people in training horses is used simply as a means to avoid proper education of the horse, and it shows in the quality of these horses' performances. Trainers have become slaves to equipment, spending large sums of money and countless hours trying to force horses to learn with an unbelievable array of bits, bitting rings, draw reins, martingales and other paraphernalia. Many times the equipment is used improperly and inappropriately. Simply because draw reins were effective in teaching one horse to flex at the poll and lighten his forehand doesn't mean it works well for the next horse. Each piece of equipment used in training a horse should have a specific reason for being used. Don't slap something on a horse just because Joe Horsetrainer who won at the pleasure class at last week's show uses one. If you evaluate training in terms of proper cue presentation, and contingent and appropriate reinforcement of responses you can probably forego the new equipment in favor of your own common sense and ability.

Conclusion

MANY HORSEMEN feel that reading a book is no way to learn how to train a horse. And certainly in a practical sense they're right. Experience is the best teacher, and nowhere is this more true than in horse training.

But books do afford the reader knowledge and understanding which can be applied to a training situation, increasing the trainer's effectiveness in communicating with his student. And books do help us learn from other people's successes and failures. I hope this book has provided the reader with additional insight into equine learning mechanisms and how a trainer can influence the behavior of a horse through the application of basic learning principles.

A list of books and articles, both technical and non-technical, is provided for those readers who would like to delve deeper into the areas of equine learning and training. References are arranged by general topics, but many cover several areas pertinent to learning and training. This list of additional reading is regrettably incomplete. Many fine books and articles are not included, but those presented will assist the reader in obtaining more information to enhance his relationships with horses.

Additional Reading

BEHAVIORAL PRINCIPLES

Darling, E. F. 1952. "Social Life in Ungulates." Centre Nationale pour Recherche Scientifique, Paris. Vol. 34, *Structure et Physiologie des Societes Animals*, pp. 221–6.

Fiske, J. C. 1978. "A Guide to Horse Mentality." *Practical Horseman* (July).

Fiske, J. C. 1979. "Categorizing Equine Behavior and Abnormalities." *Chronicle of the Horse*, Vol. XLII, p. 18.

Fox, M. W. 1968. *Abnormal Behavior in Animals*. Saunders, Philadelphia, Pennsylvania.

Francis-Smith, K., and D. G. M. Wood-Gush. "Coprophagea as Seen in Thoroughbred Foals." *Equine Veterinary Journal*, Vol. 9, p. 155.

Frohmberg, Enid. 1970. "Psychology of the Horse" (four-part series). *Western Horseman* (Jan.–April).

Glendinning, S. A. 1974. "A System of Rearing Foals on an Automatic Calf-Feeding Machine." *Equine Veterinary Journal*, Vol. 6, p. 12.

Hafez, E. S. E. 1968. *The Behavior of Domestic Animals*. Balliere, London.

Hediger, H. 1968. *The Psychology and Behavior of Animals in Zoos and Circuses*. Dover Publications, New York.

Hull, C. L. 1943. *Principles of Behavior*. Appleton-Century-Crofts, New York.

Kiley, M. 1972. "The Vocalizations of Ungulates, Their Causation and Function." *Zier Tierpsychologie*, Vol. 31, p. 171.

Klinghammer, E. and Fox, M. W. 1971. "Ethology and Its Place in Animal Science." *Journal of Animal Science*, Vol. 32, p. 1278.

Lorenz, K. 1965. *Evolution and Modification of Behavior.* University of Chicago Press, Chicago, Illinois.

Odberg, F. O., and K. Francis Smith. "A Study on Elimination and Grazing Behavior—The Use of the Field by Captive Horses." *Equine Veterinary Journal,* Vol. 8, p. 147.

Roe, A., and Simpson, G. 1964. *Behavior and Evolution.* Yale University Press, New Haven, Connecticut.

Ryden, Hope. 1972. *Mustangs; A Return to the Wild.* Viking Press, New York.

Schafer, M. 1975. *The Language of the Horse.* Arco Publishing Co., New York.

Simpson, G. G. 1961. *Horses.* The American Museum of Natural History, Doubleday & Co., New York.

Smyth, R. H. 1966. *The Mind of the Horse.* The Stephen Greene Press, Brattleboro, Vermont.

Tinbergen, N. 1951. *The Study of Instinct.* Oxford, England.

Tinbergen, N. 1953. *Social Behavior in Animals.* London, England.

Wiechert, D. A. 1971. "Social Behavior in Farm Animals." *Journal of Animal Science,* Vol. 32, p. 1274.

Williams, M. 1974. "The Effect of Artificial Rearing on the Social Behavior of Foals." *Equine Veterinary Journal,* Vol. 6, p. 17.

PHYSIOLOGY OF THE SENSES

Breazile, J. E. 1971. *Textbook of Veterinary Physiology.* Lea and Febiger, Philadelphia, Pennsylvania.

Catcott, E. J., and Smithcor, J. F. 1972. *Equine Medicine and Surgery.* American Veterinary Publications, Wheaton, Illinois.

Granit, R. 1955. *Receptors and Sensory Perception.* Yale University Press, New Haven, Connecticut.

Knill, L. M., Eagleton, R. D., and Harver, E. 1977. "Physical Optics of the Equine Eye." *American Journal of Veterinary Research,* Vol. 38, p. 735.

Mueller, C. G. 1965. *Sensory Psychology.* Prentice-Hall, Englewood Cliffs, New Jersey.

Odberg, F. O. 1978. "A Study of the Learning Ability of Horses." *Equine Veterinary Journal,* Vol. 10, p. 82.

Prince, J. H., Diesen, C. D., Eglitis, I., and Ruskell, G. L. 1960. *Anatomy and Histology of the Eye and Orbit in Domestic Animals.* Charles C. Thomas Co., Springfield, Illinois.

Schneider, A. M. and Tarshis, B. 1975. *An Introduction to Physiological Psychology.* Random House, New York.

Sivak, J. G. and Allen, D. B. 1975. "An Evaluation of the Ramp Retina of the Horse Eye." *Vision Research,* Vol. 15, p. 1353.

Smythe, R. H. 1975. *Vision in the Animal World.* St. Martin's Press, New York.

Swenson, M. J. (ed). 1970. *Duke's Physiology of Domestic Animals.* 8th ed. Comstock Publ. Assoc. Cornell Univ. Press, Ithaca, New York.

BASIC CONCEPTS IN LEARNING

Bitterman, M. E. 1965. "Phyletic Differences in Learning." *American Psychologist,* Vol. 20, p. 396.

Bolles, R. C. 1970. "Species-Specific Defense Reactions and Avoidance Learning." *Psychological Review,* Vol. 77, p. 32.

Bolles, R. C. 1972. "Reinforcement, Expectancy, and Learning." *Psychological Review,* Vol. 79, p. 394.

Bolles, R. C. 1975. *Theory of Motivation.* Harper and Row, New York.

Bolles, R. C. 1975. *Learning Theory.* Holt, Rinehart and Winston, New York.

Breland, K. and Breland, M. 1961. "The Misbehavior of Animals." *American Psychologist,* Vol. 16, p. 681.

Brush, F. R. 1971. *Aversive Conditioning and Learning.* Academic Press, New York.

Church, R. M. 1963. "The Varied Effects of Punishment on Behavior." *Psychological Review,* Vol. 70, p. 369.

Deutsch, J. A. (ed.). 1973. *The Physiological Basis of Memory.* Academic Press, New York.

Ferster, C. B. and Skinner, B. F. 1957. *Schedules of Reinforcement.* Appleton-Century-Crofts, New York.

Garcia, J. and Koelling, R. 1966. "Relation of Cue to Consequence in Avoidance Learning." *Psychonomic Science,* Vol. 4, p. 123.

Gilbert, R. M. and Sutherland, N. S. 1969. *Animal Discrimination Learning.* Academic Press, New York.

Harlow, H. F. 1949. "The Formation of Learning Sets." *Psychological Review,* Vol. 56, p. 51.

Hempelmann, F. 1926. *Tierpsychologie vom Standpunkte des Biologen.* Leipzig.

Honig, W. K. and James, P. H. R. (eds.). 1971. *Animal Memory.* Academic Press, New York.

John, E. R. 1967. *Mechanisms of Memory.* Academic Press, New York.

Katz, D. 1948. *Mensch und Tier.* Studien zur Vergluchenden Psychologie. Zurich.

Krasner, L. and Ullman, L. P. (eds.). 1965. *Research in Behavior Modification.* Holt, Rinehart, and Winston, New York.

Miller, N. E. 1948. "Studies of Fear as an Acquirable Drive. I. Fear as Motivation and Fear Reduction as Reinforcement in the Learning of New Responses." *Journal of Experimental Psychology,* Vol. 38, p. 89.

Mowrer, O. H. 1960. *Learning Theory and Behavior.* Wiley, New York.

Seligman, M. E. P. 1970. "On the Generality of the Laws of Learning." *Psychological Review,* Vol. 77, p. 406.

Skinner, B. F. 1938. *The Behavior of Organisms.* Appleton-Century-Crofts, New York.

Spence, K. W. 1956. *Behavior Theory and Conditioning.* Yale University Press, New Haven, Connecticut.

Spence, K. W. and Spence, J. T. (eds.). 1967. *The Psychology of Learning and Motivation.* Academic Press, New York.

Tarpy, R. M. 1975. *Basic Principles of Learning.* Scott, Foresman, and Co., Glenview, Illinois.

Thorpe, W. H. 1964. *Learning and Instinct in Animals.* Methuen and Co., London.

Wagner, A. R. 1961. "Effects of Amount and Percentage of Reinforcement and Number of Acquisition Trials on Conditioning and Extinction." *Journal of Experimental Psychology,* Vol. 62, p. 234.

Washburn, M. 1930. *The Animal Mind.* New York.

Wyrwicka, W. 1972. *Mechanisms of Conditioned Behavior.* Charles C. Thomas Co., Springfield, Illinois.

SCIENTIFIC REFERENCES ON LEARNING IN THE HORSE (arranged in chronological order)

Hamilton, G. V. 1911. "A Study of Trial and Error Reactions in Mammals." *Journal of Animal Science,* Vol. 1, p. 33.

Gardner, L. P. 1933. "The Responses of Horses to the Situation of a Closed Feed Box." *Journal of Comparative Psychology,* Vol. 15, p. 445.

Gardner, L. P. 1937. "The Responses of Horses in a Discrimination Problem." *Journal of Comparative and Physiological Psychology,* Vol. 23, p. 13.

Gardner, L. P. 1937. "The Responses of Horses to the Same Signal in Different Positions." *Journal of Comparative and Physiological Psychology,* Vol. 23, p. 304.

Gardner, L. P. 1942. "Conditioning Horses and Cows to the Pail as a Signal." *Journal of Comparative and Physiological Psychology,* Vol. 34, p. 29.

Popov, N. F. 1956. "Characteristics of Higher Nervous Activity of Horses." *Zh. Vyssh. Nervn. Deyatel.,* Vol. 6, p. 718.

Bobylev, I. 1960. "A Study of the Typological Features in the Higher Nervous Activity of Race Horses." *Konevodstvo i Konnyi Sport,* Vol. 2, p. 19.

Myers, R. D. and Mesker, D. C. 1960. "Operant Responding in a Horse under Several Schedules of Reinforcement." *Journal of Experimental and Analytical Behavior,* Vol. 3, p. 161.

Warren, J. M. and Warren, H. B. 1962. "Reversal Learning by Horse and Raccoon." *Journal of Genetic Psychology,* Vol. 100, p. 215.

Dixon, J. C. 1970. "Pattern Discrimination, Learning Set, and Memory in a Pony." *The Thoroughbred Record,* Vol. 192.

Kratzer, D. D. 1971. "Learning in Farm Animals." *Journal of Animal Science,* Vol. 32, p. 1268.

Cook, J. *Equine Avoidance Learning.* University of Kentucky, Lexington, Kentucky.

Yeates, B. F. 1976. "Discrimination Learning in Horses." Master's Thesis, Texas A&M University, College Station, Texas.

Fiske, J. C. 1976. "Discrimination Reversal Learning in Yearling Horses." Master's Thesis. Texas A&M University, College Station, Texas.

Fiske, J. C. and G. D. Potter 1979. "Discrimination Reversal Learning in Yearling Horses." *Journal of Animal Science* (August).

Travis, B. 1976. "Texas A&M Experiment Probes Learning Ability in Horses." *Quarter Horse Journal* (May), p. 138.

Kratzer, D. D., Netherland, W. M., Pulse, R. E. and Baker, J. P. 1977. "Maze Learning in Quarter Horses." *Journal of Animal Science*, Vol. 46, p. 896.

Cottongim, S. T. *Positive Reinforcement in Horses.* Georgia State University, Atlanta, Georgia.

Fiske, J. C. 1979. "Behavior and Learning in the Horse." *Southwestern Veterinarian*, Vol. 32.

TRAINER PSYCHOLOGY

Grant, S. 1977. "Learning Ability in Horses—Psychology and Learning Ability." Excerpts from a lecture by J. C. Fiske, Texas A&M University, at the National Horsemen's Seminar, Fredericksburg, Virginia. *Chronicle of the Horse*, Vol. XL, p. 6.

Jones, D. 1976. *The Western Trainer.* Arco Publishing Co., New York.

Maday, St. Von. 1912. *Psychologie des Pferdes und der Dressur.* Berlin.

Miller, R. W. 1975. *Western Horse Behavior and Training.* Doubleday, New York.

Podhajsky, A. 1967. *The Complete Training of Horse and Rider in the Principles of Classical Horsemanship.* Doubleday & Co., Garden City, New Jersey.

Stewart, D. 1973. *Western Equitation, Horsemanship and Showmanship.* Vantage Press, New York.

Williamson, M. 1974. *Applied Horse Psychology.* Cordovan Corp., Houston, Texas.

EARLY EXPERIENCES AND THEIR EFFECT ON LEARNING

Krech, D., Rosenzweig, M. R. and Bennett, E. L. 1962. "Relation between Brain Chemistry and Problem Solving among Rats Raised in Enriched and Impoverished Environments." *Journal of Comparative and Physiological Psychology,* Vol. 55, p. 801.
Lorenz, K. Z. 1952. *King Solomon's Ring.* Crowell, New York.
Sluckin, W. 1965. *Imprinting and Early Learning.* Aldine Publishers, Chicago, Illinois.

BREAKING AND TRAINING THE HORSE

Chamberlin, H. D. 1973. (2nd ed.). *Training Hunters, Jumpers and Hacks.* Arco Publishing Co., New York.
Jones, D. 1968. *Practical Western Training.* Arco Publishing Co., New York.
Seunig, W. 1956. *Horsemanship.* Doubleday & Co., Garden City, New York.
Wright, G. 1962. *Horsemanship and Horsemastership.* Wilshire Book Co., North Hollywood, California.
Young, J. R. 1977. "Simplified Ground Driving." *Horseman* (May), p. 84; (June), p. 30.

(See also under Trainer Psychology: Podhajsky and Miller.)

Index

Aids (in training)
artificial, 76, 88
natural, 76, 88
See also Stimuli
Amplitude, amplification, 28, 32
Appuyer. *See* Shoulder-in; *ill.* 123
Aqueous humor, 23
Arms and hands (of rider). *See* Hands
Auricle, 30

Baer, Kathy, 60
Behavior, 14, 104
aggressive, 13
agonistic, 12–13
allelomimetic, 10
contactual, 4–6; *ill.* 5
eliminative, 7–8
epimeletic, 8–9; *ill.* 9
et-epimeletic, 9–10
ingestive, 6
investigative, 10–11
learning, 49
Behavioral patterns, 49
Behavioral studies, 49–63
Bits, 95–7, 110, 114
Blind spots, 26
Bobylev, I., 52
Bosal, 97, 100, 105, 110, 114; *ill.* 100
Breaking technique, 94–113
See also Halter breaking
Bridling technique, 99–101

Canter
described, 105–6; *ill.* 106
leads, 107
lead changes, 125–7

Chemoreceptors, 19
Cochlea, 30–1
Conditioning
avoidance, 42–3, 56, 82, 83–4
classical, 37–8
escape, 82, 83–4; *ill.* 43
instrumental, 37–8
See also Learning
Colgate University, 52
Confidence, 5–6, 35, 93
Cornea, 23
Cornell University, 50
Corpora nigra, 23
Cottongim, Suzanne Taylor, 62
Cues (in training), 47
auditory (voice), 32, 88, 91–2, 107, 116
neutral, 85
sensory, 58
tactile, 88
visual, 88

Dixon, Jane, 55–6
Dressage, 106, 115
See also Gymnastics

Ear
anatomy of, 29–31; *ill.* 29
sensitivity of, in horse, 99
Eardrum. *See* Tympanic membrane
Emotionality in horses, 15, 52, 59, 60, 132
Equipment, 95–8, 133–4
See also individual entries: Bits;
Bosal; Martingale; Reins; Saddle;
Stirrup.

145

978-0-595-37933-0
0-595-37933-8

1935387R0009

Printed in Great Britain
by Amazon.co.uk, Ltd.,
Marston Gate.